FLOWER TYPES

SPIKE　　RACEME　　CORYMB　　PANICLE　　UMBEL　　CYME

COROLLA SHAPES

ROTATE　　CAMPANULATE　　FUNNELFORM　　URCEOLATE　　SALVERFORM

TREE AND SHRUB SHAPES

LOW TRAILING　　ROUND COMPACT　　HORIZONTAL SPREADING

ERECT　　ARCHING　　UPRIGHT

CONE　　COLUMN　　WEEPING　　GLOBE　　FASTIGIATE

P9-DDY-111

herb
gardening

General Consultants:
Lisa Cadey, The New York Botanical Garden
Amy Greving and Dr. Donald Steinegger, University of Nebraska
Horticulture Department
Richard Isaacson, Minnesota Landscape Arboretum, Chanhassen, Minnesota
Richard Thurston, San Diego Wild Animal Park
Rebecca Wellborn, North Carolina Botanical Garden, Chapel Hill

Design Consultant: Cristina Spindler, Peconic River Herb Farm
Historical Consultant: Frank Anderson, former curator The New York
Botanical Garden Library
Botany Consultant: Dr. Lucile H. McCook
Enabling Garden Consultant: Eugene Rothert, Chicago Botanic Garden

herb gardening

The Robison York State Herb Garden, Cornell Plantations

Matthaei Botanical Gardens of the University of Michigan

University of California Botanical Garden, Berkeley

By Patricia Hopkinson
DIRECTOR, MATTHAEI BOTANICAL GARDENS

Diane Miske
HORTICULTURIST, THE ROBISON YORK STATE HERB GARDEN, CORNELL PLANTATIONS

Jerry Parsons
HORTICULTURIST, UNIVERSITY OF CALIFORNIA BOTANICAL GARDEN, BERKELEY

Holly Shimizu
ASSISTANT EXECUTIVE DIRECTOR, UNITED STATES BOTANIC GARDEN

With Kathy Sammis
Series Editor: Elvin McDonald
Principal Photography by Ian Adams, Dency Kane,
Stephen and Sylvia Sharnoff

Pantheon Books,
Knopf Publishing Group
New York
1994

Acknowledgments
This book was created with the help, expertise, and encouragement of a great many people. We would like to thank all the consultants who contributed so much to it, the photographers who took magnificent photographs, and Kathy Sammis who helped us write it. We also appreciate the efforts of Diane Kothe of University of California Botanical Garden, and contributing authors from Matthaei Botanical Garden: Cindy Brautigan, Lucia Brewer, Bernadine Byk, Merrill Crockett, Jamie Hove, Rosemary Hughes, Betty Jozwick, Rodger Keller, Sally McDonald, Adrienne O'Brien, Dot Owen, Judy Scanlon, Helen Schwimmer, Diane Steinhauer, and Irene Truesdell. Thank are also due to Susan Ralston, Jennifer Bernstein, Jennifer Parkinson, Ellen McNeilly, Alan Kellock, Deborah Ecker, Albert Squillace, Michelle Stein, and Deena Stein.

Project Director: Lori Stein
Book Design Consultant: Albert Squillace
Editorial Director: Jay Hyams
Associate Art Director: Eric Marshall

Library of Congress Cataloging-in-Publication Data
Herb gardening / by Patricia Hopkinson . . . [et al.] ;
principal photography by Ian Adams [et al.]. --1st ed.
p cm. –(American garden guides)
     Includes indexes
ISBN 0-679-41432-0 :
     1. Herb gardening–United States 2. Herb gardening–Canada.
3. Herbs–Pictorial works. I. Hopkinson, Patricia II. Series.
SB351.H5H353 1994   93-11362
635'.097–dc20   CIP

Manufactured in Singapore

First edition

9 8 7 6 5 4 3 2 1

NOTE: Readers are advised to be aware that many of the plants mentioned in this book have toxic, carcinogenic, or other dangerous properties. No remedies mentioned in this book should be taken as medications without proper medical advice, and no plant should ever be taken internally or used near food unless it is determined to be totally safe. Special care should be taken if children or pets frequent the areas where these plants are grown.

Opposite: Herb garden at University of Michigan's Matthaei Botanical Gardens.

contents

Allium tuberosum (Chinese chives)

The basil collection at the
National Arboretum

3. DESIGN GUIDE 168

4. TECHNIQUES 182

5. SPECIAL CONDITIONS 204

the american garden guides

The network of botanical gardens and arboreta in the United States and Canada constitutes a great treasure chest of knowledge about plants and what they need. Some of the most talented, experienced, and dedicated plantspeople in the world work full-time at these institutions; they are the people who actually grow plants, make gardens, and teach others about the process. They are the gardeners who are responsible for the gardens in which millions of visitors exclaim, "Why won't that plant grow that way for me?"

Over thirty of the most respected and beautiful gardens on the continent are participating in the creation of *The American Garden Guides*. The books in the series originate with manuscripts generated by gardeners in one or several of the gardens. Drawing on their decades of experience, these originating gardeners write down the techniques they use in their own gardens, recommend and describe the plants that grow best for them, and discuss their successes and failures. The manuscripts are then passed to several other participating gardens; in each, the specialist in that area adds recommended plants and other suggestions based on regional differences and different opinions.

The series has three major philosophical points carried throughout:

1) Successful gardens are by nature user-friendly toward the gardener and the environment. We advocate water conservation through the precepts of Xeriscaping and garden health care through Integrated Pest Management (IPM). Simply put, one does not set into motion any garden that is going to require undue irrigation during normal levels of rainfall, nor apply any pesticide or other treatment without first assessing its impact on all other life—plant, animal, and soil.

2) Gardening is an inexact science, learned by observation and by doing. Even the most experienced gardeners often develop markedly dissimilar ways of doing the same thing, or have completely divergent views of what any plant requires in order to thrive. Gardeners are an opinionated lot, and we have encouraged all participants to air and share their differences–and so, to make it clear that everyone who gardens will find his or her own way of dealing with plants. Although it is important to know the rules and the most accepted practices, it is also important to recognize that whatever works in the long run for you is the right way.

3) Part of the fun of gardening lies in finding new plants, not necessarily using over and over the same ones in the same old color schemes. In this book and others in the series, we have purposely included some lesser-known or underused plants, some of them native to our vast and wonderful continent. Wherever we can, we call attention to endangered species and suggest ways to nurture them back to their natural state of plenty.

This volume was created by horticulturists in several botanic gardens. The main portion of the book was originated by Pat Hopkinson at Matthaei Botanical Gardens in Ann Arbor, Michigan, Diane Miske at Cornell Plantation's Robison York State Herb Garden, Jerry Parsons at University of California Botanical Gardens, Berkeley (who also provided information on routine care and pests and diseases), and Holly Shimizu (who also provided information on choosing and planting herbs and on specialized gardens). The manuscript was then reviewed, and added to, by Lisa Cadey at The New York Botanical Garden, Richard Isaacson at Minnesota Landscape Arboretum, Rebecca Wellborn at North Carolina Botanical Garden, and Richard Thurston at The San Diego Wild Animal Park.

Elvin McDonald
Houston, Texas

NOTE: We have used the term "variety" in this volume in its common, rather than botanical sense, to indicate different genera, species, cultivars, as well as botanical varieties.

directors' prefaces

Cornell Plantations is the arboretum, botanical garden, and natural preserves of Cornell University. Located directly on campus, Cornell Plantations serves many audiences–faculty, undergraduate, and graduate students, researchers, photographers, and of course, the public in all its dimensions.

One of our finest gardens and collections is the Robison York State Herb Garden, which celebrates its twentieth anniversary in 1994. Provided through the generosity of the late Ellis H. and Doris B. Robison of Troy, New York, the Garden effectively serves the educational and informational needs of students and the public alike. We are pleased indeed to share the Garden's collections and information through the medium of this book.

CARL F. GORTZIG
THE ELIZABETH NEWMAN WILD
DIRECTOR OF CORNELL PLANTATIONS

Herb gardening is an exciting enterprise, as old as mankind yet still providing experiences relevant to the modern world. An antidote to the gray, sterile worlds of computer screens and fluorescent interiors, herbs are ingredients for evoking that essential spark of joy and pleasure that makes life worth getting up for: the silver beads of early morning dew on lady's mantle; the fragrance of lavender stems crushed in the hand; the musky taste of cilantro folded into curry; the bouquet of thyme in a creamy chicken sauce; mist rising over the neat geometry of a well-laid-out garden.

The Matthaei Gardens in Ann Arbor, Michigan, displays a large classical herb garden, replete with fragrance, culinary, medicinal, and drying beds, enclosed by a curved Shaker garden bench nestled against dark green yew hedges. It is an intriguing spot of refuge that can be visited time and again, every season of the year with new revelation.

For even in the age of new wave music, e-mail, and cd roms, although we live amid the cacophony of computer hums, microwave bleeps, and the spread of exhaust, somehow–perhaps especially now–herb gardens beckon with their secrets. Walk by, and you may catch a whiff. If you do, we cordially invite you to open the gate and come in.

As both staff member and director of the Matthaei Botanical Gardens, I am fortunate to have had the opportunity to participate in the growth and development of a large herb knot garden, named for the late Alexandra (Sandy) Hicks, who was an herb connoisseur and enthusiast of the most smitten sort, past editor of the Herb Society of America's quarterly journal, and founder of an herb study group at Matthaei where her persuasive curiosity, careful research, and detailed knowledge was shared by many. Our herb knot garden is an outgrowth of her original vision, and many knowledgeable members of the herb study group have contributed to this volume.

PATRICIA S. HOPKINSON
DIRECTOR, MATTHAEI BOTANICAL GARDENS
UNIVERSITY OF MICHIGAN

Culinary herbs are just one facet of the diverse world of herbs; the gardener will find many more varieties of these herbs than the supermarket shopper. *Above:* Lemon basil, one of dozens of basil varieties.

The world of herb gardening is magically varied. It offers a heady mix of fragrances and tastes, a visual tapestry of blending and contrasting colors, textures, and shapes, and a fascinating sense of connection to the past and to cultures around the world.

A DEFINITION With all their diversity, herbs are not easy to define. Botanically, an herb is an herbaceous plant, one that does not develop persistent woody stems. Herb gardeners do not take this definition literally, or they would not grow such popular woody plants as lavender, rosemary, sage, and thyme. Even full-scale trees such as the tall black birch (whose twigs and bark have been used medicinally by Native Americans) or gingko (whose leaves are important in Chinese medicine) can be considered herbs, though their size may make them inappropriate for the herb garden.

A more encompassing and widely accepted definition of an herb is a plant whose roots, stems, leaves, flowers, or fruits (including seeds and seedpods) are valued for their medicinal, savory, or aromatic qualities, or are put to some household or industrial use. But there is ambiguity here as well. Aren't vegetables used and appreciated for their flavor? Isn't the beauty of a flower useful? And what about plants without a practical use but valued for their sacred, historical, or sentimental significance–which of these should be called herbs?

We come then to a more refined, philosophical definition. Herbs enhance the pleasures or quality of life rather than being staples of life; they have some use, special significance, or historical interest apart from being purely ornamental garden plants. Basic food crops such as carrots, wheat, and potatoes are excluded from the herb garden, while unusual salad greens, traditional potherbs, and flowers with interesting histories or symbolic associations might find their way in. Accepting this broad view, Diane Miske includes an array of plants not always thought of as herbs in Cornell Plantations' Robison York State Herb Garden. Skirret, an old-fashioned root vegetable, is planted for its historical interest and because it is more a novel addition to the menu than everyday fare; acanthus is included as the inspiration for the design of the Corinthian column in the 5th century B.C., Scotch thistle as the emblem of Scotland, yellow marigolds because they denote jealousy.

To add more controversy to the task of defining an herb, some people differentiate herbs from spices in that spices, like vanilla and cinnamon, come from the tropics. Since spices are commonly thought of only as culinary seasonings, this seems an arbitrary distinction particularly because tropical plants used for fragrance, dyes, and medicines are considered herbs. To further confuse matters, sometimes one part of a plant is popularly called an herb, another part a spice–the green leaves of coriander, known as cilantro or Chinese parsley, for example, are referred to as an herb, while the ground seeds are often termed a spice. We make no clear-cut distinction and include among herbs some plants, like nutmeg and ginger, traditionally thought of as spices.

Herbs are put to many and varied uses. Perhaps the first among these is as culinary seasoning. Many herb gardeners grow the herbs they use in cooking–parsley, sage, rosemary, thyme, basil, oregano, mint, and dill are among

Previous pages: The Robison York State Herb Garden at Cornell Plantations is divided into 18 different theme beds.

the most common. Although fresh herbs are becoming increasingly available in supermarkets, the varieties on hand for gardeners are infinitely more interesting. Lemon basil, fruit salad sage, and chocolate mint are only 3 of the dozens of varieties that exist for each herb. So vast is the selection that an entire garden can be created around a single herb.

Many herbs are valued for their fragrance, enjoyed both in the garden and later in the form of scented oils, perfumes, lotions, soothing baths, sachets, and potpourris made from petals, leaves, or roots. Roses and lavenders are just 2 of the many herbs we use for their incomparable aromas.

Dye plants are another herbal specialty. A rich and varied palette of textile dyes is possible: blue from indigo, yellow from woad, red from madder. The dried leaves of henna produce a bright orange-red dye, long popular in the Middle East as a hair and skin coloring. The seeds of anatto provide a yellow dye used commercially to color food.

Fiber plants such as linen, cotton, or ramie are also sometimes included in the herb garden.

Herbs are also steeped to make teas or to flavor other beverages, both for

Left: At the University of California (Berkeley) Botanic Garden, culinary, household, and medicinal herbs are blended into the landscape; one area of the garden is devoted to a Chinese medicinal herb garden. *Below:* The herbal knot garden at Matthaei Botanical Gardens

HISTORICAL NOTES

Humans have always relied on plants for food, fuel, building material, fibers, dyes, and medicine. Folk medicine based on plants was long the only healing known to humans. Interest in the plant kingdom is understandably a constant aspect of early civilizations.

The Egyptians, Assyrians, and Babylonians compiled lists of plants and their medicinal uses; at roughly the same time similar lists were being made in India and China. The Egyptians built walled gardens, and the Mesopotamians constructed terraced gardens, such as the Hanging Gardens of Bablyon. Buddhists spread the planting of sacred groves from India to China, creating a style for naturalistic gardens in which the beauty of natural scenery was accentuated by plants arranged so as to set off their colors and fragrances.

The many contributions of the ancient Greeks to the nascent science of botany include the writings of Hippocrates, Aristotle, and Theophrastus, who systematically categorized more than 450 plants. Even more influential was Dioscorides, whose *De Materia Medica* set the pattern for the great European herbals and became the prototype of our modern pharmacopoeias. The healing virtues of plants were the primary subject of these works, but the ancient Greeks did not overlook the use of herbs in the kitchen: as early as 400 B.C. the physician Chrysippos wrote about herbs, citing basil as among his favorites.

The Romans added a great deal to the history of cooking, including the first cookbooks. They were fond of seasonings: pepper was the favorite, followed by lovage, rue, coriander, cumin, oregano, celery seed, parsley seed, bay leaf, anise, fennel, and mint. The Romans did little, however, to further botanic sciences: Pliny had nothing new to say in his *Natural History*, which is nonetheless valuable as a compilation of earlier knowledge. Much of the folk medicine repeated here passed into the folklore of Europe and the New World.

During the medieval period the medical arts came increasingly under the influence of Arabian physicians. Such men as Mesue, Serapion, Rhazes, and Avicenna revolutionized medicine. Avicenna compiled the *Canon,* a vast encyclopedia of pharmacy and curative procedures that became as respected in Europe as in Islam. In addition the Europeans were stimulated to make some advances of their own in the 12th-century compilation *Circa instans,* which became the physician's *vade mecum* for the next three hundred years. The next major botanical advance came in 1484 with the publication of Peter Schoeffer's *Herbarius Latinus,* which proved to be only the curtain raiser for his magnificent production of the revolutionary *Der Gart* of 1485. In that work the common vernacular of Germany replaced Latin, thus increasing the audience for the book. And in 1491 came the *Hortus Sanitatis,* the last herbal to be devoted exclusively to Old World plants. Then in 1530 Brunfels' *Herbarum Vivae Eicones,* or "Images of Living Plants," gave the death blow to all unrealistic, schematic representations of herbs. From then on plants were drawn from nature.

The study of plants was aided by the creation of botanic gardens, also known as physic gardens. The first such gardens were founded at Padua in 1545, Leyden in 1587, and Oxford in 1621. There were also private gardens, and new foreign plants–such as those from the New World–were eagerly collected and cultivated. John Gerard cataloged 1,030 plants in his London garden and published his famous *Herball* in 1597. The most ambitious English herbalist was John Parkinson, whose *Theatrum Botanicum* (1649) covers roughly 3,800 plants. In *The English Physician* (1651), Nicholas Culpeper revealed the chicanery of the doctors of the day who continued the employment of ancient and worthless medications. Following on these events came Louis XIV(1638-1715) and the creation of Versailles, the model for every royal garden from that time forward.

In America the Bartrams of Philadelphia and Mark Catesby prowled the forests for new horticultural specimens, introducing hundreds of new trees and plants throughout Europe and the American colonies. Before all that growth became chaotic, Linnaeus imposed a firm hand on putting things in order with his *Species Plantarum* of 1753, thus creating the definitive science of botany. Meanwhile the physic gardens of Chelsea, Paris, Montpellier, and Padua, continued to build the frontiers of medicine, botany, and horticulture, and the disciples of Linnaeus fanned out to make further discoveries and report on the plants of Asia, Africa, and the Americas.

It was not long before the American colonies entered the horticultural world, and the Prince Gardens became established at Flushing, N.Y. They were soon followed by the Parsons firm, also of Flushing, and the Caswell-Massey pharmacy of New York City, whose lotions, rinses, and cosmetic preparations remain popular today.

FRANK ANDERSON

refreshment and for their therapeutic effects. Among these are mints, borage, sweet woodruff, hops, and nettles.

Herbs serve many other household uses. Lemon balm is used as furniture polish, pennyroyal as a flea repellent, southernwood as a moth chaser, and soapwort to produce a mild soap. Other herbs are prized for their contribution to dried arrangements and wreaths.

Some herbs have industrial uses, like jojoba, whose seeds provide a top-quality lubricant. Others are important in a variety of commercial products: pyrethrum as an organic insecticide, safflower as the source of a widely used cooking oil, peppermint as a flavoring in syrups, liqueurs, candies, mouthwashes, tobacco, and toothpaste.

This brings us to another major and traditional use of herbs: medicines like feverfew (a remedy for headache), chamomile (a sedative), foxglove (a source of digitalis). The therapeutic values of many herbs were discovered early on, and some "folk remedies" were actually quite effective and led to modern-day medicines. Aspirin is only one example: in ancient times people boiled the bark of willow trees to make an antifever medicine; modern chemists isolated the active ingredient and named it salicylate, from the Latin *salix* ("willow"). No one would recommend that a person with a heart condition treat himself with digitalis from his herb garden, but the plant is often included in gardens because of its medicinal usage. This aspect of herbs should be kept in mind: many contain chemicals that can have powerful effects on the human body. Modern technology uses many of these chemicals to make medicines important to us; our forebearers used these same chemicals to make poisons (even aspirin can be poisonous, of course: a large overdose impairs the central nervous system). Care should be taken to keep children, particularly toddlers, away from potent, and potentially dangerous herbs (and from all plants). The colors, smells, and, in many cases, bite-size berries of toxic herbs could be especially appealing to toddlers, who are capable of suddenly putting plant parts in their mouths.

In many botanic gardens, herbs are grouped according to their varied uses, ethnic divisions, or historical associations, or by some more esoteric theme such as sacred herbs (plants that have some religious significance), herbs in literature (Shakespearean gardens use only plants mentioned in the bard's works), or plants that have a meaning or sentiment attached to them in the language of flowers. The herbs in Cornell Plantations' Robison York State Herb Garden are grown in the following theme beds: herbs of the ancients; herbs in literature; bee herbs; edible flowers, salad, and potherbs; herbs of Native Americans; medicinal herbs; simples and worts (old-time single-plant remedies, some effective, some included for their historical interest); culinary herbs; economic herbs (which provide oils, fibers, fragrances, flavorings, etc.); dye herbs; tea herbs; fragrant herbs; sacred herbs; tussie-mussies and nosegays; scented geraniums; and herbs with ornamental value. At the University of California Botanic Garden at Berkeley, a section is devoted entirely to Chinese medicinal herbs; other sections group herbs geographically.

Plants used for fragrance and medicines have a time-honored place in the herb garden. *Top:* Lavender ready to be used for potpourri. *Above:* Plants prepared for medicinal use by Chinese herbalists.

A BRIEF LESSON IN BOTANY

Plants are living things and share many traits with animals. Plants are composed of millions of individual cells that are organized into complex organ systems. Plants breathe (take in and expel gases) and extract energy from food; to do this they require water, nutrients, and atmospheric gases. Like animals, plants reproduce sexually, and their offspring inherit characteristics through a genetic code passed along as DNA and, unlike animals, some plants reproduce asexually.

Plants, however, can do one thing that no animal can do. Through a process called photosynthesis, plants can capture energy from the sun and convert that energy into compounds such as proteins, fats, and carbohydrates. These energy-rich compounds are the source of the energy for all animal life, including humans.

THE IMPORTANCE OF PLANTS

Because no living animals can produce the energy they need to live, all their energy comes from plants. Like other animals, we eat green plants directly, in the form of fruits, vegetables, and grains (breads and cereals), or we eat animals and animal products that were fed green plants.

The oxygen we need to live on Earth is constantly pumped out of green plants as a byproduct of photosynthesis. Plants prevent the erosion of our precious soils and hinder water loss to the atmosphere.

Plants are also an important source of drugs. Fully one-quarter of all prescriptions contain at least one plant-derived product. Aspirin, one of the most commonly used drugs, was originally isolated from the bark of the willow tree. Today, scientists are screening plants from all over the world in search of new compounds to cure cancer, AIDS, and other diseases.

THE WHOLE PLANT

Basically, a plant is made up of leaves, stems, and roots; all these parts are connected by a vascular system, much like our circulatory system. The vascular system can be seen in the veins of a leaf, or in the rings in a tree.

LEAVES

Leaves are generally flattened and expanded tissues that are green due to the presence of chlorophyll, the pigment that is necessary for photosynthesis. Most leaves are connected to the stem by a stalk, or petiole, which allows the leaves to alter their position in relation to the sun and capture as much energy as possible. Plants that have leaves year-round are often called "evergreen," while plants that lose all their leaves at one time each year are termed "deciduous."

Leaves come in an astounding variety of shapes, textures, and sizes. Some leaves are composed of a single structure, or blade, and are termed simple. Other leaves are made up of many units, or leaflets, and are called compound (see endpapers).

STEMS

Technically, a stem is the tissue that supports leaves and that connects the leaves with the roots via a vascular system. Stems also bear the flowers on a plant. Therefore, a stem can be identified by the presence of buds, which are the unexpanded leaves, stems, or flowers that will develop at a later time.

Plants that send up leaves in a rosette or clump may have stems so short that they are difficult to distinguish. Other plants, like the iris, have a stem, called a rhizome, that travels horizontally underground. Many plants of arid regions have very reduced leaves or have lost their leaves altogether in order to avoid loss of water to the atmosphere. The barrel cactus is an example of a plant that is almost entirely stem.

ROOTS

Although out of sight, roots are extremely important to the life of the plant. Roots anchor a plant in the soil, absorb water and nutrients, and store excess food, such as starches, for the plants' future use. Basically, there are two types of roots: taproots and fibrous roots. Taproots are thickened, unbranched roots that grow straight down, taking advantage of moisture and nutrients far below the soil surface. Taproots, such as carrots, store carbohydrates. Fibrous roots are fine, branching, and generally more shallow. They often form dense mats of roots, making them excellent agents of soil stabilization. Fibrous roots absorb moisture and nutrients from a shallow zone of soil and may be more susceptible to drought.

Roots obviously need to come into contact with water, but they also need air in order to work properly. Except for those adapted to aquatic environments, most plants require well-drained soils that provide them air as well as water.

VASCULAR SYSTEMS

Plants have a well-developed vascular system that extends throughout the plant body and that allows movement of water and compounds from one part of a plant to another. Once the roots absorb water and minerals, the vascular system funnels them to the leaves, where they are used in photosynthesis. Likewise, energy-rich compounds that are produced in the leaves must travel to the stems and roots to provide nutrition for further growth. The vascular system also strengthens plant tissues. Although much of the vascular system is part of the internal anatomy of a plant, some parts can be seen.

PHOTOSYNTHESIS

A green plant is like a factory that takes raw materials available in the environment and converts them into other forms of energy. In a complex series of energy transfer and chemical conversion events called photosynthesis, plants take energy from the sun, minerals and water from the soil, and gases from the atmosphere; these raw materials are converted into chemical forms of energy that are used for plant growth. These same energy-rich compounds (proteins, sugars and starches, fats and oils) can be utilized by animals as a source of food and nutrition. All this is possible because of a green pigment, chlorophyll.

Photosynthesis is an extremely complex series of reactions that takes place in the cells of leaves, the byproducts of which are connected to other reactions throughout the cell. The most basic reactions of photosynthesis occurs like this. Energy from the sun strikes the leaf surface, and electrons in the chlorophyll molecule become "excited" and

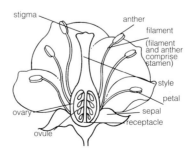

stigma
anther
filament
(filament and anther comprise stamen)
style
petal
ovary
sepal
receptacle
ovule

are boosted to a higher energy level. Excited electrons are routed through a chain of reactions that extracts and stores energy in the form of sugars. As a byproduct of electron loss, water molecules (H_2O) are split; hydrogen moves in to replenish the electrons lost from chlorophyll, and Oxygen is released, finding its way into our atmosphere. In another photosynthetic reaction, carbon dioxide from the atmosphere is "fixed," or converted into organic compounds within the plant cell. These first chemical compounds are the building blocks for more complex reactions and are the precursors for the formation of many elaborate chemical compounds.

PLANT NUTRITION

Plants require mineral nutrients from the soil, water, and the atmosphere in order to maintain healthy growth and reproduction. Macronutrients, those nutrients needed in large amounts, include hydrogen, oxygen, and carbon so essential for photosynthesis. Other macronutrients are nitrogen, phosphorus, potassium, sulfur, and calcium. Nitrogen is an important component of chlorophyll and of proteins, which are used to construct DNA, cell membranes, and other vital compounds in the cell. Phosphorus is also used in building DNA and is important in cell development. Potassium is important in the development of tubers, roots, and other storage organs. If macronutrients are in limited supply, growth and development in the plant will be strongly curtailed. Micronutrients, such as iron, copper and magnesium, are required in smaller amounts and are of variable importance to different kinds of plants.

LIFE CYCLE

Higher plants (except for ferns) begin life as a seed. Given the right set of conditions (temperature, moisture, light), a seed will germinate and develop its first roots and leaves using food stored in the seed (humans and other animals take advantage of the high-quality food in seeds when we eat wheat, rice, and corn, just to name a few). Because of the presence of chlorophyll in the leaves, the small plant is soon able to produce its own food, which is used immediately for further growth and development. As the seedling grows in size, it also grows in complexity. The first, simple root gives way to a complex root system that may include

underground storage organs. The stem is transformed into an intricate system of vascular tissue that moves water from the ground upward into the leafy part of the plant, while other tissues transport energy-rich compounds manufactured in the leaves downward to be stored in stem and root systems.

Once the plant reaches maturity, flower initiation begins. Flowers hold the sexual apparatus for the plant; their brilliant colors and glorious odors are advertisements to attract pollinators such as insects or birds. In a basic, complete flower, there are four different parts, given below. However, many plants have incomplete flowers with one or more of these parts missing, or the parts may be highly modified.

1. Sepals. The outermost part of the flower, the sepals cover the young floral buds. Although they are often green, they may be variously colored.

2. Petals. The next layer of parts in the flower, petals are often colorful and play an important role in attracting pollinators.

3. Stamens. Stamens are located next to the petals, or may even be basally fused to the petals. The stamens are the "male" reproductive parts of the flower; they produce the pollen. Pollen grains are fine, dustike particles that will divide to form sperm cells. The tissue at the end of the stamen that holds pollen is called the anther.

4. Pistil. The innermost part of the flower holds the female reproductive apparatus for the plant. The stigma, located at the tip of the pistil, is often covered with a sticky substance and is the site where pollen is deposited. The stigma is held by a floral tube, call the style. At the base of the style, the ovary holds one to many ovules, which contain eggs that represent undeveloped seeds.

Pollination is the transfer of pollen from

an anther to a stigma and is the first step in the production of seeds. Pollen can be transferred by an insect visiting the flower, by the wind, or even by the splashing of raindrops. After being deposited on a compatible stigma, the pollen grains grow into tubes that travel from the stigma down the floral tube into the ovary, depositing sperm cells to the ovules. If all goes well, sperm cells unite with the eggs inside the ovules, and fertilization takes place.

After fertilization, the entire floral structure is transformed into a fruit. Fruit can be fleshy, like an apple, or dry like a pea pod. Within each fruit, fertilized eggs develop into seeds, complete with a cache of storage tissue and a seed coat.

ANNUALS AND PERENNIALS

An annual is a plant in which the life cycle is completed in a growing season; a biennial returns the following year and then dies; a perennial is a plant that persists and produces reproductive structures year after year. The seed of an annual might germinate in the spring, produce flowers in the summer, and drop their seeds a little later; the plant itself will wither and die completely by the time winter arrives. The following growing season, seeds are the only tissue available to begin another round of the life cycle of the annual plant. In contrast, a perennial plant may die back during the winter, but some part of the plant, usually a stem or root structure, remains alive all winter. When spring comes, perennials resprout new leaves or stems from last season's plants and may also have seeds from the previous year.

These definitions are based on the biology of the plant, but do not account for the many ways that humans cultivate plants. Many of the plants that we cultivate as annuals are actually perennials in their native habitate. For example, pampas grass is a perennial, but does not survive very cold weather; in colder climates, it is grown as an annual, or dug up and brought inside for the winter.

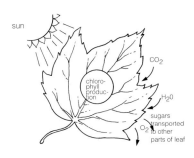

sun

CO_2

chloro-phyll production

H_2O

O_2 sugars transported to other parts of leaf

Salvia leucantha, an ornamental species in the same genus as the common culinary herb sage, creates a striking accent in herb or flower gardens. It is not used for cooking.

For the purposes of this book, we have not restricted the term *herb,* in the hope that readers will make up their own definitions as they follow their interests into the vast realm of herbs. The choice becomes enormous; those interested in unusual culinary herbs can find examples from every corner of the earth, from Italian parsley and Greek oregano to lemon grass (used in Thai cooking) and wasabi (Japanese horseradish). In addition to geography, herb gardeners can dig into history and grow the medicines of the Middle Ages and ancient Chinese dynasties, the cosmetics of Egyptian concubines, the salad greens of early American settlers.

ORNAMENTAL HERBS Although the definition of herbs excludes plants that are strictly ornamental, it does not exclude ornamental plants. Many herbs are extremely beautiful and often do double-duty in perennial or annual beds. Their herbal uses aside, coneflowers, pot marigolds, and digitalis—even roses—are old standby ornamentals that have unquestionable herbal status as well. Herbs can serve landscaping purposes as hedges (germander, lavender), edgings (betony, lady's mantle), and ground covers (sweet woodruff, wild ginger). Other plants that we consider more useful than ornamental—creeping thyme, chives, perilla—deserve a second look for their ornamental qualities. Some species of the most common herbs are less fragrant or tasty than the ones cultivated for herbal usage, but have more beautiful flowers or foliage; although ornamental sages and oreganos are not as useful in the kitchen as other, less showy, varieties, they do have a place in the herb garden.

If the gardener so chooses, landscaping with herbs can become less utilitarian and more artistic. A well-designed herb garden brimming with delicate sprays of lavender, striking combinations of green, silver, and purple foliage, vivid spikes of clary sage, and colorful rosebushes can make one forget that these plants are grown for any use other than loveliness.

BASIC NEEDS With all their multiple uses, herbs are really quite easy to grow.

Jerry Parsons

Diane Miske has a master of professional studies degree in horticulture and ornamental horticulture from Cornell University. She has worked as a horticulturist since 1985 at Cornell Plantations, where she tends to the cut-flower garden as well as the 1-acre herb garden. Diane particularly enjoys exchanging herbal knowledge with the many visitors of different cultural backgrounds who are stimulated by the garden to talk about their experiences with herbs and their memories of herbal use by their parents and grandparents. Diane finds herb gardening highly rewarding because it satisfies so many different senses and interests—herbs can be appreciated for their flavors, scents, textures, forms, and colors—and learning about the ways different cultures have used various plants at many different times in human history is endlessly fascinating.

Jerry Parsons is a horticulturist at the University of California at Berkeley Botanic Gardens. After an initial career in the business world, Jerry returned to his first interest and earned a B.S. in botany. Berkeley's herb garden is planted in theme beds and is constantly busy with visitors. Jerry particularly likes working with herbs because of their wide variety of textures and smells ("You smell good after working in the herb garden") and because an herb garden can be ever-changing—herbs grow quickly, so you can bring in new plants and have a mature garden in one season. Jerry's advice to home growers is to let the garden reflect personality and style; grow what you want, mixing color, texture, and form, and keep experimenting until you get what works best for you.

Most are very adaptable, tolerant of a wide range of conditions, and more likely to be killed off by pampering (overwatering, overfeeding) than by neglect. As a rule, herbs give best results in a good, well-drained garden soil, with a pH from neutral to slightly alkaline. Most herbs will tolerate (although not thrive in) even poor soil, but not wet areas–an indication of many herbs' Mediterranean origin in rocky but thoroughly drained soils. Another heritage of that origin is the requirement of most herbs for a lot of sun–at least 6-8 hours a day–which is what produces maximum amounts of the herbs' essential oils. To grow herbs in other-than-ideal conditions, seek out the exceptions–for example, sweet cicely and woodruff tolerate partial shade, and mint can stand more water.

Herbs generally don't need much fertilizer, although plants that are heavily harvested benefit from a sidedressing of compost and organic plant food in midseason. Most herbs don't need extensive winter protection in harsh climates, though lavenders and some sages appreciate a covering of pine branches, and some herbs like rosemary, lemon verbena, and lemon grass need to be lifted and brought inside for the winter (or grown in easily moved pots) in colder zones.

Herbs are tough and adaptable. Pat Hopkinson, one of our horticulturists, wanted to keep her young children from trampling her bonsai and delphiniums. So she set up a sandbox in another garden area and surrounded it with lemon balm and spearmint, edged by sage, parsley, basil, oregano. The herbs were showered with shovelfuls of sand and stomped unheedingly all summer–and bounced back unhesitatingly and repeatedly. Even so, gardeners should not assume that they can neglect their herbs, particularly the ones that are native to regions very different from our own. As Rebecca Welbourne of the North Carolina Botanical Garden points out, since they are not grown in their native habitats, they must be helped to adapt– a moderate amount of

Pat Hopkinson, with a B.S. in horticulture from Penn State, has been at the University of Michigan's Matthaei Botanical Garden since 1983. Its herb garden was established in the early 1980s as a formal knot garden; its signature plant is the lavender, lushly growing in hedges. Pat is excited about the upcoming expansion of the Matthaei herb garden into four new theme beds, formally arranged yet with a warm Mediterranean feel. Pat finds the garden draws visitors who are interested in herbs for culinary and health reasons and that an herb garden offers a wonderful sensory experience of touch, smell, and taste. Herbs are rewarding, says Pat, because they're so easy to grow: "Herbs are literally weeds, if you have the right habitat."

Holly Shimizu, assistant executive director of the United States Botanic Garden, considers horticulture and gardening to be both her profession and her passionate hobby. Since graduating from the Temple University Ambler School of Horticulture, and Pennsylvania State University, she has studied and worked all over the United States, as well as in England, Germany, Belgium, and Holland. As first curator of the National Herb Garden in the U.S. National Arboretum, she made significant contributions toward the development of the garden. Holly and her husband, landscape architect Osamu Shimizu, actively create gardens at their home near Washington, D.C., for their family. As supervisory horticulturist of the U.S. Botanic Garden, she works on both indoor and outdoor exhibits and loves teaching people about new plants, gardening trends, and techniques.

SCIENTIFIC NOMENCLATURE

Botanists and horticulturists use a binomial, or two-name, system to label the over 250,000 species of living plants. Because the names are in Latin form, this system crosses both time and language barriers and allows people all over the world to communicate about plants. Occasionally, a scientific name will be changed by scientists; these changes reflect additions to our knowledge about the plant.

A scientific name is made up of the genus (singular; genera is plural) and the species, as in *Achillea millefolium*. The genus is always first and is always capitalized. The species name follows the genus and is generally not capitalized. If another Latinized name follows the genus and species, it denotes a subspecies, such as a subset or variety.

Cultivated plants are often selected for a particular attribute, such as leaf or flower color or resistance to disease. These selections are given a cultivar, or cultivated variety, name in addition to the genus or species. Cultivar names are capitalized and in single quotations, such as 'Summer Pastels' or 'Rose Beauty'.

Hybrids are plants resulting from sexual reproduction between two different kinds of plants. A hybrid may be denoted by an "x" such as *Thymus* x *citriodorus*.

Many plants have common names as well. In fact, most familiar plants have too many common names, creating a problem in communication–for example, *Monarda didyma* is called beebalm, bergamot, and Oswego tea. But it has only one correct scientific name.

PLANT SELECTOR 2

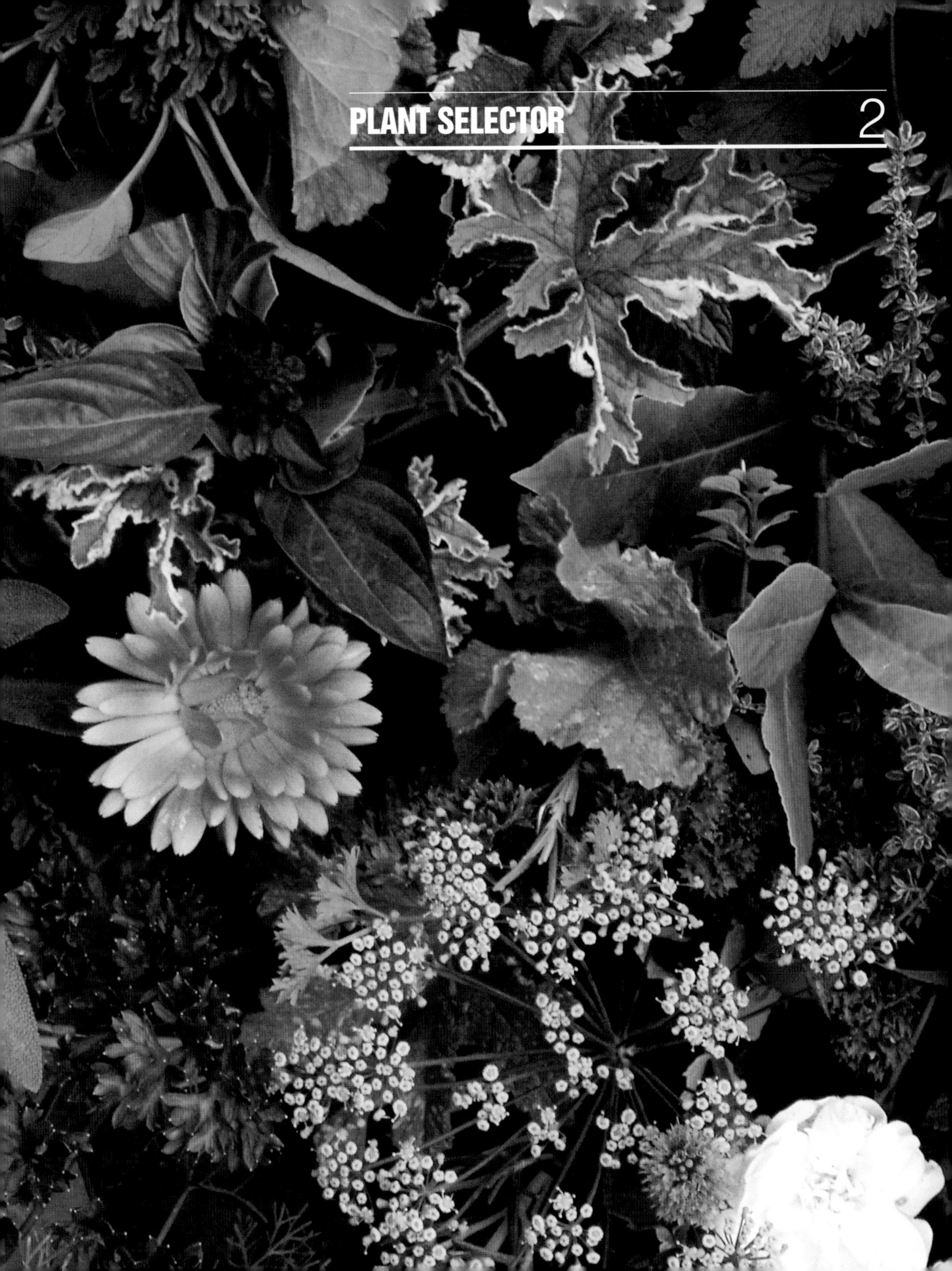

Herbs in this volume are arranged according to their Latin or scientific names. Here are the Latin names of some common herbs:

Basil: *Ocimum*
Beebalm: *Monarda*
Catnip: *Nepeta*
Celery: *Apium*
Chervil: *Anthriscus*
Cilantro/Coriander: *Coriandrum*
Dill: *Anethum*
Garlic, Chives: *Allium*
Fennel: *Foeniculum*
Lavender: *Lavandula*
Lemon grass: *Cymbopogon*
Lemon verbena: *Aloysia*
Marjoram: *Origanum*
Mint: *Mentha*
Mustard: *Brassica*
Oregano: *Origanum*
Parsley: *Petroselinum*
Sage: *Salvia*
Scented Geranimum: *Pelargonium*
Tarragon: *Artemisia*
Thyme: *Thymus*

Gardeners don't always enjoy every part of the gardening process–but finding a great new herb is pure pleasure for just about everyone. Since thousands of different varieties and cultivars are currently being sold, and nurseries, botanists, and private gardeners all over the world are busy finding and creating more, there will never be a shortage of new plants to discover. Moreover, new methods of transportation and communication are making it easier for us to find and use herbs that are common in other parts of the world. The key is finding out which ones are right for you.

This plant selector chapter is designed to give you basic information about herbs to grow in your own garden. For information on techniques like how to plant or how to start seeds indoors, see Chapter 3; for information on how to design a garden, see Chapter 4. In this chapter, you will find portraits of individual herbs. Our gardening experts have selected about 200 varieties that work well for them; they mixed some common, easy-to-find selections with others that you might not know about, but should. Gardeners from other botanic gardens around the country added varieties that do well in their regions.

When deciding which herbs to grow, ask yourself:

1. Do I want to specialize in a particular type of herb, such as medicinals or Shakespearean herbs? Do I want herbs to use for cooking or potpourri? There is, of course, no reason not to mix types.

2. What is my climate zone? Do I live in the right geographical region for this plant? If you live in a warm region, you may be able to grow cumin, but not French tarragon, which requires a cooler climate. If you are not sure about your climate zone, talk to your county extension service, local nursery, or botanic garden. But don't forget that your site is unique; it has its own "microclimate," and conditions may be different from those 2 blocks away let alone at the nursery 10 miles down the road. Even within your own yard, the climate in a sheltered spot near the house might be different from the site on the other side of a hill. (See page 184 for information on choosing a site, and Chapter 5 for information on growing herbs in difficult climates.)

3. How much care will this plant need? And how much time do I wish to spend caring for it? Is it susceptible to a disease that is rampant in my area? Will it need staking? Pruning? Extra watering? How much care is it worth? You can grow almost anything if you are willing to take the time to pamper it.

4. Can I find the plants and seeds I want in regional catalogs and local nurseries? Regionally grown plants are already acclimated to your climate and will be easier to care for.

Answer these questions honestly. It's easy to fudge–but the plant will know. Much heartache and wasted effort can be saved by putting the right plants in the right place right from the start.

CHOOSING PLANTS

When choosing plants, you will find dozens or even hundreds of varieties available for each herb. Every gardener has his or her personal favorites; one gardener's heaviest yielder is another's certain failure. A species that yields beautiful blooms for dried arrangements may not provide the taste desired by a gardener who wants to cook with it. We have listed varieties that have worked for our gardeners; the only way to find the ones that will work for you is to try them yourself. If you find a plant you love that seems only marginally suited to your climate, plant it—and see if it grows.

The U.S. Department of Agriculture has prepared this map, which separates the country into climate zones; many seed companies use these zone numbers to indicate where a particular variety will survive the winter. Find out what zone you're in, and pay attention to the growers' recommendations—but remember that climate zone is only one part of the picture.

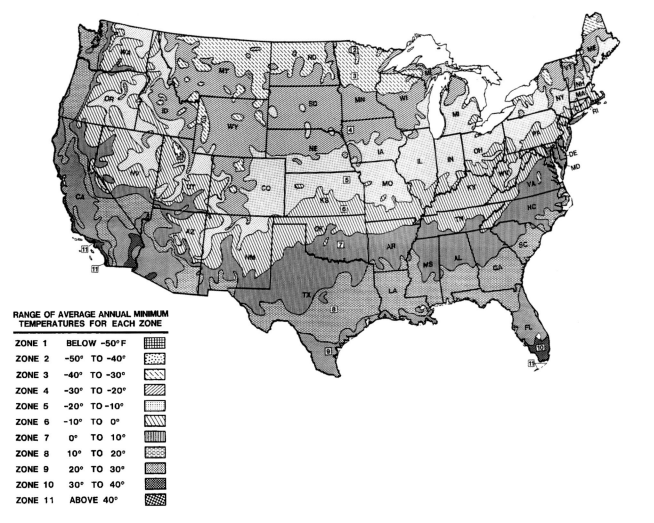

RANGE OF AVERAGE ANNUAL MINIMUM TEMPERATURES FOR EACH ZONE

ZONE 1	BELOW −50°F
ZONE 2	−50° TO −40°
ZONE 3	−40° TO −30°
ZONE 4	−30° TO −20°
ZONE 5	−20° TO −10°
ZONE 6	−10° TO 0°
ZONE 7	0° TO 10°
ZONE 8	10° TO 20°
ZONE 9	20° TO 30°
ZONE 10	30° TO 40°
ZONE 11	ABOVE 40°

HERBS USED IN COOKING

Agastache foeniculum, anise hyssop, 28
Agastache mexicana, Mexican hyssop, 29
Agastache rugosa, Korean hyssop, 29
Allium cepa , Egyptian onion, 31
Allium sativum, garlic, 33
Allium schoenoprasum, chives, 34
Allium triococcum, ramp, 34
Aloysia triphylla, lemon verbena, 36
Althaea officinalis, marsh mallow, 36
Anethum graveolens, dill, 37
Angelica archangelica, angelica, 38
Anthriscus cerefolium, chervil, 41
Apium graveolens, leaf celery, 41
Artemisia dracunculus, tarragon, 42
Asarum canadense, wild ginger, 44
Borago officinalis, borage, 47
Brassica nigra, black mustard, 48
Calendula officinalis, calendula, 51
Capsicum annuum, pepper, 53
Capparis spinosa, caper bush, 51
Carthamus tinctorius, safflower, 53
Carum carvi, caraway, 54
Chenopodium capitatum, strawberry blite, 56
Cichorium intybus, chicory, 60
Coix lacryma-jobi, Job's tears, 62
Coriandrum , coriander/cilantro, 64
Crithrum maritimum, samphire, 64
Crocus sativus, Saffron crocus, 67
Cryptotaenia japonica, mitsuba, 67
Cymbopogon citratus, lemon grass, 68
Cynara cardunculus, cardoon, 68
Dianthus caryophyllus, clove pink, 70
Elsholtzia ciliata, Vietnamese balm, 73
Eryngium foetidum, culantro, 75
Ferula assa-foetida, asafetida, 75
Foeniculum vulgare, fennel, 76
Ginkgo bilboa, ginkgo, 81
Helianthus annuus, sunflower, 82
Hibiscus, hibiscus, 82
Hierochloe odorata, sweetgrass, 85
Houttuynia cordata, houttuynia, 85
Humulus lupulus, hops, 87
Hyssopus officinalis, hyssop, 87
Laurus nobilis, bay, 88
Lavandula, lavender, 90
Levisticum, lovage, 92
Linum usitatissimum, flax, 94
Lippia graveolens, Mexican oregano, 94
Melissa officinalis, lemon balm, 97
Mentha, mint, 98
Momordica charantia, balsam pear, 102
Monarda didyma, beebalm, 102
Myrrhis odorata, sweet cicely, 104
Nigella sativa, black cumin, 106
Ocimum, basil, 108
Origanum, oregano, 110
Origanum marjorana, marjoram, 114
Pelargonium, scented geranium, 116
Perilla frutescens, perilla, 118
Petroselinum crispum, parsley, 120
Pimpinella anisum, anise, 121
Plectranthus amboinicus, Cuban oregano, 124
Poliomintha Mexican oregano, 126
Polygonum odoratum, Vietnamese coriander, 126
Portulaca, purslane, 128
Poterium , salad burnet, 128
Pycnanthemum muticum, mountain mint, 132
Rosa rugosa, rugosa rose, 135
Rosmarinus officinalis, rosemary, 137
Rumex, sorrel, 139
Salvia, sage, 139
Sambucus canadensis, elder, 143
Satureja hortensis, summer savory, 145
Satureja montana, winter savory, 145
Sesamum indicum, sesame, 149
Tagetes, marigold, 151
Thymus, thyme, 154
Trachyspermum copticum, ajowan, 157
Tulbaghia violaceae, society garlic, 157
Wasabia japonica, wasabi, 162
Zingiber officinale, ginger, 162

HERBS USED IN SALADS

Agastache foeniculum, anise hyssop, 28
Agastache mexicana, Mexican giant hyssop, 29
Agastache rugosa, Korean anise hyssop, 29
Allium cepa, Egyptian onion, 31
Allium sativum, garlic, 33
Allium schoenoprasum, chives, 34
Aloysia triphylla, lemon verbena, 36
Althaea officinalis, marsh mallow, 36
Anethum graveolens, dill, 37
Angelica archangelica, angelica, 38
Anthriscus cerefolium, chervil, 41
Atriplex hortensis, orach, 45
Borago officinalis, borage, 47
Brassica nigra, black mustard, 48
Calendula officinalis, calendula, p,51
Capsicum annuum, pepper, 53
Carum carvi, caraway, 54
Chenopodium capitatum, strawberry blite, 56
Cichorium intybus, chicory, 60
Crithmum maritimum, samphire, 64
Cynara cardunculus, cardoon, 68
Foeniculum vulgare, fennel, 76
Helianthus annuus, sunflower, 82
Hyssopus officinalis, hyssop, 87
Malva sylvestris, malva, 94
Mentha, mint, 98
Momordica charantia, balsam pear, 102
Monarda didyma, beebalm, 102
Myrrhis odorata, sweet cicely, 104
Ocimum, basil, 108
Perilla frutescens, perilla, 118
Petroselinum crispum, parsley, 120
Pimpinella anisum, anise, 121
Poterium, salad burnet, 128
Rosa rugosa, rugosa rose, 135
Rumex, sorrel, 139

Ruta graveolens, rue, 139
Salvia, sage, 139
Sambucus canadensis, elder, 143
Sesamum indicum, sesame, 149
Tropaeolum majus, nasturtium, 157
Viola odorata, violet, 160

HERBS USES FOR TEAS/BEVERAGES

Agastache foeniculum, anise hyssop, 28
Agastache mexicana, Mexican giant hyssop, 29
Agastache rugosa, Korean anise hyssop, 29
Aloysia triphylla, lemon verbena, 36
Arctostaphylos, bearberry, 42
Borago officinalis, borage, 47
Calamintha nepeta, calamint, 49
Chrysanthemum balsamita, costmary, 58
Cymbopogon citratus, lemon grass, 68
Dianthus caryophyllus, pink, 70
Elsholtzia ciliata, Vietnamese balm, 73
Ephedra sinensis, joint fir , 73
Foeniculum vulgare, fennel, 76
Glycyrrhiza glabra, licorice, 81
Hierochloe odorata, sweetgrass, 85
Malva sylvestris, malva, 94
Marrubium , horehound, 96
Matricaria recutita, chamomile, 97
Melissa officinalis, lemon balm, 97
Mentha, mint, 98
Monarda didyma, beebalm, 102
Nashia, moujean tea, 104
Nepeta, catnip, 106
Ocimum, basil, 108
Pelargonium, scented geranium, 116
Petroselinum crispum, parsley, 120
Pycnanthemum muticum, mountain mint, 132
Rosa rugosa, rugosa rose, 135
Rosmarinus , rosemary, 137
Salvia, sage, 139
Sambucus canadensis, elder, 143
Satureja viminea, Jamaican mint bush, 146
Solidago odora, Goldenrod, 149
Thymus, thyme, 154

HERBS USED FOR FRAGRANCE/POTPOURRI

Acorus, sweet flag, 28
Aloysia triphylla, lemon verbena, 36
Angelica archangelica, 38
Artemisia , wormwood, 42
Calendula officinalis, calendula, 51
Carthamus tinctorius, safflowerr, 53
Chenopodium botrys, ambrosia, 56
Dianthus caryophyllus, clove pink, 70
Elsholtzia ciliata, Vietnamese balm, 73
Galium odoratum, woodruff, 78
Geranium, cranesbill, 79
Hesperis matronalis, dame's rocket, 82

Hierochloe odorata, sweetgrass, 85
Hyssopus officinalis, hyssop, 87
Iris germanica, orris root, 87
Lavandula, lavender, 90
Levisticum, lovage, 92
Malva sylvestris, malva, 94
Melissa officinalis, lemon balm, 97
Mentha, mint, 98
Monarda didyma, beebalm, 102
Myrrhis odorata, sweet cicely, 104
Ocimum, basil, 108
Pelargonium, Geranium, 116
Perovskia atriplicifolia, Russian sage, 118
Pogostemon cablin, patchouli, 126
Rosa rugosa, rugosa rose, 135
Rosmarinus, rosemary, 137
Salvia, sage, 139
Santolina chamaecyparissus, santolina, 143
Thymus, thyme, 154
Vetiveria zizanioides, vetiver, 160

HERBS USED FOR DRIED ARRANGE-MENTS/CRAFTS

Achillea, yarrow, 26
Acorus, sweet flag, 28
Alchemilla, lady's mantle, 31
Allium cepa, Egyptian onion, 31
Allium schoenoprasum, chives, 34
Amorpha canescens, leadplant, 37
Artemisia, wormwood, 42
Asclepias tuberosa, butterfly, 44
Baptisia, false indigo, 45
Borago officinalis, borage, 47
Carthamus tinctorius, safflower, 53
Celosia argentea, cockscomb, 54
Chenopodium botrys, ambrosia, 56
Coix lacryma-jobi, Job's tears, 62
Galium verum, lady's bedstraw, 78
Hierochloe odorata, sweetgrass, 85
Laurus nobilis, bay, 88
Lavandula, lavender, 90
Mentha, mint, 98
Nigella sativa, black cumin, 106
Ocimum, basil, 108
Origanum, oregano, 110
Papaver somniferum, opium poppy, 114
Perovskia atriplicifolia, Russian sage, 118
Pycnanthemum muticum, mountain mint, 132
Rosa rugosa, rugosa rose, 135
Ruta graveolens, rue, 139
Salvia, sage, 139
Santolina chamaecyparissus, 143
Solidago odora, goldenrod, 149
Tanacetum vulgare, tansy, 151
Viola odorata, violet, 160

PINK FLOWERS

Achillea, yarrow, 26
Allium schoenoprasum, chives, 34
Althaea, marsh mallow, 36
Arctostaphylos, bearberry, 42
Calamintha nepeta, calamint, 49
Dianthus caryophyllus, pink, 70
Echinacea, coneflower, 72
Echium lycopsis, bugloss, 72
Fumaria officinalis, fumitory, 78
Hyssopus officinalis, hyssop, 87
Geranium, cranesbill, 79
Hyssopus officinalis, hyssop, 87
Impatiens balsamina , garden balsam, 87
Malva sylvestris, malva, 94
Monarda didyma, beebalm, 102
Origanum, oregano, 110
Pelargonium, geranium, 116
Platycodon, balloon flower, 124
Poterium, salad burnet, 128
Pulmonaria, lungwort, 129
Pycnanthemum muticum, mountain mint, 132
Rosa rugosa, rugosa rose, 135
Salvia, sage, 139
Satureja hortensis, summer savory, 145
Satureja montana, winter savory, 145
Symphytum officinale, comfrey, 150
Viola odorata, violet, 160

WHITE FLOWERS

Achillea, yarrow, 26
Aconitum, monkshood, 26
Agastache foeniculum, anise hyssop, 28
Allium cepa, Egyptian onion, 31
Allium schoenoprasum, chives, 34
Aloysia triphylla, lemon verbena, 36
Anthriscus cerefolium, chervil, 41
Arctostaphylos, bearberry, 42
Calamintha nepeta, calamint, 49
*Calendula,*calendula, 51
Capparis spinosa, caper bush, 51
Carum carvi, caraway, 54
Cimicifuga racemosa, cohosh,, 60
Coffea arabica, coffee, 60
Colchicum autumnale, meadow saffron, 62
Coriandrum, coriander/cilantro, 64
Crithum maritimum, samphire, 64
Crocus sativus, saffron crocus, 67
Dianthus caryophyllus, pink, 70
Echinacea, coneflower, 72
Galium odoratum, woodruff, 78
Gaura lindheimeri, white gaura, 79
Hesperis matronalis, rocket, 82
Houttuynia cordata, houttuynia, 85
Hyssopus officinalis, hyssop, 87
Impatiens balsamina , balsam, 87
Iris germanica, orris root, 87
Lilium brownii, brown's lily, 92
Lippia graveolens, Mex. oregano, 94

Marrubium , horehound, 96
Matricaria recutita, chamomile, *97*
Melissa oficinalis, lemon balm, 97
Mespilus germanica, medlar, 101
Monarda didyma, beebalm, 102
Myrrhis odorata, sweet cicely, 104
Myrtus communis, myrtle, 104
Nashia, moujean tea, 104
Nepeta, catnip, 106
Nigella sativa, black cumin, 106
Ocimum, basil, 108
Origanum, oregano, 110
Origanum marjorana, marjoram, 114
Panax quinquefolius, ginseng, 114
Pelargonium, geranium, 116
Pimpinella anisum, anise, 121
Platycodon, balloon flower, 124
Polygonum odoratum, Vietnamese coriander, 126
Pulsatilla vulgaris, pasque flower, 130
Salvia, sage, 139
Sambucus canadensis, elder, 143
Satureja hortensis, summer savory, 145
Satureja montana, winter savory, 145
Stachys officinalis, betony, 149
Tagetes, marigold, 151
Thymus, thyme, 154

RED/ORANGE FLOWERS

Althaea, marsh mallow, 36
Asclepias tuberosa, butterfly, 44
Atriplex hortensis, orach, 45
Calendula, calendula, p,51
Carthamus tinctorius, safflower, 53
Dianthus caryophyllus, pink, 70
Hibiscus, hibiscus, 82
Impatiens balsamina , balsam, 87
Monarda, beebalm, 102
Poterium, salad burnet, 128
Punica, pomegranate, 130

BLUE/PURPLE/LAVENDER FLOWERS

Aconitum, monkshood, *26*
Agastache foeniculum, anise hyssop, 28
Agastache mexicana, Mexican hyssop, 29
Agastache rugosa, Korean hyssop, 29
Allium schoenoprasum, chives, 34
Amorpha canescens, leadplant, 37
Angelica archangelica, 38
Asarum canadense, wild ginger, 44
Baptisia australis, 45
Bletilla striata, bletilla, 47
Borago officinalis, borage, 47
Cichorium intybus, chicory, 60
Colchicum autumnale, meadow saffron, 62
Crocus sativus, Saffron crocus, 67
Cynara cardunculus, cardoon, 68
Dianthus caryophyllus, pink, 70
Echinacea, coneflower, 72
Echium lycopsis, bugloss, 72

Glycyrrhiza glabra, licorice, 81
Hesperis matronalis, rocket, 82
Hyssopus officinalis, hyssop, 87
Impatiens balsamina , balsam, 87
Iris germanica, orris root, 87
Lavandula, lavender, 90
Linum usitatissimum, flax, 94
Mentha, mint, 98
Monarda didyma, beebalm, 102
Nepeta, catnip, 106
Nigella sativa, black cumin, 106
Ocimum, basil, 108
Origanum, oregano, 110
Pelargonium, geranium, 116
Perovskia atriplicifolia, Russian sage, 118
Platycodon, balloon flower, 124
Polemonium, Jacob's ladder, 126
Poliomintha longiflora, Mexican oregano, 126
Prunella grandiflora, self-heal, 129
Pulmonaria , lungwort, 129
Pulsatilla vulgaris, pasque flower, 130
Punica, pomegranate, 130
Rosmarinus, rosemary, 137
Salvia, sage, 139
Satureja montana, winter savory, 145
Stachys officinalis, betony, 149
Succisa pratensis, devil's bit, 150
Symphytum officinale, comfrey, 150
Teucrium, germander, 152
Thymus, thyme, 154
Trachelium, throatwort, 157
Tulbaghia, society garlic, 157
Veronia, ironweed, 160
Viola odorata, violet, 160

YELLOW/GOLD FLOWERS

Achillea, yarrow, 26
Aconitum, monkshood, 26
Allium trioccum, ramp, 34
Aloe vera, aloe, 34
Althaea, marsh mallow, 36
Anethum graveolens, dill, 37
Anthemis tinctoria, marguerite, 38
Asclepias tuberosa, butterfly, 44
Atriplex hortensis, orach, 45
Brassica nigra, black mustard, 48
Calendula, calendula, 51
Carthamus tinctorius, safflower, 53
Chrysanthemum balsamita, costmary, 58
Crithmum maritimum, samphire, 64
Crocus sativus, Saffron crocus, 67
Dianthus caryophyllus, pink, 70
Ferula assa-foetida, asafetida, 75
Foeniculum vulgare, fennel, 76
Galium verum, lady's bedstraw, 78
Helianthus annuus, sunflower, 82
Hibiscus, hibiscus, 82
Humulus lupulus, hops, 86
Impatiens balsamina , balsam, 87
Isatis tinctoria, woad, 88
Levisticum, lovage, 92

Mandragora, mandrake, 96
Matricaria recutita, chamomile, 97
Pimpinella anisum, anise, 121
Ruta graveolens, rue, 139
Santolina, santolina, 143
Senecio aureus, liferoot, 146
Solidago odora, goldenrod, 149
Tagetes, marigold, 151
Tanacetum vulgare, tansy, 151
Viola odorata, violet, 160

RED/PURPLE/BRONZE FOLIAGE

Anthriscus cerefolium, chervil, 41
Arctostaphylos, bearberry, 42
Atriplex hortensis, orach, 45
Buxus sempervirens, boxwood, 49
Carum carvi, caraway, 54
Foeniculum vulgare, fennel, 76
Houttuynia cordata, houttuynia, 85
Ocimum, basil, 108
Perilla frutescens, perilla, 118
Rehmannia, Chinese foxglove, 133
Ricinus, castor bean, 133
Salvia, sage, 139

SILVER/GRAY/BLUE FOLIAGE

Allium schoenoprasum, chives, 34
Amorpha canescens, leadplant, 37
Anethum graveolens, dill, 37
Artemisia dracunculus var. sativa, French tarragon, 42
Baptisia, false indigo, 45
Borago officinalis, borage, 47
Calamintha nepeta, calamint, 49
Capparis spinosa, caper bush, 51
Celosia argentea, cockscomb, 54
Chenopodium botrys, ambrosia, 56
Coix lacryma-jobi, Job's tears, 62
Crithrum maritimum, samphire, 64
Cynara cardunculus, cardoon, 68
Dianthus caryophyllus, pink, 70
Fumaria officinalis, fumitory, 78
Gaura lindheimeri, white gaura, 79
Lavandula, lavender, 90
Linum usitatissimum, flax, 94
Marrubium , horehound, 96
Mentha, mint, 98
Nepeta, catnip, 106
Ocimum, basil, 108
Origanum, 110
Perovskia atriplicifolia, Russian sage, 118
Platycodon, balloon flower, 124
Poterium, salad burnet, 128
Pulmonaria, lungwort, 129
Pycnanthemum muticum, mountain mint, 132
Rosmarinus, rosemary, 137
Ruta graveolens, rue, 139
Salvia, sage, 139
Santolina chamaecyparissus, 143
Satureja hortensis, summer savory, 145
Stachys byzantina, 149
Thymus, thyme, 154

Achillea is included in herb gardens for its ancient herbal use. Today, it is loved for its vividly colored, long-lasting flowers: hybrids of *A. millefolium* come in lavenders, reds, and pinks; *A. filipendulina* and other species have produced yellow varieties. Among the most popular cultivars is 'Moonshine', shown above, which has lemon-yellow flowers that brighten the garden throughout the summer—and then dry beautifully for wreaths and dried flower arrangements.

ACHILLEA MILLEFOLIUM YARROW *Asteraceae (Sunflower family)*

PERENNIAL Yarrow is a hardy, weedy perennial native to Europe now commonly found growing wild in North America. It has been used medicinally for centuries—its ancient pedigree is clear from its generic name, *Achillea*: the Greek hero Achilles is said to have used yarrow to heal wounded soldiers at Troy. Today yarrow is grown for its lovely, flat-headed flower clusters and interesting foliage. The leaves and flowers have a distinctive aroma.

CULTURE Yarrow is easy to grow and can take much abuse. Select healthy stock with lots of growth from the center, or propagate from root division in spring or fall. Space plants 1-1½ feet apart in full sun and rich, well-drained soil. Yarrow does not like soggy ground or very humid air. Cooler growing temperatures yield a longer season of bloom. Fertilizer, frost protection, and mulching are not necessary for yarrow. Yarrow is sometimes bothered by a lace bug that leaves a stippling on the plant; if ignored, the bug departs without doing any serious damage.

Yarrow flowers are excellent for cutting and dry well, keeping good color and form. Harvest flowers for drying while in full bloom, before any brown shows. After blooming, cut flower stems as low as possible to encourage a second bloom in the fall. Foliage sometimes becomes unattractive by mid-July. Prune out yellow leaves and, if necessary, cut foliage back; new growth will fill in. Yarrow spreads quickly by runners and reseeds easily; deadhead before it goes to seed to control its invasive tendencies.

USES Yarrow is included in herb gardens because of its traditional medicinal use, but it is most popular for its flowers, which are used dried in arrangements; the growing plants are often used in landscaping.

VARIETIES Yarrow species grow from 18 inches to 5 feet tall. Common yarrow (**A. millefolium**) has feathery grayish-green leaves and, usually, white flowers. Other varieties have lavender, pink, and red blooms. Woolly yarrow (**A. tomentosa**) has fuzzy green, low-growing foliage and works well in rock gardens, while fernleaf yarrow (**A. filipendulina**) grows to 4 feet with deep green, fernlike leaves. Both have yellow flowers. Garden mace (**A. decolorans**) has spicy leaves that are used to flavor soups and salads. (MATTHAEI)

ACONITUM MONKSHOOD *Ranunculaceae (Buttercup family)*

PERENNIAL Monkshood gets its common name from the hooded shape of its large, showy blue flowers, similar to a monk's cowl. *A. carmichaelii* is native to the Szechuan region of China; it is used as a narcotic and as a topical anesthetic ointment in Chinese and homeopathic medicine, but it is too powerful for the home gardener to use. *A. napellus* is the source of the drug aconite; it was formerly used to make a deadly poison (Shakespeare's Romeo killed himself with a cup of it).

CULTURE Monkshood grows best in partial or full shade in a moist, rich soil. At the University of California Botanical Garden at Berkeley, in mild, foggy summers, gardeners are able to grow the plant in full sun. Start from rhizome divisions, planted in early spring about 1 foot apart and 3-4 inches deep;

ACHILLEA MILLEFOLIUM (YARROW) Plant 18 inches to 5 feet high with narrow, flat leaves up to 8 inches long, flowers in summer to early fall, flat flower heads up to 6 inches in diameter. Hybrids come in pinks, yellows, reds, and lavenders. Full sun. Zones 3-10. Not heat-tolerant.

ACONITUM CARMICHAELII (MONKSHOOD) Erect, clump-forming plant up to 4 feet tall with cleft, dark green foliage and purple flowers arranged in panicles. Flowers in late summer to early fall. Full sun to partial shade Zones 2-9. Not heat-tolerant.

ACORUS CALAMUS 'VARIEGATUS' (SWEET FLAG) Grassy plant 2-3 feet tall with ¾-inch-wide, 2-foot-long striped green and yellow leaves and thick, fleshy flower stalk. Sun or shade. Zones 3-10.

AGASTACHE FOENICULUM (ANISE HYSSOP) Branched plant 3-4 feet tall with serrated leaves and cylindrical spikes of blue flowers. Flowers late summer to early fall. Full sun to partial shade. Zones 5-9.

Aconitum napellus is the source of aconite, the poison Romeo used to kill himself. *Above:* 'Bicolor', a particularly attractive hybrid. 'Alba', a white form, is also available.

plants started from seed will take 2-3 years to flower and germinate sporadically. Monkshood must be kept moist, so mulch it. Fertilizer applied as the growing season begins is beneficial and will keep the plants growing vigorously. At season's end, cut plants back to the ground.

VARIETIES Both *A. carmichaelii* and *A. napellus* grow to 4 feet, so they are wonderful planted at the back of a bed. Since they usually flower in late summer and early fall, they are good choices for color in the fall garden. Wolfsbane (*A. lycoctonum*) has yellow flowers and is familiar from many folktales (old superstition held that it repelled werewoles). At North Carolina Botanical Garden, *A. napellus* grows well in shade, then flowers and dies; it must be repropagated or repurchased every year.

CAUTION Although *Aconitum* varieties are used in many medicinal preparations, they are extremely poisonous. (BERKELEY)

ACORUS CALAMUS SWEET FLAG *Araceae (Arum family)*

PERENNIAL Also known as calamus root, sweet flag grows wild in marshy areas of North America. Native to the Northern Hemisphere, it has narrow, reedlike 2-foot-high leaves and a thick, fleshy flower stalk. The entire plant has a spicy, lemony scent.

CULTURE Grow sweet flag in the marshy conditions it prefers: alongside pools, in bog gardens, in moist areas. Choose field-grown plants with strong, upright growth, or propagate by division of the rhizome. Set out in early spring 12-15 inches apart, in full or partial sun and moderately fertile loam. Sweet flag is not fussy; it will grow in a wide array of conditions, so long as it has moisture. It's very hardy. Only minimal pruning is required; cut back old flowers and leaves as they brown. Sweet flag is not prone to disease or insect problems. In Berkeley, it goes through a dormant period every winter.

USES In earlier times, sweet flag was used as a tonic to increase the secretion of gastric juices. Today, neither dried rhizome nor essential oil of sweet flag is allowed in food in the United States because the leading component of the essential oil is said to be carcinogenic. Dried rhizomes, however, as well as dried leaves are used in potpourris, and the dried seed heads are an interesting addition to floral arrangements. Native Americans of the Great Lakes region weave fragrant sweet flag baskets, and those of Penobscot, Maine, believed it had protective and healing powers.

VARIETIES For variegated sweet flag, grow **'Variegatus'** of either *A. calamus* (2-3 feet tall) or *A. gramineus* (Japanese sweet flag, 6-12 inches). The variety **'Pusillus'** is a dwarf, 5-inch plant that's good for massing. (SHIMIZU)

AGASTACHE FOENICULUM ANISE HYSSOP *Lamiaceae (Mint family)*

PERENNIAL This native plant goes by several other names: blue giant hyssop, fennel giant hyssop, fragrant giant hyssop.

CULTURE Anise hyssop is easily grown in most garden soils, in full sun to partial shade. It can, however, be killed in heavy soil by wet winters, and mildew fungi can be a problem in hot, wet summers. Anise hyssop will bloom the first year from seed when started indoors in mid March. Transplant to the garden 18 inches apart after danger of frost is past, or sow directly in the garden in fall. You can also propagate from stem cuttings, taken anytime during the growing season, or division of clumps in the spring. To renew old plantings, divide every 3-5 years. Anise hyssop self-sows freely.

USES Anise hyssop is a versatile, useful garden plant. Use the fresh or dried strongly anise-flavored leaves as a tea or culinary seasoning. The abundantly produced edible spikes of blue-violet flowers are also anise-flavored and sweet; they are particularly good in fruit salad, make a beautiful addition to the perennial border, and dry well. Flowers and leaves are a good addition to potpourris, birds like the seeds, and the plant's abundant nectar yields an excellent honey. Native Americans used it medicinally and as a flavoring.

VARIETY There is a white-flowered cultivar named **'Snow Spike'**. (CORNELL)

AGASTACHE MEXICANA MEXICAN GIANT HYSSOP *Lamiaceae (Mint)*

PERENNIAL Though native to Mexico, this plant is not a true hyssop of the genus *Hyssopus*. Mexican giant hyssop will not survive below 23° F., which makes it hardy only in Zones 9 and 10. Its tubular rosy purple flowers appear on showy 4-inch-long spikes from late summer to frost.

CULTURE Mexican giant hyssop will grow in full sun in most garden soils. You can treat it as an annual, as it grows very easily from seed, and blooms the first year. Start seeds indoors in mid-March, and set out plants 12 inches apart. Plants can be dug, potted, and brought inside, or stem cuttings can be taken to keep over the winter.

USES The leaves of Mexican giant hyssop have a strong lemon-mint taste. Fresh or dried, they make a wonderful tea and are also a good culinary seasoning. The flowers make a flavorful addition to salads or punches and can be used as an attractive edible garnish. (CORNELL)

AGASTACHE RUGOSA KOREAN ANISE HYSSOP *Lamiaceae (Mint family)*

PERENNIAL Native to China, Japan, Vietnam, and Laos, Korean anise hyssop is similar to *A. foeniculum*. It is an attractive plant when in flower.

CULTURE Grow *A. rugosa* in full sun in a rich, moist soil. While the plant looks best with regular watering, it will tolerate slightly dry conditions. Start from seed sown in the fall, or propagate by cuttings early in the season. Houseplants can be set out in the early spring. If purchasing plants, look for healthy, well-rooted and -branched specimens with good foliage. Space plants 1½-2 feet apart. Mulch to conserve moisture. Regular applications of fertilizer throughout the growing season will keep plants looking their best. Left to itself, *A. rugosa* will grow 4-6 feet high; pinch back and prune if you want to restrain this growth.

USES Korean anise hyssop makes a nice anise-flavored tea and is an interesting seasoning on salads. Medicinally, it has been used to clear fevers and strengthen the stomach. (BERKELEY)

Anise hyssop *(Agastache foeniculum)* shown growing with fennel *(Foeniculum vulgare)*. These 2 plants have similar flavors.

AGASTACHE MEXICANA (MEXICAN GIANT HYSSOP) Branched plant 2 feet tall with oval leaves and 4-inch spikes of red-dish purple flowers. Flowers in summer. Full sun. Zones 9-10.

AGASTACHE RUGOSA (KOREAN ANISE HYSSOP) Erect plant 4-6 feet tall with oval leaves and spikes of purple flowers. Flowers in late summer to early fall. Full sun. Zones 5-9.

ALCHEMILLA MOLLIS (LADY'S MANTLE) Plant 1-2 feet tall with gray-green toothed leaves up to 6 inches wide and lime green flowers. Flowers in late spring to early summer. Full sun to partial shade. Zones 3-9. Not heat-tolerant.

ALLIUM CEPA VAR. VIVIPARUM (EGYPTIAN ONION) Plant 2-3 feet tall with cylindrical leaves and white flowers. Full sun. Zones 3-9.

ALCHEMILLA MOLLIS LADY'S MANTLE *Rosaceae (Rose family)*

PERENNIAL The Latin name *Alchemilla* means "little magical one," a reference to the plant's purported magical properties. The common name comes from the similarity of the herb's leaves to the scalloped edge of a cloak. Lady's mantle is native to Europe.

Today, low-growing lady's mantle is popular as an edging plant, its leaves spilling out attractively over walks or paths. It combines well with purple-leafed plants, such as bronze fennel and throatwort, and fits neatly under tall herbs like angelica. It is particularly lovely after rainfall.

CULTURE Lady's mantle is easy to grow. Propagate by root division, or purchase healthy clumps with many dense, fresh, clean leaves. Established plants seed themselves readily, and seedlings transplant or weed out easily. Set out plants in spring, 1-1½ feet apart. Leaves of transplants may wilt but will be quickly replaced by fresh new leaves. Lady's mantle looks best grown in rich, moist soil with partial shade, although it will tolerate other conditions (it thrives in full sun at Cornell Plantations). Deadheading keeps the plant looking its best and prevents overseeding. A monthly application of a high-nitrogen fertilizer is beneficial, but not necessary in most garden soils. Lady's mantle seems to have few diseases or pests. Plants will go semidormant in mild climates, dormant in harsher areas (such as Cornell) but no frost protection is required.

USES Although lady's mantle makes an excellent dried flower, its primary reason for inclusion in the herb garden is its many traditional medicinal uses—the fresh root was used to stop bleeding, and a tea made from its leaves was taken to cure disorders of the female reproductive organs and as a heart tonic.

VARIETY *A. alpina,* a smaller species, is suitable for the rock garden.

ALLIUM ONION *Liliaceae (Lily family)*

The onion family consists of over 400 species, most of them rhizomes or bulbs, and most having a strong odor and flavor. Many members of this family also produce delicate flowers. Chives, shallots, and garlic are all widely used in cooking and have long held a place in the herb garden.

ALLIUM CEPA VAR. VIVIPARUM EGYPTIAN ONION *Liliaceae (Lily family)*

PERENNIAL Egyptian (also called top, multiplier, tree, and walking) onion seems to grow in reverse. It produces small bulblets on top of its flower stems; its vertical stems make it an attractive landscape plant. The origins of this Lily family member are unknown; the plant is known only in cultivation.

CULTURE Egyptian onion will tolerate partial shade, but does best in full sun and a rich, well-drained, moist soil. To start, plant the bulblets from the stem tops in the summer after they form, setting 12 inches apart. Left to themselves, the top-heavy stems will eventually fall to the ground, and the bulblets will root and sprout shoots. You can divide these up and move them to a new spot. You can also plant the individual bulbs that form in the soil, or divide established clumps in the spring (this should be done every 3-4 years to renew old clumps). Cut back yellowed old stems that have fallen to the ground; a new flush of fresh greens will grow.

Garlic plants (above) are tall and leafy and have edible, coiled white flower heads. Although they are attractive, they do emit a strong odor that some people do not like. Garlic is reputed to repel pests from other herbs and vegetables; although this is a widely accepted theory, it has never been scientifically proven. Recent medical studies have shown that garlic prevents a number of diseases and reduces blood cholesterol levels if eaten raw or taken as garlic-oil capsules. Although it may not prove to be the panacea that some people are hoping for, this plant does seem to provide significant benefits.

ALLIUM FISTULOSUM (WELSH ONION) Multiple shoots with many flowers. Plant in early spring for summer harvest. Full sun. Zones 3-9.

ALLIUM SATIVUM VAR. OPHIOSCORODON (SERPENT GARLIC) Flower stalks 2-4 feet high form a tight coil; spreading, broad green leaves, rounded cloves. Matures in spring and fall. Full sun. Zones 3-9.

ALLIUM AMPELOPRASUM (ELEPHANT GARLIC) Tall flower stalks with large, showy, white flowers; 4-6 very large cloves. Full sun. Matures in spring and fall. Zones 3-9.

ALLIUM SPHAEROCEPHALICON (ROUND-HEADED GARLIC) Large heads with many purple flowers on stalks 2½-3 feet tall. Full sun. Matures in spring and fall. Zones 3-9.

USES Young Egyptian onion plants can be harvested like scallions, pick bulblets after they develop but before they sprout. Use Egyptian onion leaves in
cooking for an onion flavor. You can pickle the bulblets, sauté them whole,
cream them, or add them to sauces for a delicate onion flavor.
VARIETY *A. cepa ascalonicum* (shallot) produces small bulbs with mild onion flavor. They are often used as green onions, though they store well. (CORNELL)

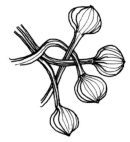

ALLIUM FISTULOSUM WELSH ONION *Liliaceae (Lily family)*
PERENNIAL Native to China and Japan, Welsh onions (also called Japanese
bunching onions) produce green-stemmed bulbs on hollow stalks from early
spring until frost. They are often used in place of onions.

Welsh onions produce seeds in their second year of growth. To propagate,
sow seeds or root cuttings. Welsh onions do best in rich soil, but will survive
in almost any type of soil; they will also tolerate shade. Plant in spring or fall,
but bulbs will not be produced until spring if the seed does not have time to
germinate before frost.

ALLIUM SATIVUM GARLIC *Liliaceae (Lily family)*
PERENNIAL Although garlic has long been cultivated and is widely naturalized,
its origins are uncertain. This bulb is made up of 4-15 bulblets, or cloves,
enclosed in a papery sheath.
CULTURE Garlic will grow in partial shade, but it produces the biggest bulbs in
full sun, in rich, deep, moist, well-drained soil. To plant, split a bulb apart and
set individual cloves 2-4 inches deep and 4-6 inches apart in the fall or earliest
spring. The further apart they are set, the bigger the bulbs will be. Keep
weed-free, and water during dry weather. Cut off or bend back flower stalks
as they form; this hastens development and promotes larger growth of bulbs.
According to some sources, garlic is a valuable companion plant, as it repels
many insects on a variety of vegetables and even blackspot and mildew on
roses. To harvest, dig bulbs after the leaves wither, in late summer or early fall.
Spread bulbs out and dry in the shade for several days. Then braid leaves
together and hang, or remove leaves and store bulbs in an old nylon stocking
or net bag. Store in a cool, dark, dry place.
USES Crushed and chopped cloves are widely used in cooking, and the green
leaves can be finely chopped and added to salads. Garlic has the reputation of
warding off colds and flu if eaten regularly, and also has antiseptic properties.
VARIETIES *A. s.* **var.** *ophioscorodon* (serpent garlic) is an interesting variety. Its
flower scapes form 1 or 2 coiled loops before the flowers develop; the loops
gradually straighten out. The cloves have a milder flavor.
A. ampeloprasum (elephant garlic–also called great-headed garlic, wild leek, and
Levant garlic) is native to Europe, North Africa, and Asia. Its flower scapes
grow to 3 feet or more, with many rose-pink flowers in large spherical heads.
Elephant garlic produces giant bulbs that are distinctly milder than those of
A. sativum. When planting elephant garlic, space cloves 1 foot apart. (CORNELL)
A. sphaerocephalicon (round-headed garlic) is useful in cooking and is also deco-

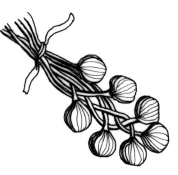

Braided garlic is traditional, practical,
and decorative. Hang the plant,
including its stalks, until it is fully dry.
Then braid as shown; the garlic will
retain its flavor for months if hung in
a cool, dry area.

You pay homage when and where you can. I love the smell of the bulb as the earth opens and releases it in harvest, an aroma that only those who grow garlic and handle the bulb and the leaves still fresh from the earth can know. It is a smell richer and more vibrant than what most people think of as garlic. Anyone who gardens knows these indescribable presences—not only of fresh garlic, but onions, carrots and their tops, parsley's piercing signal, the fragrant exultation of a tomato plant in its prime, sweet explosions of basil. They can be known best and most purely on the spot, in the instant, in the garden, in the sun, in the rain. They cannot be carried away from their place on the earth. They are inimitable. And they have no shelf life at all.
FROM *A GARLIC TESTAMENT*, BY STANLEY CRAWFORD

Above: Chives

rative. Large heads with many purple flowers are produced on tall stalks, 2½-3 feet high. Mass plantings add great form and color to any herb garden. If you allow the seed heads to ripen, the plant will reseed itself. (BERKELEY)

ALLIUM SCHOENOPRASUM CHIVES *Liliaceae (Lily family)*
PERENNIAL Chives, native to Europe and Asia, grow in clumps, with numerous long, thin, grasslike and hollow leaves. Small, round lavender flowerheads appear on tall stalks in early summer. Plants are decorative, making a good border, and are good companions to carrots, grapes, roses, and tomatoes. According to some gardeners, they repel Japanese beetles and black spot on roses, scab on apples, and mildew on cucurbits; this has not been proven.
CULTURE Chives tolerate a wide range of growing conditions, accepting full sun to partial shade. Sow seed in spring, indoors or out, or divide existing clumps every 3-5 years in spring or fall. Space plants 12 inches apart. Chives self-sow prolifically; cut off seed heads before they mature to control this. When harvesting, snip leaves off to just above ground level; they do not dry well–preserve by chopping and freezing. Chives make good windowsill plants, as they do not die down or go into dormancy. Pot up a clump anytime during the growing season, or pot volunteer seedlings in late summer or early fall. Indoor chives need at least 5 hours of direct sunlight or 12 hours of bright artificial light per day and will not produce as prolifically as those grown outdoors.
USES Chopped leaves are added to salads, sauces, soups, and spreads, imparting a mild onion flavor; they can also flavor vinegar. Flowers are attractive and flavorful sprinkled on salads and soups. Leaves produce a yellow or yellow-green dye of excellent fastness. Cut flowers are attractive fresh or dried.
VARIETIES *A. schoenoprasum* **var.** *sibericum* (giant chives) is taller, and has a more robust flavor. *A. tuberosum* (garlic chives, also known as Chinese chives, Oriental garlic, Chinese leeks, and gow choy) are taller than regular chives, with numerous star-shaped white flowers that appear in late summer and early fall. Cut flower stalks before seeds mature, or a multitude of seedlings will sprout and can become a nuisance. The leaves have a mild garlic flavor. Seed stalks can be used in dried arrangements, but should be allowed to dry thoroughly to avoid a strong odor. (CORNELL)

ALLIUM TRICOCCUM RAMP *Liliaceae (Lily family)*
PERENNIAL Ramp, native to the moist woodlands of eastern-to-midwestern North America, has a potent odor; it is used to flavor wild game. These small rhizomes spread slowly. They do best under light shade, in acid soil, with a mulch of compost. They need to be watered only during dry spells.
CAUTION Ramp resembles poisonous lily of the valley. Do not confuse them.

ALOE VERA ALOE *Aloeaceae (Aloe family)*
PERENNIAL Aloe—a striking plant native to tropical and semi-tropical regions of Africa and the Mediterranean—has been used as a healing plant since the Greek and Roman eras. This easily-grown pot plant is often found on win-

ALLIUM TUBEROSUM (CHINESE CHIVES) Clumps of long thin leaves, 2-3 feet tall with star-shaped white flowers in late summer or early fall. Full sun. Zones 3-9.

ALOE VERA (ALOE) Gray-green toothed rigid leaves, 1-2 feet long, forming rosettes 2-3 feet tall, 1½-2 feet wide. Yellow flowers in spring and summer. Full sun or partial shade. Zones 9-10. Heat-tolerant.

ALOYSIA TRIPHYLLA (LEMON VERBENA) Plant 3-5 feet tall (taller if grown outdoors in warm climates) with willow-shaped leaves; small white flowers from summer to fall. Full sun. Zones 9-10; usually grown as an annual or indoors.

ALTHEA OFFICINALIS (MARSH MALLOW) Tall, thick stems, 5 feet tall, with heart-shaped leaves 6-8 inches long and red, pink, yellow, or maroon flowers 3-5 inches long. Double forms are available. Flowers in summer and early fall. Full sun. Zones 2-10. Not heat-tolerant.

Hollyhock is often confused with *Althaea;* it is closely related, but is actually *Alcea officinalis.* Hollyhock has been used to soothe bee stings, but is not as important medicinally as marsh mallow. 'Nigra', an almost-black cultivar, is shown above.

dowsills, within easy reach for use on minor cuts and burns.

CULTURE This rampant grower can be grown as a pot plant if good friable soil and a pot with good drainage are available. Indoors, a sunny window is best, but this tough plant will withstand less than optimum conditions. It is best to water pots well, and then allow the soil to dry out almost completely between waterings. Occasional fertilizing with an all-purpose houseplant fertilizer encourages good growth. Repot and divide once a year to keep size manageable. Aloe can be grown outdoors, but only in areas with very mild winters. Aloes relish a summer outdoors where the pot can be sunk into a sunny situation for an accent plant in a herb garden.

USES Widely used in skin-care products, aloe is a fine remedy for minor burns and skin irritations, insect bites, and poison ivy. Simply cut off a portion of a leaf and apply the aloe juice to the affected skin. Aloes are used widely for their moisturizing and softening properties. (MINNESOTA)

ALOYSIA TRIPHYLLA LEMON VERBENA *Verbenaceae (Verbena family)*

SHRUB Lemon verbena, sometimes called "queen of the lemons," is a tropical shrub native to Central and South America that was introduced to Europe by Spanish explorers. It is widely grown in gardens, greenhouses, and homes for its unparalleled fresh lemony scent and essential oils.

CULTURE In warm climates, lemon verbena is grown in the garden year-round, in full sun and a rich, moist, humus-rich soil. It makes a sizable shrub, forming a good background for other herbs. Pinch tips to keep plant full and bushy. Feed regularly every 2 weeks from late winter through summer with a liquid fertilizer. Lemon verbena is hardy to 10° F.; in areas where winter temperatures drop lower, it's grown in a tub and brought indoors during the cold season; prune branches back when bringing it in. Since the leaves will drop off after the plant is returned to the house, pick them first for use in potpourris, sachets, and teas. New leaves will come in late winter; until then, keep in a cool spot and water sparingly. Grown indoors, lemon verbena has yellow-green foliage; outdoors, gray-green.

Lemon verbena is usually propagated by stem cuttings of half-ripened wood taken in summer before flowering. It is quite susceptible to whiteflies and red spider mites, especially in the greenhouse. As a preventive measure, wash the foliage weekly with lukewarm water. With proper care—a sunny window and a weekly shower bath—lemon verbena will live a long time as a houseplant, imparting its delightful scent to your home.

USES In addition to its fragrant essential oils, which are used for perfumes, herbal baths, powders, soaps, and potpourris, lemon verbena also makes an excellent hot or iced tea, alone or mixed with other herbs. Fresh leaves can be used in flavoring salads, jellies, and desserts. (MATTHAEI)

ALTHAEA OFFICINALIS MARSH MALLOW *Malvaceae (Mallow family)*

PERENNIAL Marsh mallow is striking, with full, lobed foliage and flower spikes to 5 feet tall. It's a favorite of visitors to the herb garden at Matthaei

Botanical Gardens because of the large flowers and unusual seedpods. Native to Europe, it is now naturalized in moist areas in the eastern United States.
CULTURE Marsh mallow is easy to grow. It starts well from seed or from root divisions taken in the fall. It needs full sun and likes poor, light soil that's moist to wet. It does not like hot, dry summers or clay soil. (Although it tolerates clay soil at Berkeley as long as it is kept moist. And it grows in the heat at North Carolina Botanical Garden, though not as lushly.) Space plants 2 feet apart; because of its size, a single specimen may be sufficient. Marsh mallow is very hardy, dying back to the ground for the winter, and is not bothered by insects or disease. It tends to get shabby-looking by late August; prune back as seeds form. Larger plants need support from string and a ring of stakes.
USES Marsh mallow has many uses, historical and current. The original marshmallow confection was made from the plant root. Young, tender leaves can be added to salads, and roots can be boiled, then fried with butter and onions. Medicinally, marsh mallow was valued for its soothing qualities–for irritations and inflamations of the skin, throat, eyes, lungs, and urinary organs; the name *althaea* comes from a Greek word meaning "to cure." (MATTHAEI)

AMORPHA CANESCENS LEADPLANT *Fabaceae (Pea family)*

SHRUB Also known as false indigo, this is an attractive, drought-tolerant herb with deep roots, silvery gray foliage, and clusters of small, deep-red-violet flowers. It blooms from July to September throughout the Great Plains.
CULTURE Leadplant is an easy plant to grow, provided you don't kill it with kindness. It prefers full sun and moist, well-drained soil and grows from 2-5 feet tall depending on amount of moisture.
USES Leadplant was used for its astringent qualities by many Native Americans. Its flowers can be dried for use in everlasting bouquets. (NEBRASKA)

ANETHUM GRAVEOLENS DILL *Apiaceae (Parsley or Carrot family)*

ANNUAL Dill, native to southwestern Asia and the Mediterranean, is grown mostly for the many culinary uses of its leaves and seeds; but its feathery foliage and tall, broad flower heads make it an attractive garden plant as well. Standard dill reaches 3 feet in height; newer varieties are shorter.
CULTURE Grow dill from seed sown directly in the garden in early spring, with seedlings thinned to 6-18 inches apart. Dill seeds itself readily, coming up year after year, but it doesn't transplant well because of its long taproot. Because dill doesn't last long, going to seed quickly, resow every few weeks throughout the season for a steady supply. Dill needs full sun and a rich, well-drained, slightly acidic soil. Water regularly, especially in the heat of summer. For best leaf production, keep flower blooms cut off. Preserve leaves by freezing; they lose flavor quickly when dried. Harvest seed heads just before they turn brown, placing them in paper bags until the seeds drop. In very hot climates, like that of the North Carolina, sow seeds in early spring and late summer for a fall crop; midsummer crops do not germinate well.
USES Dill is used in a great many recipes, particularly sauces for seafood and

Dill (shown above with fennel) has served a number of purposes over the years, some of them contradictory. In the 18th century it was given to babies to lull them to sleep, and to small children to keep them awake in church. Further back in history, Romans fed it to gladiators to ease digestion, and one herbal stated that chewing dill seed "aswageth the blasting and griping torment of the stomach."

ANGELICA

Like a surprising number of plants, angelica was unknown to the ancients. Although found in the northern and temperate regions of Europe and eastward all the way to the Himalayas, it does not seem to have attracted attention until the 15th century and first appeared in European herbals in the early 1500s. Its name reflects the legend that an angel revealed its special virtues to a monk during a time of plague. Angelica wasn't believed to cure the plague but protect against it; a piece of root was held in the mouth as an antiseptic. In Germany it was known as the root of the holy ghost and was believed to eliminate the effects of intoxication and also render witchcraft harmless. In England, where it was also known as bellyache root, dried angelica roots were made into a powder and mixed into wine to "abate the rage of lust in young persons." The plant was also given symbolic qualities: angelica stands for magic and poetic inspiration. Angelica is used in perfumery and is the source of a yellow dye. Its stalks are also eaten: raw in Lapland, blanched and served on buttered bread in England. The stalks have long been candied as a confection (known as angelica), and angelica is used in the liquor industry in gin, chartreuse, Benedictine, and vermouth. A sweet, fortified wine made in California is known as Angelica, but this probably relates more to angelic effects than to any herb's flavor.

poultry. Green seeds can be used in salads. Mixed with fennel and caraway seeds, it makes a fine after-dinner "mint" and aids digestion.
VARIETY Slow-bolting **'Tetra'** does well even in hot climates. (MATTHAEI)

ANGELICA ARCHANGELICA ANGELICA *Apiaceae (Parsley or Carrot family)*
BIENNIAL OR SHORT-LIVED PERENNIAL A tall, dramatic native of Europe, Asia, and Greenland, angelica has stout hollow stems, striking foliage, and very showy green flowers in rounded clusters borne over a long season.
CULTURE A hardy, sturdy plant, angelica requires moisture but no other care. Grow in partial to full shade in moderately rich, moist soil. Shelter plants from hot afternoon sun. Start from fresh seed, no more than 3 months old; collect ripe seed in late summer and sow in early autumn. Transplant in early spring before the taproot becomes established. Space plants 3 feet apart. Add mulch and water as needed to keep soil moist but not soggy. Biennial angelica produces foliage the first year and stems and flowers the second. It dies back in the winter (no frost protection is necessary). You can extend the life of the plant by cutting flowers before seeds form. Angelica is not bothered by weeds; it grows well in the wild surrounded by other plants. Pruning is not necessary, but remove lower leaves if they wither.
USES All parts of this aromatic plant are used fresh, as teas, in salads, as a flavoring, and candied. The roots and fruits yield angelica oil, which is used in perfume, confectionery, medicine (especially Asian medicine), and as a flavoring for liqueurs (such as angelica).
VARIETY *A. gigas* (Korean angelica) is an exquisite ornamental introduced to the United States in the early 1980s. All parts are a rich purple, including the deep-toned flowers. It's an excellent contrast for finely textured tall grasses and combines well with colorful perennials. (BERKELEY)

ANTHEMIS TINCTORIA DYER'S MARGUERITE *Asteraceae (Sunflower)*
PERENNIAL *Anthemis* is also known as golden marguerite and yellow or dyer's chamomile–"chamomile" because it's related to the perennial form of that herb, *A. nobilis* (now called *Chamaemelum nobile,* see page 55); and "dyer's" because its flowers yield a distinctive yellow dye, and its foliage a pale green dye. Its large, solitary flowers display in many shades of yellow, and its finely divided leaves have an unusual acrid odor. The plant is native to Europe. Dyer's marguerite is an excellent ornamental, covered with richly colored flowers, well-suited for cutting from June through late October.
CULTURE *A. tinctoria* grows best in full sun, in any well-drained, fertile, moist soil. While this is a perennial herb, the center of the plant tends to die out as it becomes increasingly mature. To maintain best appearance, treat this as an annual, allowing it to self-sow or dividing it yearly. Purchase young, well-branched plants free from any center dying out, and set out in spring. Or start from seed sown in late summer or early fall. If you wish to select for a certain color, propagate by cuttings. The plants will get fairly large and bushy, so space 1-2 feet apart. A mulch will keep out weeds, and a fertilizer applied at

AMORPHA CANESCENS (LEADPLANT) Shrub 2-5 feet tall with gray compound leaves and spikes of violet flowers 3-6 inches long in summer. Sun or partial shade. Zones 2-8.

ANETHUM GRAVEOLENS (DILL) Lacy, blue-green plant 3-5 feet tall (some new varieties are shorter) with clusters of yellow flowers on hollow stems. Flowers summer through early fall. Full sun.

ANGELICA ARCHANGELICA (ANGELICA) Imposing plant 4-6 feet tall with compound leaves and umbels of small greenish-white flowers. Flowers in summer. Full sun or partial shade. Zones 4-9.

ANTHEMIS TINCTORIA (DYER'S MARGUERITE) Strong stems 1 1/2-3 feet tall with finely dissected green leaves and bright yellow flowers 1½ inches long. Flowers in late spring to early fall. Full sun. Zones 3-10. Not heat-tolerant.

ANTHRISCUS CEREFOLIUM (CHERVIL) Plant up to 12 inches tall and 18-24 inches wide with fernlike, bright green leaves. Cool-weather annual. Full sun or partial shade.

APIUM GRAVEOLENS 'PAR-CEL' (CUTTING CELERY) Plant 2-3 feet tall with leaves that taste like celery. Full sun. 60 days to maturity.

ARCTOSTAPHYLOS UVA-URSI (BEARBERRY) Evergreen shrub or ground cover with small leaves that turn red in fall, pinkish flowers in spring, and bright red berries in summer. Partial shade. Zones 2-7.

ARTEMISIA ABSINTHIUM 'POWIS CASTLE' (WORMWOOD) Bushy plant 2-3 feet tall with feathery silver-gray foliage forms a mound 2-3 feet wide. Foliage grows in summer. Full sun. Zones 4-10. Not heat-tolerant.

regular intervals during the growing season will keep the plant flowering over a longer period. If you allow plants to dry out to the point of wilting, they will look ragged and unsightly. Although dyer's marguerite is very resistant to disease, it is sometimes susceptible to aphids. At The New York Botanical Garden, this plant is fertilized only once a season, if at all; gardeners find that it keeps a stronger, less floppy shape and reflowers more abundantly when deadheaded, and grows to about 2½ feet tall and wide after a few years.

USES Dyer's Marguerite is a source of yellow and pale green dyes. (BERKELEY)

ANTHRISCUS CEREFOLIUM CHERVIL *Apiaceae (Parsley or Carrot family)*

ANNUAL Chervil is an attractive garden herb, grown for its lacy, fernlike foliage that resembles anise or parsley in taste. Native to Europe and western Asia, chervil makes a neat edging and a fine container plant, with tiny white flowers borne in clusters during the summer. The foliage and stems turn pinkish, then red, in the fall.

CULTURE Grow chervil in filtered shade in warm climates, full sun in cool ones; it does not like to be baked in hot sun. Rich, light, well-drained garden soil is best. Sow seed directly in place in early spring or fall; choose seedlings with dark green leaves in sturdy rosettes. Thin seedlings to 9-12 inches apart. Young leaves, the most flavorful, will be ready to harvest in 6-8 weeks. For a steady supply, make several plantings a few weeks apart from spring through early fall. Keep flower clusters pinched out to encourage leaf production. If you leave a few flowers to mature, plants will self-sow. Harvest the outer leaves, and center leaves will continue to grow.

USES The subtly anise-parsley-flavored leaves are a refreshing, spicy addition to salads as well as soups, sauces, and egg dishes. They are an important ingredient in *fines herbes*, as chervil enhances the flavor of herbs it is combined with. While chervil can be dried or frozen, fresh leaves are most flavorful; in cooked dishes, add just before serving. (SHIMIZU)

APIUM GRAVEOLENS LEAF CELERY *Apiaceae (Parsley or Carrot family)*

BIENNIAL Leaf, French, or Chinese celery is sold as *A. g.* **var.** *secalinum* and *A. g.* **'Parcel'**. Its appearance and growth habit are similar to those of Italian parsley, and its foliage has the characteristic look and pungent taste of celery. Leaf celery is native to Europe and temperate Asia.

CULTURE Leaf celery is treated as an annual and is started fresh from seed each year. Give it full sun and a well-drained but moisture-retentive soil. Start seed indoors in early spring and transplant to garden after danger of frost is past. Space plants 10-12 inches apart, and keep well-watered in dry weather. Pick leaves as needed for fresh use; they do not dry well. It is grown without any problems under a variety of weather conditions at Cornell Plantations.

USES The leaves are used as a flavoring, especially for soups and stews, and a garnish. (CORNELL)

Many *Artemisia* varieties have silvery foliage that contrasts beautifully with more deeply colored plants. *Above: A.* 'Powis Castle' with purple asters.

The genus *Artemisia* was named for Artemis, goddess of the Moon, and is sacred to her because of its silvery foliage. The nearly 400 members of the species include the common sagebrush (*A. tridentata*), also called the big sagebrush, and the white sage (*A. ludoviciana*). Native Americans used these plants in purification ceremonies and tied them into bundles, sometimes along with other herbs, to form smudge sticks. *A. annua*, known as sweet Annie, is used dried in wreaths and flower arrangements. Harvested when flowering, the plant has a wonderful sweet, fruity fragrance. It is used in Chinese medicine, as is *A. sinensis,* which is dried and rolled into cigar-shaped sticks by the Chinese and used in the practice of moxibustion, which uses heat to treat the pressure points involved in acupressure and accupuncture. The sticks are lit and applied at the pressure points to produce a scab. (LISA CADEY, THE NEW YORK BOTANICAL GARDEN)

ARCTOSTAPHYLOS UVA-URSI BEARBERRY *Ericaceae (Heath family)*

SHRUB Also known as kinnikinick, this low-growing, trailing evergreen shrub reaches about 1 foot high; its rounded dark green leaves make it an attractive ground cover, although it grows slowly under less than ideal conditions. Its white bell-shaped flowers appear from May to July, followed by red berries in autumn that are supposed to be a delicacy for bears.

CULTURE Bearberry prefers a sandy or rocky acidic soil; its range is from Canada down to southern New Jersey. In the southern heat, it struggles and usually dies; it can be grown in a pot if given its preferred conditions.

USES Bearberry is used medicinally in problems of the urinary system and general toning of this system. Native Americans used its leaves in smoking mixtures, and made a tea from the berries. (NEW YORK)

ARTEMISIA DRACUNCULUS VAR. SATIVA FRENCH TARRAGON

Asteraceae (Sunflower family)

PERENNIAL Also known as estragon or "little dragon," for its serpentine roots, tarragon is prized for the distinctive, pungent flavor and aroma of its narrow leaves. Do not confuse French tarragon with regular tarragon, which is taller and more vigorous, but tasteless.

CULTURE Tarragon grows in full sun or partial shade. Well-drained soil is essential; it is less likely to survive the winter in poorly drained sites. Tarragon rarely flowers and does not set seed, so it must be propagated by division (in early spring, before new leaves are 4 inches high), by stem cuttings (in spring or summer; they root slowly), or by root cuttings in early spring or fall. Space plants 20 inches apart, and keep them bushy and erect by pinching back. To maintain vigor and flavor, divide established plants every 2-3 years in the spring. In cold areas tarragon needs a winter mulch applied after the ground has frozen. As a companion plant, tarragon is said to enhance the growth of most vegetables. To grow indoors, pot up a division in the fall and leave it outdoors in the cold for 2-3 months before bringing it inside. Indoors, provide 16 hours of lighting per day. Don't overwater; allow to dry out for a day or two between waterings. Apply half-strength fertilizer twice a month.

Tarragon suffers from fungal diseases. For this reason, well-drained soil is a must. Cuttings of French tarragon must be kept moist but never wet, and good air circulation is a must.

USES Tarragon is widely used in cooking. Leaves are best used fresh; cut sprigs as needed. If drying, handle carefully, as the leaves bruise easily and lose some flavor. You can also freeze whole sprigs. Do not confuse French with Russian tarragon (*A. dracunculoides*), which is grown from seed and has inferior flavor. *Tagetes lucida* (see page 151) is a substitute in warm climates.

VARIETIES Many other varieties of *Artemisia* exist; they are often used in the herb garden, but they are not culinary herbs. Wormwoods (**A. pontica** or **A. absinthium**) are members of the same genus and are used in dried arrangements, wreaths, and potpourris; they have been used medicinally since ancient times, and Dioscorides recommended them as a remedy for intoxication. **A.**

ARTEMISIA DRACUNCULUS VAR. SATIVA (TARRAGON) Plant 1-2 feet tall plant with supple stems and narrow blue-green leaves. Begins growth in late spring. Full sun. Zones 4-6.

ASARUM CANADENSE (WILD CANADA GINGER) Plant 6-8 inches wide with 6-inch heart-shaped leaves in pairs; brownish flowers in spring. Partial to full shade. Zones 2-9.

ASCLEPIAS TUBEROSA (BUTTERFLY WEED) Clump-forming stems, 1-2½ feet tall, with leaves 2-4 inches long and bright orange flowers in tight 2-inch umbels. Flowers in summer. Full sun. Zones 3-10. Heat-tolerant.

ATRIPLEX HORTENSIS (ORACH) Plant can grow to 4-6 feet tall and 2-3 feet wide but is usually smaller. Red, gold, and green varieties are available. Full sun.

DYES

The colors of the past–often very bright–were obtained using natural dyes made of plants, animals, and various naturally occurring minerals. The Chinese, Persians, and Indians used natural dyes many centuries ago, and the Egyptians created particularly brilliant colors. Among the earliest of these dyes was indigo, a blue color obtained from plants of the genus *Indigofera*–Egyptian mummies have been discovered wrapped in indigo-dyed cloth. Dyes like indigo were made by letting macerated plants ferment in vats. In some cases the dye required the use of a mordant, a chemical used to fix the dye in cloth. Cloth to be dyed would be treated first with the mordant and then the dye, or the mordant and dye could be applied together; changing the mordant changed the resulting color.

Opposite: The dye garden at the National Arboretum in Washington, D.C., contains many brightly colored annuals, including cosmos (which yields an orange dye when combined with a chrome mordant, yellow when a tin and cream of tartar mordant is used); marigolds (yellow); and zinnias (yellow).

lactiflora is the only species grown for its flowers; it looks nice in the back of a border. Many other artemisias have ornamental silver-gray foliage, including *A. ludoviciana* (white sage) and *A. stelleriana* (dusty miller). *A. schmidtiana* '**Silver Mound**' tolerates heat more than most varieties. (CORNELL)

ASARUM CANADENSE GINGER, WILD CANADA *Aristolochiaceae*

PERENNIAL This is not the tropical plant that produces the knobby root familiar in Oriental cooking, although it can be used as a substitute for that ginger. Native to North America, it grows from New Brunswick south to North Carolina and Missouri. It is a low-growing plant with large, glistening, heart-shaped leaves up to 6 inches across. The 1-inch purplish flowers are hidden under the leaves; finding them is a fun challenge for children.

CULTURE Wild ginger does best in partial sun in a woodsy or humus-rich soil that's slightly alkaline. It needs moisture to grow well, and favors the cool night temperatures of spring and fall. Propagate by root division in autumn, or set out purchased plants in early spring. Buy specimens with good, strong growth or, if it's too early in the spring for leaves to have emerged, strong crown and roots. Plant no more than 1 inch deep, and add a mulch of compost. Water while plants are establishing themselves and during periods of extreme drought. Few weeds will grow through established wild ginger. Slugs may be a problem in very moist conditions.

Wild ginger is a good, low-maintenance ground cover. It's an excellent choice for a shaded terrace or rock garden and for a naturalized garden.

USES This herb was used by Native Americans for its ginger flavor.

VARIETY *A. europaeum* (European ginger) is evergreen, with shiny, more leathery leaves than the Canada wild ginger. (SHIMIZU)

ASCLEPIAS TUBEROSA BUTTERFLY WEED *Asclepiadaceae (Milkweed)*

PERENNIAL Milky-juiced butterfly weed is native to North America. It is grown in the herb garden as an ornamental, notable for its brilliant orange flowers and attractiveness to butterflies, especially the monarch. It is seen along roadsides in many parts of North America.

CULTURE An undemanding plant, butterfly weed does not require fertilizing, frost protection, or pruning; it is drought-resistant; and it is seldom bothered by insects or disease. Start from seed in spring or fall, or purchase plants if available; once established, it will self-sow. Grow in full sun and sandy soil, spacing plants 12 inches apart. Because it has a taproot, butterfly weed does not transplant well. It's a good idea to mark where butterfly weed is planted, as there is no sign of it during the winter, and it comes up late in the spring. Plants grown in pots do not overwinter well outside. Sow either in late winter to plant in spring, or in summer to plant in fall. Spray with warm water to control spider mites; chemicals might kill butterfly larva.

Butterfly weed is most effective planted in masses and is especially pretty interplanted with Shasta daisies and orange cosmos.

USES Butterfly weed makes an excellent cut flower, and its long, slim seedpods can be dried in the fall for ornamental use. It was valued as a medicine by Native Americans, and continues to be used medicinally in illnesses of the respiratory system.

VARIETY New varieties now come in reds and yellows. ***A. incarnata*** (swamp milkweed) is a common perennial plant so beloved of the monarch butterfly and its larva that the insect is sometimes known as the milkweed butterfly. Like other members of the Milkweed family, the plant produces a milky sap. Growing 2-4 feet tall, swamp milkweed prefers a moist site and produces pretty umbels of soft pink or rose-colored flowers. Keep this plant from taking over your garden by picking the attractive pods (and using them in dried arrangements) before they burst open and release their fluffy seeds. (MATTHAEI)

ATRIPLEX HORTENSIS ORACH *Chenopodiaceae (Goosefoot family)*

ANNUAL Also known as mountain spinach, orach is grown for its tender young leaves. It grows to 6 feet and can be very ornamental, particularly the colored varieties. It is native to Asia and naturalized in North America.

CULTURE Orach requires a rich, moisture-retentive soil and full sun. It is best started from seed sown directly in the garden in late fall or early spring. Do not cover seeds with soil; they require light for germination. For a continuous supply of fresh, young leaves, make successive sowings every 2 weeks from spring through early summer. Pinch out flower heads as they appear to encourage growth of new leaves, and pinch plants back to promote bushiness. Irrigate freely during dry periods; otherwise, orach will bolt to seed. It self-sows profusely.

USES Young leaves can be eaten fresh in salads or cooked like spinach. They become tough and inedible as they mature. Orach is often cooked with sorrel to counteract sorrel's acid flavor. It also has a variety of medicinal uses and is the source of a blue dye.

VARIETIES *A. hortensis* has green leaves. For dark reddish leaves, plant **A. h. 'Rubra'**; for yellow green leaves, plant **'Aurea'**; for coppery leaves, plant **'Cupra'**. (CORNELL)

BAPTISIA FALSE INDIGO *Fabaceae (Pea or Pulse)*

PERENNIAL Also called wild indigo, this U.S. native grows in the wild in light woods and in open places where the soil is moist. With its lupinelike flowers, baptisia is a fine addition to the flower border, meadow, native plant garden,

Among the colors obtained from natural plant dyes are:

Plant	Mordant	Color
Dandelion	Alum	Light yellow
Dandelion	None	Purple, red
Elderberry	Alum	Blue, lilac
Elderberry	Chrome	Purple
Golden rod	Alum	Yellow , tan
Golden rod	Chrome	Old gold
Madder	Alum /tartar	Lacquer red
Madder	Chrome	Garnet red
Meadowsweet	Alum	Black
Nettle	Alum	Greenish-yellow
Nettle root	Alum	Yellow
Orach	Alum	Blue
Safflower	Alum	Yellow
Saffron	Alum	Yellow
Tansy	Alum	Yellow green
Thyme	Alum	Gray
Thyme	Tin	Yellow
Tumeric	Ash extract	Yellow
Tumeric	Citric acid	Brown
Tumeric	Safflower	Scarlet
Weld	Alum	Lemon yellow
Willow	Alum	Rose

BAPTISIA TINCTORIA (FALSE INDIGO) Bushy plant 2-4 feet tall with oval blue-green leaves and racemes of yellow flowers in early summer. Zones 3-10. Heat-tolerant.

BLETILLA STRIATA (BLETILLA) Underground bulb produces 3-5 pleated leaves 8 inches long with wiry stems with purple flowers. Flowers in early summer. Partial shade. Zones 8-10.

BORAGO OFFICINALIS (BORAGE) Plant 1½-3 feet tall with limp, oval gray-green leaves and very ornamental blue flowers. Full sun. Flowers in summer.

BRASSICA NIGRA (BLACK MUSTARD) Plant 4-6 feet tall with narrow leaves and branches of flowers followed by seedpods. Flowers in early summer. Full sun. Self-sowing annual.

or those sometimes difficult transitional areas between formal gardens and woodlands. The most popular and tallest species is **B. australis**, the wild blue false indigo. **B. tinctoria** is the source of a blue dye.

CULTURE Wild blue indigo performs best in full sun or just a little shade and favors deep, reasonably fertile, well-drained soil, with a light application of complete fertilizer in early spring to offset poorer soils. Start in the garden in spring or fall from seed; fall-sown seed will overwinter before germination occurs. Protect young plants with winter mulch the first season. Baptisias resent disturbance, so dig to propagate by division only when really necessary, in early spring before growth begins. Retain at least 3 eyes per division, and shorten the roots to 3-4 inches. Unless you want the fruits, you can shear the plants into rounded or domed shapes for a bulky shrublike design effect. Powdery mildew may be a problem in areas that are shaded or have poor air circulation.

USES In addition to its traditional use as a dye, indigo flowers are good for cutting, and the inflated seedpods are useful for dried arrangements. (MATTHAEI)

BLETILLA STRIATA BLETILLA *Orchidaceae (Orchid family)*

PERENNIAL Bletilla's straplike leaves arise from tubers, and it produces clusters of 3-6 orchidlike purple flowers with a yellow- and brown-spotted lip. The plant is native to China and Indochina.

CULTURE Bletilla grows best in partial shade in a well-drained, rich, moisture-retentive soil. Propagate by tuber division, or purchase plants with firm tubers, good growth, and undamaged leaves. Plant tubers just below the soil surface at the beginning of the growing season. A regular application of a balanced fertilizer will increase vegetative growth, which will also improve flowering. Keep plants well watered but not waterlogged. Cut off old leaves when the plants begin to go dormant, and cut back on the water when the plants go into dormancy. Bletilla will take some freezing; mulch if the ground will remain frozen for any length of time. Probably because it is native to an area in China with very high elevation, this is the hardiest of the orchids; it is not hardy in either Philadelphia or Michigan. At the The University of California at Berkeley Botanic Garden, it survived 3 days at 15° F. and a week at 23°.

USES The tuber is used in Chinese medicine as a remedy for external bleeding. (BERKELEY)

BORAGO OFFICINALIS BORAGE *Boraginaceae (Borage family)*

ANNUAL Borage is a highly ornamental garden herb. At the peak of its growth, the bushy, round plant seems enveloped by a blue haze, from the abundant clusters of sky-blue star-shaped flowers on its many-branched stems. This namesake of the Borage family is native to Europe, Asia Minor, and North Africa and has spread to North America.

CULTURE Borage grows best in full sun in fairly rich, light, porous soil. Sow seed directly in the garden after danger of frost, or earlier indoors in individual pots. (Some gardeners find it does not like to be moved; at Cornell

Bletilla, which is used in Chinese medicine, is one of the hardiest of orchids.

KNOT GARDENS

Although we usually refer to knot gardens as Elizabethan, they were actually first created by East Indian Moguls, who built them as part of their elaborate estates. Explorers brought the idea back to England in the middle of the 16th century, where gardeners at the physic gardens believed the tight patterns would protect the plants from cold. Simultaneously, gardens in Europe were becoming more highly designed, perhaps as a result of French monarch Charles VIII's love of Italian garden design, which incorporated parterres, tightly trimmed hedges, and plants that, according to one source, "ranged in regular lines," like soldiers at a procession. Cardinal Wolsey, who built Hampton Court for England's Henry VIII, entrenched the style by including elaborate knots in the landscape. Different styles of knots quickly became popular in France and England. French knot gardens were likely to be enclosed in sheared boxwood hedges and contained flowers as well as herbs; English knots often included hedges of fragrant lavender and rosemary that were used to dry linen; they were more geometric than the French versions. For more information on how to create a knot garden, see pages 176-77.

Plantations, borage has been started indoors and transplanted when small without any problems.) Thin or set plants 12-18 inches apart. Borage self-sows readily; be prepared for many seedlings in the fall (these will overwinter) and the following spring. Keep plants free from invasive weeds. Without a lot of trimming back during the summer, borage gets leggy. Cutting full heads when you want flowers encourages bushiness. By early September, plants are huge and straggly and will soon die down; remove them from the garden.

USES Borage seeds are a source of GLA (Gamma Lineolinic Acid), which is sometimes used to alleviate symptoms of premenstrual syndrome. Borage is a useful companion plant in the vegetable garden. It attracts bees needed especially for pollination of tomatoes, squashes, and strawberries. Flowers, stems, and leaves have a pleasant cucumber flavor. Young leaves can be cooked as greens or used in tea; the stiff white hairs will disappear. Flowers are ornamental in drinks and salads and make lovely candied decorations.

VARIETY 'Alba' is an attractive white-flowering form. (BERKELEY)

BRASSICA NIGRA BLACK MUSTARD *Brassicaceae (Mustard family)*

ANNUAL Native to Europe and Asia, mustard is widely naturalized in North America, where fields of its bright yellow flowers are a familiar early summer sight. While common mustards can be annoying weeds, *B. nigra*–along with white mustard, *B. hirta*–is grown commercially for its seeds, which are used in combination with other ingredients to make the well-known condiment.

CULTURE Start mustard from seed, sowing in the spring or, for a spring harvest of seeds, in autumn. Plants will self-sow freely and grow like weeds. Thin seedlings to 9 inches apart. Seedpods appear in late summer; collect seeds as soon as pods turn from green to tan, before the pods burst and the

seeds scatter. Air-dry seeds for a few weeks, then store.
USES Young leaves add a pungent flavor to salads and are sometimes cooked as strong-flavored greens. Seeds yield an oil that is a counterirritant; whole or ground, seeds are used alone or with other ingredients to flavor foods and produce the condiment.

BUXUS SEMPERVIRENS BOXWOOD *Buxaceae (Box family)*

SHRUB A broadleaf shrub with dense evergreen foliage, boxwood is native to southern Europe and Asia. Not itself an herb, it has been grown for centuries as a border and hedge, particularly as a low edging to establish orderly patterns in formal herb knot gardens.
CULTURE Boxwood will grow in full sun or partial shade; in hotter climates, it does best with partial shade. It needs well-drained soil but does not like drought. When purchasing plants, look for vigorous roots, lots of branches, and a healthy green color. Set out in spring or fall, spacing as appropriate for the variety. Apply a mulch of well-rotted manure (chicken manure is best) or leaf mold to keep roots cool. Be sure to scratch the mulch into the soil so that roots do not develop in this top layer. Do not surface cultivate, as boxwood has shallow roots. Trim back as needed to maintain the size and shape you want. Boxwood does not need supplemental applications of fertilizer or winter protection. Applying lime in autumn every 2-3 years can be beneficial.

To propagate boxwood, take stem cuttings in autumn and stick them in sand, or a well-drained cutting mixture, and place outside in a nursery or protected area over winter. They will root slowly.
VARIETIES Many varieties of boxwood are available. *B. sempervirens* (common boxwood) has dark green, glossy leaves. In mild climates, larger varieties grow in undulating mounds or tall hedges. The dwarf variety **suffruticosa** has been common in American herb gardens since colonial times; also called "edging box," it's the variety usually used in knot gardens. In northern climates, boxwood tends to brown out at the tips in the winter; some varieties even turn a ghastly yellow green. For these regions, the best boxwood to grow is *B. microphylla* **var. *koreana***, especially the cultivar **'Green Gem'**. This is a slow-growing, hardy dwarf plant (maximum size 2 feet) whose deep green foliage keeps its color throughout the winter. **'Kingsville Dwarf'** is a suberb small, slow-growing cultivar. **'Winter Beauty'** turns a wonderful bronze-red in winter. (MATTHAEI)

CALAMINTHA NEPETA LESSER CALAMINT *Lamiaceae (Mint family)*

PERENNIAL Growing 1-2½ feet tall, calamint makes an excellent border or edge-of-walkway plant, so its fragrance can be enjoyed. Its round-toothed leaves and white to pink flowers, borne on erect stems, blend beautifully with other garden perennials. It also grows happily in nooks and crannies and rock gardens. It is native to southwest and south-central Europe.
CULTURE Calamint is best started from cuttings. Once established, it is fairly short-lived for a perennial, but will reseed itself. Plant in early to mid spring, 12 inches apart, in a warm, sunny, well-drained site, in average garden loam.

BUXUS SEMPERVIRENS 'VARDAR VALLEY' (BOXWOOD) Evergreen shrub 2-4 feet tall with dark, shiny leaves 1-1½ inches long. Full sun, partial shade in warm climates. Zones 4-8.

CALAMINTHA NEPETA (LESSER CALAMINT) Bushy plant 1-2½ feet tall with toothed grayish oval leaves and small pink or white flowers. Flowers in summer. Full sun.

CALENDULA OFFICINALIS (CALENDULA) Plant 1-2 feet tall with glossy dark green long oval leaves and bright yellow-gold flower heads 1-2 inches long with many petals. Flowers spring and fall. Full sun to light shade.

CALENDULA ARVENSIS (FIELD MARIGOLD) Many-branched annual, 12 inches tall, 18 inches wide, with 1-inch golden, daisylike flowers. Full sun.

Calamint benefits from a mulch of sand or fine pine chips. Apply only low to moderate amounts of fertilizer or water. Cut back once or twice during the growing season; cut leaves can be used for making tea. Calamint has no notable disease or pest problems.

USES Calamint leaves are used to make tea. Romans rubbed the plant over meat to sweeten it; in medieval times, calamint was used to induce sweating and to calm colic. Edmund Spenser refers to it in *The Faerie Queen*: "The aged nourse had gathered rew and calamint."

VARIETIES A calamint with larger, more strongly toothed leaves and bright pink flowers is **C. grandiflora**. The variegated cultivar **'Bert's Beauty'** has an attractive mottled leaf that combines well with perennial flowers. (SHIMIZU)

CALENDULA OFFICINALIS CALENDULA *Asteraceae (Sunflower family)*

ANNUAL An old garden favorite also known as pot marigold, calendula is treasured for its free production of bright yellow and orange flowers over a long season. Gardeners at the U.S. Botanic Garden in Washington, D.C., have found that it does not like hot summers, so they use it as a spring or fall annual. Although calendula is originally from southern Europe, it is perfectly hardy in North America.

CULTURE Calendula is very easy to grow and makes a colorful border or edging. Sow seed in April or May in the North when the soil temperature is at least 60° F., in fall and winter in the South and Pacific Coast. Calendula seed holds its germination for only a year, so use fresh seed. Thin to 9-10 inches. Calendula will grow in almost any garden soil, doing best in full sun. Flowers begin to appear in June in the North and continue until hard frost. At North Carolina Botanical Garden, plants are cut back and usually rebloom in fall; they sometimes survive the winter. To keep it blooming freely, deadhead spent blossoms or make successive sowings. The flowers close at night and open again at dawn. If the ripened seeds are allowed to scatter, they will furnish a supply of new young plants at the beginning of the next season.

USES The young leaves of pot marigold can be eaten fresh in salads or cooked like spinach. The flower petals with their sweet and saline taste are used in salads, soups, teas, and as garnish. They are also used as a saffron substitute to color cheese, butter, rice dishes and cakes. The petals are used fresh or spread in a single layer to dry. The blooms make fine cut flowers. In Europe, calendula flowers are used for salves, lotions, shampoos, and baby products. (MATTHAEI)

VARIETY An interesting variation is **C. arvensis** (field marigold), an ornamental, many-branched annual that grows to 12 inches tall and spreads to 18 inches. It has dainty, golden, daisylike flowers 1 inch across, about ⅓-¼ the size of *C. officinalis* flowers. (CORNELL)

CAPPARIS SPINOSA CAPER BUSH *Capparaceae (Caper family)*

SHRUB The caper bush is a prickly shrub native to the Mediterranean region, with a rounded, slightly arching habit. Its lovely white flowers fade quickly but produce masses of showy red stamens. It can be grown as a container

Two of the most popular shrubs in the herb garden are *Buxus* (boxwood) and *Berberis* (barberry). Each comes in a wide range of sizes, from compact dwarf varieties to tall varieties that can be used as hedges. Barberry leaves are gold, green, or dark red; boxwoods are various shades of green. They can be used as backdrops, as edgings, and as accents. They have always been valued for their use in knot gardens.

CAPPARIS SPINOSA (CAPER BUSH) Bush 2-3 feet high with slightly upright, arching habit; blue-green leaves and white flowers with red stamens in summer. Zones 7-10.

CAPSICUM ANNUM (PEPPER) Low-growing bushy plant with bright green leaves and red, yellow, or green fruit ranging in length from less than 1 inch to 8 inches. Fruits mature in summer. Full sun.

CAPSICUM ANNUM 'LONG RED CAYENNE' (HOT PEPPER) Spreading plant produces twisted, pointed dark green and bright red peppers, 5 x ½ inches. Very hot. Yields 70 or more peppers per plant. Full sun. 70 days to maturity.

CARTHAMUS TINCTORIUS (SAFFLOWER) Branched plant 3 feet high with finely toothed leaves and round orange-yellow flowers in midsummer. Full sun.

plant and looks particularly nice with its branches cascading over a rock wall.
CULTURE In warmer regions, caper bush can be grown outdoors, but in
northern areas it needs the shelter of a greenhouse. It is happy in the rocky
soil of its origins and needs full sun and an average amount of water. To
keep it neat, cut back previous years' growth to 2-3 inches each winter.
USES Flower buds are picked when young and tender (before they are close
to opening), pickled in vinegar, and sold as capers. (BERKELEY)

CAPSICUM ANNUM PEPPER *Solanaceae (Nightshade family)*
PERENNIAL The sweet or hot, red or green peppers grown in the vegetable garden and used in the kitchen are native to warm areas of the Americas; the
small hot varieties are often grown in herb gardens. They are not related to
the ground black and white pepper we use for seasoning, which come from
Far East peppercorns. Peppers exist in a wide variety of sizes, shapes, colors,
and degrees of hotness. Small-fruited compact types are often grown as ornamental pot plants. All peppers are interesting additions to flower beds and
borders. Although often perennial in hot climates, peppers are most often
grown as annuals.
CULTURE Purchase seedlings from a nursery, or start your own from seed
indoors 8-12 weeks before the last spring frost. Wait several weeks after that
date to set plants outside. Choose varieties that are well adapted to your
growing conditions, especially cool or long and hot summers. While peppers
need hot weather to set fruit, flowers can drop in daytime temperatures over
90° F. or nighttime temperatures below 60° F. Space plants according to the
height they'll attain, which depends on your growing season. Keep well-
watered and also well-drained. Container plants will do well indoors.
USES Hot peppers are used as is and also dried and ground for a variety of culinary uses; they are also used in a topical cream for athritis pain.
VARIETIES Hot varieties useful for chili are **'Jalapeño'** and **'Long Red Cayenne'** and
the somewhat milder **'Anaheim'** and **'Hungarian Wax'**. An ornamental variety
'Purple Venuzuelan' has purple foliage, flowers, and fruit; if pinched back at 6
inches tall, they grow to a height of 2½ feet.

CARTHAMUS TINCTORIUS SAFFLOWER *Asteraceae (Sunflower family)*
ANNUAL Native to the Mediterranean countries, safflower (also known as false
saffron) is now widely cultivated around the world both for the oil extracted
from its seeds and for its flowers, which are used in dyeing and also as a substitute for the expensive flavoring saffron. Safflower's flowers and spiny-
toothed leaves give the plant a thistlelike appearance. It is a short-lived plant.
CULTURE Safflower is grown from seed. Its small woody root does not run deep
in the soil, so it is best to sow the seed where transplanting won't be necessary.
Plants prefer a warm, sunny spot with light soil and a fairly dry summer climate. Seed catalogs often offer "saffron" seed. This is actually safflower seed;
true saffron is a bulb, or corm. The orange-red flowers appear in July.
USES The flowers can be dried and powdered to make a saffron substitute;

mixed with finely powdered talc, they make a rouge. Fresh flower petals yield dye colors ranging from yellows to red. Flowers are also used as a scent in pot-pourris and look nice dried as well. (BERKELEY)

CARUM CARVI CARAWAY *Apiaceae (Parsley or Carrot family)*

BIENNIAL Caraway, native to Europe and western Asia, is now naturalized in North America. It produces a 12-inch mound of finely divided, carrotlike leaves the first season after sowing; these are hardy to Zone 3. Early the following summer, 2-foot flower stems appear topped by umbels of white flowers. Oblong seeds ripen in mid- to late summer, and then the plant begins to die.

CULTURE Full sun and deep, fertile, well-drained soil are best for caraway, although it will tolerate light shade and heavy soil. Because of its long taproot, it does not transplant well. Seed directly in the garden anytime from very early spring through late summer. Caraway self-sows readily. Space plants 6-12 inches apart, and water during dry periods. Watch for slugs and snails. Caraway does not grow well near fennel.

USES Caraway seeds have a licorice-flavored tang and are widely used in bread, cheese, cake, cookies, and many other dishes. You can add fresh young leaves to salads and soups, and the thick taproot can be prepared and eaten like parsnips or carrots. Cut stalks when seeds begin to turn brown, checking frequently to catch them before they fall. Dry in paper bags for a few weeks, and check for insects before storing. One large caraway plant produces about ⅓ cup of seed.

VARIETIES A newly available annual strain of caraway supposedly produces double the crop of the common biennial variety. Sown in March or April, its seeds are ready to harvest in August or September. Another benefit of this strain is that its seeds do not shatter when mature, making it easier to harvest. Tuberous caraway, or earth chestnut (**C. bulbocastanum**; sometimes sold as **Bunium bulbocastanum**) is grown for both its seeds (used like common caraway) and its bulbous, tuberous roots, which taste like chestnuts and are boiled and eaten like potatoes. You can harvest the roots in late summer or early fall from spring-sown seeds, or in the second season after you've collected the ripened seed. (CORNELL)

CELOSIA ARGENTIA CELOSIA, COCKSCOMB *Amaranthaceae*

ANNUAL Also known as quail grass, the cockscomb form of celosia gets its name from its dense, striking flower spikes, which are flat, like the comb of a rooster, or pyramid-shaped, with deep and wide flower heads. It is native to southern China, India, Sri Lanka, Africa, and the Americas. Since celosia flowers in late summer and fall, it's a dramatic addition for color, form, and texture late in the season.

CULTURE Celosia prefers full sun; although it will grow in any type of soil, it does best in rich, well-drained, moist soil. It grows easily from seed, best started in the fall. Seedlings will appear in the spring; thin to 1 foot apart. Mulch will help retain moisture, and fertilizer applied regularly during the growing season will keep plants looking their best. Leave plants in the garden until seeds have ripened and dropped to the ground, so you will have new seedlings next spring.

USES Flowers can be dried for everlasting bouquets. Chinese herbalists use the seeds for painful swollen eyes, blurred vision, and cataracts. (BERKELEY)

CHAMAEMELUM NOBILE CHAMOMILE *Asteraceae (Sunflower family)*

PERENNIAL A creeping herb, chamomile is native to the British Isles, western Europe, North Africa, and the Azores. Growing just 3-12 inches high (though sometimes up to 3 feet in cultivation), with small, daisylike flowers, the whole plant is fragrant. It has traditionally been planted as a lawn substitute or ground cover for walkways because the plant releases a sweet apple scent when crushed.

CULTURE Chamomile likes full sun and a light and well-drained soil with moderate amounts of water. It will grow well in partial shade, but will not flower as much. Set out transplants or seedlings in spring or fall, spacing 12-18 inches apart and adding a light mulch. Keep weed-free, and cut back old flowers.

While perennial chamomile makes a good ground cover, it does jump around a bit. Transplant seedlings in spring to the places you want the plant to grow. Chamomile is effective in combination with roses, and it's great planted in corners and containers, nooks and crannies. You can also grow a chamomile seat that will give off a wonderful apple fragrance when you sit on it. A chamomile lawn, however, tends to be difficult to keep; it will not succeed unless summers are cool.

USES Flowers and young leaves are used to make a tea that supposedly helps

HERBAL TEAS

Humans have been steeping fragrant leaves and flowers in boiling water to produce tea for many thousands of years. One version of the origin of tea holds that Confucius invented it so that his disciples would boil their water before drinking it. Dioscorides (c. A.D. 100) recommended the use of medicinal teas, and his advice was followed by later herbalists, such as Parkinson and Culpeper.

Hundreds of plants have been used to make herbal teas (which are also called tisanes); some, such as mints and lemon balm, for their flavor, some, such as chamomile and throatwort, for their soothing qualities. Many people prefer blends. Most parts of the plant–seeds, roots, leaves, berries, flowers, even twigs and branches–can be steeped for tea, but it is important to remember that many plants are poisonous: don't use a plant for tea unless you know it is safe. And don't use metal teapots or saucepans: use enamel or earthenware.

Among the herbs used for tea:
Agrimony: a tea substitute
Angelica: used with lemon and honey to treat colds
Basil: for digestive problems
Borage: a good "pick me up"
Catnip: used to treat colic
Clove: a nausea treatment
Costmary: used by colonists to make "Sweet Mary" tea
Dandelion used for tea and wine
Fennel: digestive problems
Hyssop: used for tisanes
Lemon verbena, lemon balm: make pleasing lemony teas
Nettle: sometimes mixed with ginger and hyssop
Rosemary: used in the treatment of headaches and colds
Sage: makes a full-bodied tea used as a tonic or for fevers
Thyme: once used to treat indigestion
Yarrow: popular with early settlers for a host of complaints

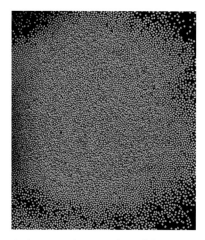

Quinoa, another member of the *Chenopodium* genus, is an important food crop in the Andes Mountains of South America. Its seeds can be eaten fresh, but are usually dried and cooked as a cereal. It thrives in the southern and southwestern United States, and many economists predict that it will become popular in the Northern Hemisphere in the coming years.

induce sleep. In former times, it was reputed to cure just about every ailment imaginable, and to keep other plants planted near it healthy as well. Annual chamomile, *Matricaria recutita,* is considered by some to be more effective.

VARIETIES 'Treneagne' does not bloom; **'Plena'** has double white blooms. (SHIMIZU)

CHENOPODIUM AMBROSIOIDES EPAZOTE *Chenopodiaceae (Goosefoot)*

SHORT-LIVED PERENNIAL Epazote is a standard, strong Mexican seasoning also known as American wormseed, Spanish tea, and Mexican tea; it is native to tropical America, now naturalized in North America, Europe, and Asia.

CULTURE Epazote is grown as an annual or short-lived perennial. In Zone 5 it persists 3 or 4 years, yielding a continual supply of self-sown seedlings. It is an attractive plant, with tiny green flowers borne in dense, leafy, drooping spikes during the summer. Grow epazote in full sun and well-drained soil, with plants spaced 12-24 inches apart. Sow seeds indoors or outdoors in early to mid spring. Epazote can also be grown as a container plant. Pick fresh leaves as needed throughout the summer after plants become established; you can also dry leaves on trays for storage.

USES Epazote's strongly scented, coarsely toothed leaves are irreplaceable in Mexican cooking, used for light seasoning and always added to beans soon after cooking begins to blend flavors well. Oil from the seeds was once used to expel intestinal parasites, hence the name wormseed. Caution: dosages of the oil can easily be toxic. A strong, nonedible "tea" made from the whole plant is used in tropical America to swab floors and porches as an insect and worm larvae deterrent. (CORNELL)

CHENOPODIUM BOTRYS AMBROSIA *Chenopodiaceae (Goosefoot)*

ANNUAL Also called Jerusalem-oak and feather geranium, ambrosia is native to Europe, Asia, and North Africa, but has naturalized in parts of North America. An intensely fragrant plant, its glandular hairs release essential oils when touched or crushed. Ambrosia was known as the food of the Greek gods; the word *ambrosial* means sweet-smelling or delicious.

CULTURE Ambrosia grows easily from its fine seed sprinkled on well-prepared, well-drained soil in a sunny place; thin seedlings to 12 inches. The annual plants will self-sow year after year, but ambrosia is not weedy.

USES A flower-arranger's friend, ambrosia develops graceful, arching plumes of golden flowers with feathery foliage that resembles miniature oak leaves. These 2-foot sprays make a nice foil in the garden for bright fall flowers and easily dry to a pleasing tawny shade when cut (after seeds develop) and hung for use in dried arrangements. Leaves and seeds can be used as a blender in sachets and potpourris. (CORNELL)

CHENOPODIUM CAPITATUM STRAWBERRY BLITE *Chenopodiaceae*

ANNUAL Also known as Indian paint, strawberry blite is native to Europe and now naturalized in North America. The fleshy, bright red, berrylike fruit clusters ripen in September from dense flower heads. The fruits have a flavor

CARUM CARVI (CARAWAY) Plant forms 12-inch mound of carrot-like foliage. Clusters of flat white blossoms appear during the second summer followed by seeds. Full sun to light shade. Zones 3-4.

CELOSIA ARGENTIA (CELOSIA, COCKSCOMB) Plant 3 feet tall with silvery-white leaves in erect or drooping spikes. Full sun. Flowers in late summer and fall.

CHAMAEMELUM NOBILE (CHAMOMILE) Creeping plant, 3-12 inches tall and 12 inches wide, with finely divided lacy leaves and small white daisylike flowers. Blooms in late spring through late summer. Full sun to partial shade. Zones 3-8.

CHENOPODIUM AMBROSIOIDES (EPAZOTE) Plant 2-3½ feet tall with coarsely toothed leaves. Full sun, partial shade.

NEW NAMES

Scientific nomenclature is the most accurate way of referring to plants; each plant is given a name that is accepted by the entire world. However, occasionally scientists discover that groupings within families were erroneous. New techniques of looking at plants produce information that makes it necessary to revise entire genera. This has recently occurred within the genus *Chrysanthemum.* Many plants that were grouped under this genus have now been separated into separate genera, including *Tanacetum* and *Leucanthemum. Chrysanthemum parthenium* is is now *Tanacetum parthenium* and *Chrysanthemum balsamita* is now *Tanacetum balsamita.*

somewhat resembling mulberries.

CULTURE Strawberry blite will grow in conditions ranging from full sun to partial shade. Sow seed indoors in mid to late April, or directly outdoors after danger of frost is past. Space plants 10-12 inches apart; it will self-sow.

USES Strawberry blite is grown for its edible leaves and fruit. The toothed, triangular leaves are eaten raw or cooked, like spinach.

OTHER SPECIES *Chenopodium bonus-henricus* (Good King Henry), also called mercury, shoemaker's heels, allgood, and wild spinach, grows best in full sun, but will tolerate light shade. It prefers deep, well-cultivated, fertile, humus-rich soil. Propagate by division, or sow seed indoors or outdoors in early spring; once established, the plant will self-sow. Space plants 12 inches apart. Water during dry periods to maintain succulent growth. Cut off spent flower spikes and old, yellowing foliage to promote fresh young leaf growth. Divide and replant every 5-6 years in early spring or fall. Allow plants grown from seed 1 year to develop before beginning to harvest. Good King Henry's coarse, arrow-shaped leaves are glossy and dark green and are eaten when young like spinach, raw or cooked. The flavor is blander than spinach, but the iron content is higher; leaves are also rich in vitamins. The flower spikes, which should be picked just as they begin to open, can be steamed and eaten like broccoli; the pencil-thick shoots, which should be cut below ground when 5 inches high, can be used like asparagus. (CORNELL)

CHRYSANTHEMUM BALSAMITA COSTMARY *Asteraceae (Sunflower)*

PERENNIAL Costmary is native to southern Europe and western Asia; its name is formed by the Latin word *costus,* meaning "fragrant root," and Mary–according to medieval legend, it was the balsam with which Mary Magdalene washed Jesus' feet. Costmary has small daisy-like flowers with white ray petals. Its leaves have a strong camphorlike scent.

CULTURE Costmary grows well in full sun in average, well-drained soil; once established, it does well in dry soil. It's best propagated by division of its rhizome; it also spreads rapidly via these rhizomes. Set out new plants in the spring when the ground is warm, spacing 1-2 feet. The plant dies back over the winter in cold climates, and comes back in the spring. Frost protection isn't needed. Costmary can be susceptible to chewing insects such as grasshoppers, but the damage is usually cosmetic, not life-threatening. Aphids on stem tips can be controlled with insecticidal soap.

This herb tends to get leggy and look unkempt, and its stems do not always remain upright. Keep the plant cut back, and grow it in an inconspicuous spot in the garden. At North Carolina Botanical Garden, the plant is not allowed to flower at all and remains attractive throughout the season.

USES Costmary is also known as alecost, because it was used in brewing ale, and as bible leaf, because leaves of the plant were used as bookmarks in Bibles and were chewed on during sermons for their stay-awake flavor. (MATTHAEI)

CHRYSANTHEMUM PARTHENIUM FEVERFEW *Asteraceae (Sunflower)*

PERENNIAL This bushy plant is native to southeastern Europe but is now found in North and South America. When parts of the plant are rubbed or crushed they give off a strong, bitter smell.

CULTURE Feverfew is easily started from seed. You can also propagate it by dividing established plants into fairly large pieces in March, or from cuttings taken from young shoots with a heel attached, planted out from October to May. Set plants about 1 foot apart. Feverfew is not a fussy grower, tolerating some shade, most soils, and dry (but not very moist) conditions. Feverfew plants are easily injured by hoes, so you should hand-weed. Because feverfew freely self-seeds, it is apt to escape from the garden; cutting off old heads will prevent this. To keep the plant's leafy growth looking neat, cut back hard, to within 1 inch of the base, before the season's active growth starts. Feverfew is very disease-free and has a lifespan of 2-3 years. In hot climates, it benefits greatly from partial shade.

USES Feverfew's common name comes from its traditional use to lower body temperature in fevers. Today, it's grown for the profusion of daisylike flowers it bears; it blends particularly well with roses. It is currently being researched as a cure for migraine.

VARIETIES The variety **'Flore Pleno'** is double-flowered, with dark green leaves. The variety **'Avrea'**, with its beautiful lime yellow leaves, contrasts nicely at the front of planting beds with dark green or gray green foliage plants such as lady's mantle and lavender. (BERKELEY)

Illustration from a 15th century herbal shows Dioscorides, Pliny, and other renowned herbalists.

EARLY HERBAL MEDICINE

Archaeological evidence suggests that people have been using plants as medicine since earliest times: a 60,000-year-old Neanderthal gravesite yielded remains of plants with known medicinal properties, and lists of plants used as medicines have been found in the earliest written records. Hammurabi, king of Babylonia from 1728 to 1686 B.C., left a code of laws that includes reference to medicinal plants that are still used in modern medicine. Hippocrates, known as the father of modern medicine, listed nearly 400 medicinal plants, but it was Dioscorides who set the pattern for the future study of plants. While traveling as a surgeon in the Roman army of the emperor Nero he collected information on plants and their uses and wrote a work, *De Materia Medica*, that remained standard for centuries. Unfortunately, those who followed Dioscorides studied Dioscorides and not nature: for fifteen hundred years he was the unquestioned authority in both medicine and botany. Many of the famous herbals (most of which were written between 1470 and 1670) were based at least in part on Dioscorides, but their fanciful and often superstitious descriptions of the magical powers of plants did not necessarily further the science of medicine. The drugs used in today's modern medicine may seem unrelated to ground-up plant parts, but in truth many still contain the active ingredients of plants, and the synthetic chemicals used in others are based on plant chemistry.

COFFEE

Coffee's early history is shrouded in legend. Known in Ethiopia before A.D. 1000, it was probably first used as a food: the fruit was crushed, mixed with fat, and molded into a ball to make an easily portable food for nomads. Later, a wine was made from the fermented husks and pulps; the wine was known as *kahwah*, and that name–the origin of our *coffee*–was later applied to a drink made from the ground and roasted beans. Despite early suppression on religious and political grounds, this drink had become the universal beverage of the Arabs by the 15th century. It was firmly opposed by Italian churchmen, who called it "the wine of Islam" and detested it as the drink of infidels. Pope Clement VIII Christianized coffee, and by the mid 17th century it had spread throughout Europe. Coffee was brought to the New World around 1668 and became a staple American beverage after the Boston Tea Party rendered tea unpatriotic.

CICHORIUM INTYBUS CHICORY *Asteraceae (Sunflower family)*

PERENNIAL Native to North Africa, Europe, and Asia, chicory has been naturalized in North America and is common along roadsides. The lovely blue flowers close by noon, about 5 hours after they open. The plant grows 3-4 feet tall with coarsely toothed leaves at the base and arrow-shaped leaves toward the top. Flowers appear in midsummer in groupings of 2-3.

CULTURE Chicory will tolerate total neglect, but prefers a light alkaline soil (pH 7.0 or above) deeply dug to produce good roots. It can be propagated by seed or transplants; thin seedlings to about 1 foot apart. Chicory will reseed in the garden, so cut off old flowers if you don't want it to reseed. Blanched heads, also known as Witloof chicory or Belgian endive, are produced by forcing the roots. To do so dig the roots in autumn, cut off most of the leaves and about 1 inch of root. Store in a cool, dry place for at least 3 months, then replant outside (or in a cellar) in sandy compost with heavy mulch. Harvest before the sun hits the new growth.

USES Chicory has traditionally been added to coffee to soften the flavor; roasted chicory roots can be used to make a coffee substitute. The leaves are used fresh or cooked like spinach.

VARIETIES Witloof varieties are used to produce the blanched heads; Magdeburg or Brunswick varieties produce the roots used as a coffee substitute. (SHIMIZU)

CIMICIFUGA RACEMOSA BLACK COHOSH *Ranunculaceae (Buttercup)*

PERENNIAL Black cohosh is found growing native in deciduous woods under partial to full shade. It produces creamy white flowers in racemes on stalks up to 3 feet tall (5-8 feet in New York, Massachusetts, and Connecticut); it is a stunning plant.

CULTURE Black cohosh can be grown in shade or full sun but it grows more vigorously in sun. It can be propagated by root division in late fall or early spring (in warm climates, root division can be done throughout the winter). Plant 2½-3 feet apart in regular garden soil and mulch well. Fertilize just prior to and during the flowering period. If the plant is grown in full sun, leaves may turn brown in late summer; cut leaves to the ground.

USES Black cohosh has long held a reputation for relaxing areas of smooth muscle, such as the respiratory and female reproductive systems. The root has been used to soothe coughing and menstrual cramping. (NORTH CAROLINA)

COFFEA ARABICA COFFEE *Rubiaceae (Madder)*

SHRUB Coffee is a large shrub to small tree usually pruned down to a small to medium shrub. It is native to tropical Africa and Ethiopia. In the United States, coffee is grown outdoors only in the deep South, where a summer mulch helps. Elsewhere, it's grown as a potted houseplant. It easily withstands the low light of northern greenhouse winters.

CULTURE Fresh coffee seed, kept warm and wet, germinates well and grows quickly. Start seeds singly in small pots in fall or winter, in slightly acid soil.

CHENOPODIUM CAPITATUM (STRAWBERRY BLITE) Plant 1½ feet tall produces dense flower heads and bright red berrylike fruit. Full sun to partial shade.

CHRYSANTHEMUM BALSAMITA (COSTMARY) Plant 12 inches tall with gray-green leaves and 3-foot-tall flowerstalks with insignificant yellow flowers. Blooms in late summer.

CHRYSANTHEMUM PARTHENIUM (FEVERFEW) Many-branched plant 2-3 feet tall with many small, white, daisylike flowers. Full sun to partial shade. Zones 5-9.

CICHORIUM INTYBUS (CHICORY) Clumps of rangy stems, 3-5 feet tall, with toothed leaves and sky-blue ray flowers. Root is used herbally. Flowers in summer. Full sun or partial shade. Zones 4-10.

PRONUNCIATION
Now I shall be compelled to disappoint any who want to know which is "correct," *'erb* or *herb,* by declaring that all the facts in the history of these words have nothing to do with correctness. Correctness is, and has always been, solely a matter of general agreement in cultivated habits of speaking. . . . Those who prefer *'erb* can rightly feel proud of preserving a well-founded tradition; those who prefer an unmistakably well-aspirated *herb* can justly feel they are at least not old-fashioned. But I hope that both parties agree in liking herbs.
JOHN KENYON, IN
THE HERBARIST, 1953

Grow in filtered sun or light shade, at moderate (65° F.-80° F.) temperatures. Keep somewhat moist in spring and summer, slightly dryer (but never completely dry) in fall and winter. Maintain humidity, and apply a balanced fertilizer regularly in spring and summer. Top pruning is often needed to control height.

Coffee bushes are not hard to grow and are quite disease- and insect-resistant. However, a really attractive specimen needs close attention to temperature, light, and watering. Brown leaf edges are usually the result of fertilizer burn; too high a temperature caused by too much sun causes burned spots.

At the University of California Botanical Garden at Berkeley, coffee bushes attract mealybugs so significantly that they are sometimes used as indicators for mealybugs in the greenhouse.

USES People grow coffee bushes not to supply household caffeine needs but as attractive potted plants with glossy green leaves, fragrant white flowers, and red berries. (MATTHAEI)

COIX LACRYMA-JOBI JOB'S TEARS *Poaceae (Grass family)*

ANNUAL The colorfully named Job's tears is an easily grown grass; native to Africa and Asia, it's now cultivated in warm countries of both the Old and New Worlds.

CULTURE Job's tears is grown from seed, or from seedlings, planted in mid spring when the soil warms up. This plant needs a long, hot summer if it is to flower and produce seeds; in cool climates, seeds should be started in late winter. Sow seeds 1 inch deep, and space seedlings 14 inches apart. Grow in full sun, in average garden soil. Job's tears requires moderate amounts of water; it does not tolerate drought. It isn't much bothered by disease or pests. Cut back leaves or pull up plants late in the growing season after they die down.

USES Although Job's tears is grown in some countries for food and medicine, it is mainly appreciated for its seeds. Of a beautiful pearly gray color, mottled or striped, globular or oval, the seeds are used to make necklaces and rosaries; some sources indicate that they can be ground into a flour for bread or used to make beer. Because of its height (3-4 feet), Job's tears is good for the back of the border. It is appropriate for an Asian herb garden, and it's fun for kids, who can make jewelry from the seeds. (SHIMIZU)

COLCHICUM AUTUMNALE MEADOW SAFFRON *Liliaceae (Lily family)*

PERENNIAL Also known as autumn crocus, meadow saffron resembles, but is not, the true crocus. It produces clusters of lovely, large, lavender crocuslike flowers in the fall. Foliage appears in the spring and dies down by midsummer. *Colchicum* is native to central and southeastern Europe, growing in damp meadows, marshes, roadsides, banks, and woods.

CULTURE To grow this freely flowering herb, plant corms 3 inches deep and 3 inches apart in July or August in a sandy soil enriched with decayed manure or leaf mold. Favored locations are moist beds, rockeries, shrubberies, and borders in full sun. Propagate by dividing the corms during the dormant sea-

CIMICIFUGA RACEMOSA (BLACK COHOSH) Wiry stems 3-8 feet tall with divided dark green leaves and wandlike racemes of white flowers. Flowers in summer. Full sun or partial shade. Zones 3-10. Not heat-tolerant.

COFFEA ARABICA (COFFEE) Evergreen shrub or small tree 15-40 feet tall (usually kept smaller) with 6-inch-long glossy dark green leaves, pure white corolla-type flowers, and round deep red fruit. Often grown as a houseplant. Full sun. Zone 10.

COIX LACRYMA-JOBI (JOB'S TEARS) Grows over 3 feet tall, with flat bladelike leaves, and white to bluish gray seeds, sometimes mottled or striped.

COLCHICUM AUTUMNALE (MEADOW SAFFRON) Conical corms produce 3-8 green leaves, up to 1 foot long, in spring, and showy white, lavender, or purple flowers with 1-4 petals and yellow anthers. Flowers in fall. Zones 5-9.

Coriandrum sativum is used in 2 ways. Its seeds are ground to make coriander, a spice used in curry and many other recipes. Its leaves, called cilantro or Chinese parsley, are indispensable in Mexican, Chinese, Thai, Cambodian, and Mediterranean cuisines.

son, usually June and July. Fertilizer applied when the leaves appear is beneficial. The plants do not need frost protection.

USES Caution: the corms and seeds are highly poisonous (they yield the drug Colchicine, used for the treatment of gout); grow and use this plant only for its autumn display of flowers. (BERKELEY)

COMPTONIA PEREGRINA SWEETFERN *Myricaceae (Bayberry family)*

SHRUB Sweetfern is a strongly aromatic deciduous shrub that grows about 3 feet tall with a fernlike habit and long, rounded, fernlike leaves. However, it's not actually a fern; rather, it's a member of the Bayberry family. The flowers are not showy, and the fruits resemble small, slender cones. Sweetfern grows in dry or sandy soils, and it starts easily from seed, division, or layers. It makes a wonderfully fragrant plant for the wild garden.

USES Native Americans used it as a beverage and poisoning and to stop bleeding. (NEW YORK)

CORIANDRUM SATIVUM CORIANDER/CILANTRO *Apiaceae (Parsley)*

ANNUAL An ancient herb native to southern Europe and Asia, coriander is now grown throughout temperate regions of the world.

CULTURE As it doesn't transplant well, sow coriander directly outdoors as early in the spring as possible, or even the previous fall to lie dormant under snow cover. Choose a light, fertile soil and a sunny position, although coriander will accept some early morning or late afternoon shade. Thin seedlings to 4 inches. Coriander has a reputation for repelling aphids, both from itself and from nearby plants.

Harvest coriander seeds as soon as they ripen in late summer, or they will scatter and self-sow. Grown for the foliage, cilantro is trickier, as the plant has a great tendency to go quickly to seed in hot weather and has a very short lifecycle. Cilantro is not widely available on the East Coast and in the Midwest, though it's common in the West. Sow seed early, so plants grow in cooler weather; provide plenty of moisture; make successive sowings; harvest young leaves from the top several inches of the plant to encourage new growth; and snip out the central stalk as soon as it appears, to prevent seed formation.

USES The sweet, aromatic seeds of this herb are called coriander and are widely used for flavoring. The pungent leaves are called cilantro or Chinese parsley and are a distinct, principal seasoning in many Mediterranean, Chinese, Thai, Cambodian, and Mexican dishes. Use the oval, toothed young leaves for cooking, not the mature, feathery ones.

VARIETY 'Santo', a slow-bolting form, is available from Nichols Seeds (see source list). (MATTHAEI)

CRITHMUM MARITIMUM SAMPHIRE *Apiaceae (Parsley or Carrot family)*

PERENNIAL Samphire is native to the rocky coasts of Europe. Its name comes from an Old French word meaning "St. Peter's herb"—the name Peter comes from a Greek word for "rock." Samphire is famous for growing in out-of-the-

COMPTONIA PEREGRINA (SWEETFERN) Shrub 3-4 feet tall with fernlike habit and aromatic, rounded, fernlike leaves. Fruit resembles small slender cones. Full or partial shade. Zones 2-8.

CORIANDRUM SATIVUM (CORIANDER/CILANTRO) Plant 1½-2½ feet tall with slender stems, lacy foliage, and tiny white flowers in summer. Full sun.

CRITHMUM MARITIMUM (SAMPHIRE) Plant 1-2 feet tall with compound leaflets and small, yellow or white flowers. Full sun. Zones 8-10.

CROCUS SATIVUS (SAFFRON CROCUS) Flattened corm produces 8-inch-long leaves and lavender, white, or reddish purple flowers with red stigmata. Stemless. Leaves stay green until following spring. Full sun or partial shade. Zones 6-9.

CRYPTOTAENIA JAPONICA (MITSUBA) Leafy plant grows up to 3 feet tall in moist, partially shaded setting, 2 feet tall in sun. Space 12-18 inches apart.

CYMBOPOGON CITRATUS (LEMON GRASS) Clumps of tapered grass 4-6 feet tall, bright green. Full sun to light shade. Zones 8-10.

CYNARA CARDUNCULUS (CARDOON) Arching stalks with large, spiny, silvery gray leaves with white undersides and purple thistlelike flowers that open from artichokelike buds. Full sun. Flowers in summer. Perennial in Zones 9-10.

DIANTHUS CARYOPHYLLUS (CLOVE PINK) Stem 1-3 feet tall with blue-green leaves 3-6 inches long and flowers 1-4 inches long, often double, in red, white, pink, purple, yellow, or spotted colors. Flowers in summer. Partial shade. Zones 6-10, evergreen in Zones 7-9.

way, dangerous places, and those brave enough to go in search of it often risked their lives. Shakespeare refers to this in *King Lear*: "Halfway down hangs one who gathers samphire, dreadful trade!" (The herb was used as a relish for meat in his era). Samphire's blue-gray leaves are fleshy, its flowers inconspicuous.

CULTURE True to its origins, samphire likes a seaside garden best. It's hardy in Zones 8-10; in colder zones, treat it as a tender perennial (at Cornell Plantations it is dug up and brought inside). Grow in full sun, in warm weather, and in sandy or gravely soil. Samphire will rot if the soil is too wet. Start from seed, rooted cuttings, or division, in mid to late spring. Space plants 12 inches apart. If mulching, avoid compost and use sand instead. In cold areas, protect from frost with pine needles. It is a favorite of gophers; if they are a problem in your area, take precautions.

USES Samphire leaves are eaten in salad or as a condiment and are also added to vinegar and used as capers. Although not often grown, samphire has potential as an ornamental in a mixed border or rock garden, and it looks good in container combinations. (SHIMIZU)

CROCUS SATIVUS SAFFRON CROCUS *Iridaceae (Iris family)*

PERENNIAL Saffron is the world's most costly seasoning because it's produced from the golden stigmas of the saffron crocus's lilac flowers, and 60,000 flowers are needed to produce 1 pound of saffron. It is probably native to Asia Minor and Greece.

CULTURE Saffron grows from a flattened corm. Its crocuslike flowers appear in late September, and the grasslike leaves can stay green until the following spring and are an attractive feature in the winter garden (though they don't survive in Michigan). Select firm corms and plant in full sun in late summer ½-1 inch apart and 2 inches deep. Soil should be well-pulverized, neither poor nor heavy clay. Water during the growing season, which begins in September, but keep saffron dry during the summer months; planting in a well-drained area will help. Apply a general fertilizer when growth begins in the fall, and mulch in areas where heavy freezes occur. Be sure to plant saffron in an area where its late-September-blooming flowers will not be obscured by other plants. Divide every few years as the corms naturally multiply underground.

USES Saffron was prized as a dye by the ancients. A small amount added to food produces a delicious flavor and lovely yellow color, perhaps most notably in Spanish paella. Use only the anthers; corms are poisonous. (BERKELEY)

CRYPTOTAENIA JAPONICA MITSUBA *Apiaceae (Parsley or Carrot family)*

PERENNIAL Mitsuba, sold as *C. canadensis* and also known as Japanese parsley, Japanese wild chervil, honewort, and white chervil, is native to Austria, North America, and eastern Asia.

CULTURE In its natural shaded habitat of woodlands, ravines, and riverbanks, mitsuba grows to 3 feet high; cultivated in full sun a garden setting at Cornell Plantations, it grows only 2 feet tall. Mitsuba does best in partial shade in a

SAFFRON

Few herbs come to us trailing as much history as saffron. Homer wrote of the "saffron-robed morn," saffron grew in Solomon's garden, and saffron-scented essences were showered over the heads of spectators seated in Rome's Colosseum. Saffron is made from the dried stigmas of the true crocus (*Crocus sativus*)–the stigmas must be picked by hand, and a great many (the numbers given vary) are needed to make a very small amount. These dried stigmas yield saffron powder, used as a flavoring–and coloring agent–in food, especially in Mediterranean cooking. Saffron powder was also the source of the principal yellow dye of the ancient world. Saffron's golden color, exotic perfume, and unique taste have given it a primary place over the centuries. It was everywhere in Rome: women dyed their hair with it, it was used to dye the garments of priests and nobles, it was an ingredient in perfume, and theaters and public places were strewn with saffron flowers. The Roman poet Lucan wrote that blood spurts from a man bitten by a serpent "in the same manner as the sweet-smelling essence of saffron issues from the limbs of a statue." When Rome fell, saffron disappeared from most of Europe–it was unknown in England during the Dark Ages–and its return to northern Europe is recorded in various legends. For example, a pilgrim is said to have smuggled saffron back into England by hiding a stolen bulb in the hollow of his palmer's staff. Saffron enjoys great popularity as a seasoning and coloring for food and is still used as a dye for the robes of Buddhist monks.

rich soil with plenty of moisture. Sow seeds outside as soon as soil can be worked in the spring, or inside in late winter or early spring, setting out late in the spring. Thin or space about 1 foot apart. Successive sowings will insure a continual supply of fresh young leaves, which you can pick as needed for fresh use.

USES Mitsuba is commonly cultivated in Japan, where its tender young leaves and leafstalks are used fresh or blanched for flavoring, fresh as a garnish like parsley, or cooked (lightly) like spinach. Its edible roots are fried. (Cornell)

CYMBOPOGON CITRATUS LEMON GRASS *Poaceae (Grass family)*

PERENNIAL Lemon grass is a large-growing, clump-forming plant that originated in the tropics of southern India and Ceylon.

CULTURE Lemon grass is not grown from seed. Instead, purchase strong-growing, young potted plants, or divide established clumps in the spring. You can also try rooting stems of lemon grass sold sometimes in food markets, but they will grow slowly and reluctantly. This tropical plant will grow outdoors only in the South and West Coast of the United States, where plants should be spaced 2-3 feet apart. At North Carolina Botanical Garden, lemon grass has survived 5 winters; it is mulched well, and gardeners bring some indoors each year "just in case." In cooler climates lemon grass must be grown as a potted plant and wintered indoors. At Cornell Plantations, it is planted in the spring; in the fall it is dug up, potted, and cut back to about 2 inches from its base and spends winter in the greenhouse. Grow in full sun to light shade, in well-drained, slightly acidic sandy loam. Lemon grass likes lots of water, especially in the summer (an organic mulch is helpful), and warm to hot temperatures. Apply a balanced fertilizer during spring and summer, but hold back on feeding in winter.

USES The wonderful lemon flavor of lemon grass has made it a staple of Oriental cooking. When the leafy bases of mature stems are stewed or steamed with food, they add a delicious, interesting lemony flavor. Don't try to eat the tough stems, however; discard before serving. It also makes a pleasant tea and a refreshing herbal bath. (Matthaei)

CYNARA CARDUNCULUS CARDOON *Asteraceae (Sunflower family)*

PERENNIAL Cardoon is a gorgeous, bold ornamental, native to southern Europe and the Mediterranean region. It grows to 6 feet, with large, spiny leaves up to 3 feet long, and produces beautiful, purple thistlelike flowers.

CULTURE Cardoon is easy to grow, in full sun, warm temperatures, and rich soil. Plants need abundant moisture to avoid pithy or hollow stalks. Where tender, grow as an annual, sowing seeds in midspring (plants can withstand light frost), and setting seedlings 2 feet apart, with some compost enrichment. As plants grow, cut back old leaves and flowers. Although cardoon is not supposed to be winter-hardy in Zone 7, it can sometimes withstand heavy frost if covered with pine needles through the winter.

USES The blanched leaf stalks and roots are eaten like celery and endive. This striking plant, with its bold gray foliage, is extremely attractive in a border, a

DIGITALIS PURPUREA 'GIANT SHIRLEY' (FOXGLOVE) Stalks 3-4 feet tall with rows of hood-shaped flowers. Flowers in summer. Full sun or partial shade. Zones 3-10. Not heat-tolerant.

ECHINACEA PURPUREA (CONEFLOWER) Sturdy branching stems 2-5 feet tall with long, dark green leaves and showy daisy-like flowers up to 6 inches across, with drooping rays ranging from white to purplish pink. Flowers in summer. Full sun. Zones 3-10. Heat-tolerant.

ECHIUM LYCOPSIS (VIPER'S BUGLOSS) Shrubby plants with narrow gray-green leaves covered in prickly hair, in rosettes and funnel-shaped blue flowers. Blooms in spring and late summer. Full sun.

ELSHOLTZIA CILIATA (VIETNAMESE BALM) Plant 2 feet tall with oval leaves and tubular purple flowers. Blooms in late summer.

cottage garden, or an edible/ornamental garden.

VARIETIES The species **C. scolymus** (globe artichoke) is very similar to cardoon, except its leaves are not as spiny. The receptacle of the flower-head bud and the thick base of the scales around the flower of the globe artichoke are boiled and eaten as a vegetable. (SHIMIZU)

DIANTHUS CARYOPHYLLUS CLOVE PINK *Caryophyllaceae (Pink family)*

PERENNIAL Native to southern Europe, *D. caryophyllus* is the true carnation. It's grown for its attractive, blue-green foliage and (in the best varieties) its warm, spicy-sweet, clove-tinged scent–hence the common name of clove pink.

CULTURE Clove pink is suitable for Zones 6-9; it is evergreen in Zones 7-9, and sometimes survives the winter in Zone 5. It requires full sun and well-drained, alkaline soil. It will not tolerate poorly drained soil, especially in winter, and it does not like too much water or climates with extremely hot summers. Start from rooted cuttings or layering, and set plants out in early spring 12-15 inches apart. At Berkeley Botanic Garden, clove pink seeds itself all over the herb garden. A mulch of sand or pine chips is beneficial. Once established, keep old flowers cut back. Rotate planting sites to avoid foliar diseases and crown rot.

At North Carolina Botanical Garden, clove pink is planted inside the holes of cinder blocks; this provides excellent drainage, and the blocks add alkalinity to the soil.

USES Clove pink flowers are edible after the bitter tips are removed and are used in salads, fruit dishes, and sandwiches as well as in potpourris and vinegar. Clove pinks are attractive interplanted with roses. Some of the old-fashioned varieties are best for flavor and fragrance. For use as an herb, be sure to select a clove-scented variety. (SHIMIZU)

DIGITALIS FOXGLOVE *Scrophulariaceae (Figwort family)*

BIENNIAL AND PERENNIAL Foxglove is an essential component of cottage gardens; a drift of these flowers blooming in a lightly shaded woodland garden is a memorable sight. Common foxglove, **D. purpurea,** is one of the most ornamental of the genus.

CULTURE Although foxgloves will grow in full sun in the North, they are at their best in light shade on the edge of woodlands or among shrubs. In hotter climates, shade is essential, and additional water is necessary during dry periods. Plant in spring or fall in well-drained, organically rich soil that never dries out. An organic mulch is advisable in the summer, and winter protection helps prevent heaving and discourages crown rot. Fertilize lightly in early spring. Propagate perennial varieties by division in spring; biennials such as *D. purpurea* will self-sow, or you can collect and sow ripe seed. Deadheading may encourage a second flush of bloom, at the expense of seed production. Japanese beetles and slugs often require control, while poor air circulation encourages attacks of powdery mildew.

USES Foxglove has been grown for medicinal purposes since the Middle Ages.

Opposite: The coneflower is among the most beautiful of native American plants. It blooms almost all summer and tolerates drought and poor soil. Useful for its beauty, it also shows promise as a source of potent drugs for use with AIDS and other afflictions. Almost 25 percent of the drugs we use are based on plants; promoting the survival of an endangered plant species may preserve it for a life-saving use in the future.

CHINESE HERBALISM

The history of China begins in myth with tales of legendary emperor-deities who created the basic elements of Chinese civilization. Three of these emperors formed a triad of medicine gods: Shen Nung, Fu Hsi, and Huang Ti. Shen Nung, said to have lived from 3737 to 2697 B.C., was a deity of medicine, pharmacy, and agriculture. He is credited with having compiled the *Pen-Ts'ao* ("Herbal"), the oldest Chinese medical text. Based on the accumulation of centuries of earlier folk uses of plants, this work lists 365 medical preparations, almost all of them herbal. Huang Ti, also known as the Yellow Emperor and said to have reigned from 2697 to 2595 B.C., prepared his own herbal, *Huang-Ti Nei-ching* ("The Yellow Emperor's Classic of Internal Medicine"). The emperors themselves may be legendary, but the works are real (obviously written much later and only attributed to the ancient sages), and the information in them is surprisingly accurate. For example, the *Pen-Ts'ao* extols the healing virtues of *ma-huang*, a leafless desert vine, claiming that a tea made of the vine will improve circulation, reduce fevers, aid urinary problems, calm coughing, and, most of all, relieve pulmonary or bronchial problems. The plant in question is ephedra, but only during the 1920s did scientific investigation establish the value of ephedrine in relieving the discomforts of asthma, hayfever, and the common cold.

Today, it is grown for its beauty in the garden, and *D. purpurea* yields the heart stimulant digitalis. It is highly poisonous.

VARIETIES 'Giant Shirley' ('Shirley Hybrids') and 'Excelsior Hybrids' are the best-known of the hybrid strains. The strawberry foxglove, **D. x mertonensis**, and the straw or small yellow foxglove, **D. lutea**, are perennial.

ECHINACEA PURPUREA CONEFLOWER *Asteraceae (Sunflower family)*

PERENNIAL Native to North America, coneflower gets its common name from the arrangement of the florets of its showy, daisylike flowers around a prominent center "cone."

CULTURE Start coneflower from root division, or purchase plants (choose larger ones; small seedlings will take time to flower). Plants from seed will take 2-3 years to flower. Set out in the spring, spaced 1-1½ feet apart. Coneflower needs full sun and deep, light, loamy soil. It can stand somewhat dry conditions and does best with 2 or 3 applications of balanced fertilizer during the growing season. It's a good idea to mark the location of seedlings the first few years, since the plant dies back to the ground in the winter.

Coneflower is a fine source of cut flowers, blooming from July to October. Cutting off old flower heads will increase and extend the flowering season.

USES Coneflower was long used by Native Americans for medicinal purposes and is now regaining its importance because extracts from its roots (and from other parts of the plant) have been found to be effective in strengthening the immune system.

VARIETIES *E. angustifolia* is the 2-foot species of coneflower seen in most herb books, but *E. purpurea*, 5-foot purple coneflower, is the more showy variety. 'White Lustre' is an attractive white cultivar. **E. pallida** is a 3-foot type with rose-purple or white flowers. (BERKELEY)

ECHIUM LYCOPSIS VIPER'S BUGLOSS *Boraginaceae (Borage family)*

ANNUAL This curiously named plant, native to Europe but now naturalized in North America, is often found growing on walls and in gravel pits; it is a showy plant covered with prickly hairs. Its seed resembles a viper's head, which, according to the Doctrine of Signatures, is a sign of it ability to treat snakebite; the word *bugloss* means "ox's tongue," a reference to the roughness of the leaves. Its flowers, borne on curved spikes, open pink and turn blue.

CULTURE Viper's bugloss grows best in full sun and warm temperatures, in dry, well-drained soil. Start from fresh seed in fall or early spring, or buy small, vigorous plants with healthy stems and set out in spring 18 inches apart. Protect these small plants from any remaining frosts. Gravel or sand added to the soil will boost drainage. Plants appreciate an application of all-purpose fertilizer as the growing season starts. Water only enough to keep plants from wilting. Prune off dead shoots. Viper's bugloss is a self-sowing annual; allow plants to die back and go to seed, and you will have fresh plants the next year.

Viper's bugloss is effective planted so as to spill over a rock wall. It's also good with low gray foliage plants, which show off its attractive pink and blue

flowers. **E. vulgare** is a larger variety, though dwarf cultivars exist.
USES The plant was once used medicinally, particularly as a treatment for snakebite; it is now grown for its historical interest. (BERKELEY)

ELSHOLTZIA CILIATA VIETNAMESE BALM *Lamiaceae (Mint family)*

ANNUAL Native to central and eastern Asia, Vietnamese balm's leaves have a vibrant lemon scent with sweet floral undertones.
CULTURE Seeds are not readily available; purchase plants and grow them in well-drained soil. In Zone 5, there is not a long enough frost-free season to achieve flowering outdoors, so the plant is dug up and moved indoors at Cornell Plantations, and its beautiful spikes of purple flowers are enjoyed in November. Then the plants follow the natural life cycle of annuals, and die. Cuttings taken in August also flowered and then died. Plants in the greenhouse do not produce seeds (perhaps because they lack insect pollinators), so new plants must be purchased each spring. (Commercial suppliers buy bundles of the herb at Oriental markets, root the shoots, and sell them.)
USES Vietnamese balm leaves make an excellent tea, alone or blended with other herbs, and can be used for cooking in any dishes where their lemon flavor is wanted. The lemony leaves are also a fine addition to potpourri.
VARIETY The species **E. stauntonii** (mint shrub or mint balm) has minty leaves used to make tea. Like *E. ciliata*, it produces lilac flowering spikes but is hardy to Zone 4, its woody stems dying back to the ground over the winter. (CORNELL)

EPHEDRA SINENSIS JOINT FIR *Ephedraceae (Ephedra)*

SHRUB Joint fir is a profusely branched, low-growing shrub native to dry areas of northern China and Mongolia.
CULTURE Joint fir can be difficult to get established, so purchase vigorous, strongly growing plants and set 1 foot apart in midspring. The plant will

Above: Ephedra sinensis, **prepared by an Oriental herbalist for medicinal use.** *Below left: Ephedra* **growing at the Berkeley Botanical Garden.**

EPHEDRA SINENSIS (JOINT FIR) Spreading shrubby plant, 6-24 inches tall, with slender jointed stems, small green flowers in early summer. Full sun. Zones 4-10.

ERYNGIUM FOETIDUM (CULANTRO) Spiny-toothed leaves with cilantrolike aroma, small green flowers. Full sun, tolerates partial shade. Zones 8-10.

FERULA ASSA-FOETIDA (ASAFETIDA) Mounds of feathery light green foliage, 4-7 feet tall, with umbels of small yellow flowers. Flowers in summer. Full sun. Zones 6-9.

FOENICULUM VULGARE (FENNEL) Light green feathery foliage with solid stems, reaching 4-6 feet high with clusters of yellow flowers. Flowers July-October. Full sun. Zones 6-9.

spread and root where branches touch the ground; these can be divided or removed. Once established, joint fir is easy to maintain and hardy (frost protection is not necessary; however, it does not survive winter at Michigan's Matthaei Botanical Gardens). It will grow in any soil, from its native poor, rocky conditions to a rich loam. It prefers full sun but will tolerate (just) a little shade. Keep the soil around newly planted joint fir moist, but not wet; settled plants prefer dryish conditions. While joint fir does not require fertilizer, a light application at the beginning of the growing season will keep the plant looking good. Prune to the size you want.

USES The plant is named for its slender jointed stems, which are used in Chinese herbal medicine as a remedy for asthma, hayfever, and circulatory ailments. *Ephedra* is the source of the widely used drug ephedrine.

VARIETIES Species with similar properties that may be more available include **E. sinica**, **E. vulgaris**, and **E. nevadensis**. The latter is known as Mormon tea, because the Mormons made an herbal brew from it. At Cornell Plantations, **E. equistina**, a native of Siberia and China, is grown. (BERKELEY)

ERYNGIUM FOETIDUM CULANTRO *Apiaceae (Parsley or Carrot family)*

TENDER PERENNIAL Culantro, native to tropical America, is also known as spiny cilantro, false coriander, recao de monte, and spiritweed. It produces strongly scented, spiny, toothed leaves and spikes of green flowers; the leaves have a flavor similar to cilantro (coriander).

CULTURE Culantro grows best in full sun, although it will accept partial shade. It prefers a moderately fertile, well-drained soil. Start from seed anytime for potted plants. To grow as an annual outdoors in cold regions, start seeds indoors in late winter and transplant to the garden after danger of frost is past. Space plants 6-8 inches apart. Dig and bring inside for the winter, or start new plants from seed once again the following year.

USES Culantro leaves are used like bay leaves, added during cooking to impart their characteristic flavor, then removed before serving. Commonly used to flavor soups, culantro is indispensable in Latin American cooking and has also been adopted by Southeast Asian cooks. It has also been a highly regarded folk remedy for high blood pressure. (BERKELEY)

FERULA ASSA-FOETIDA ASAFETIDA *Apiaceae (Parsley or Carrot family)*

PERENNIAL Also called food of the gods and devil's dung, this native of Afghanistan and eastern Persia bears yellow flowers in large umbels. Since it grows up to 7 feet tall, it is a very strong and bold-looking garden plant, especially useful for backgrounds.

CULTURE Asafetida grows very quickly with the right conditions. It prefers a rich, well-drained soil and accepts full sun to partial shade. It likes lots of water when it's actively growing, less after it's full grown. It does not tolerate wet, soggy conditions in the fall and early winter when it's becoming dormant. Start from fresh seed in late spring or early fall; plants are hard to find. Plants can be propagated by root division in May or June. Plant seeds or root

COMPANION PLANTING

Many gardeners have observed that some plants, when growing near other specific plants, will either benefit or harm each other. For centuries, gardeners have employed the practice of "companion planting," pairing plants in order to reap these benefits.

Science has not been quick to validate these practices, mostly because extensive research has not been done. Many of the theories of companion planting are dismissed as folklore, despite the experience of thousands of gardeners. It has never been scientifically proven that the alleged deterrent herbs actually do the job–but that does not mean that it never will be proven. Try it–and see if it works for you. Among the herbs used to repel pests and diseases:

•All members of the onion (allium) family; said to repel many insects and to reduce weeds.

•Marigolds, which are said to repel nematodes (scientific experimentation on this theory has shown it to be true, but has also shown that a huge number of marigolds is needed to accomplish minimal results).

•Basil; said to deter asparagus beetles and to enhance the growth of peppers and tomatoes.

One aspect of companion planting that scientists have not tried to dispute is the space it saves. Interplanting small, fast-growing herbs among vegetables makes use of otherwise wasted space. Herbs planted among vegetable beds–particularly richly colored basils or perillas–also add an ornamental and orderly note.

Fennel complements other plants in both its flowering stage (shown at top, with mountain mint, *Pycnanthemum muticum*), and its lacy foliage stage (shown above with Shasta daisy).

crowns just below the soil surface. Mulch to keep the plant moist during the growing season. Cut plants back to ground level when dormant, and provide winter protection in areas with hard frosts or freezes. Asafetida will appreciate a regular application of fertilizer during the growing season.

To obtain resin, dig roots in June, slash them, and store in the shade 4-5 weeks. Scrape off the resin that leaks out.

USES Resin from asafetida roots is a staple in Indian and Persian cooking; only a tiny amount is used, owing to its bitter, acrid taste. (BERKELEY)

FOENICULUM VULGARE FENNEL *Apiaceae (Parsley or Carrot family)*

PERENNIAL A native of the Mediterranean region, fennel is often grown for its anise-flavored seeds and young leaves. It has feathery green leaves and umbels of yellow flowers.

CULTURE Grow fennel in full sun (partial shade in warm climates) and average, well-drained soil; it will not survive in a wet site. Sow seed outdoors in fall or early spring, thinning to 10-12 inches. Because of its thick taproot, fennel does not transplant well. Watch for aphids. Although it has never been proven, fennel is said to have a damaging effect on bush beans, caraway, tomatoes, and kohlrabi, and is harmed by coriander and wormwood.

At North Carolina Botanical Garden, fennel grows as a perennial; gardeners collect seeds in the summer and let the plant die back naturally in winter.

USES Fennel was once considered a remedy for failing eyesight (a tea made from its leaves can be used as a compress on swollen eyes) and was long considered an aphrodisiac, but its most enduring and popular use is in cooking. Fennel leaves and seeds have myriad culinary uses. Leaves have a delicate flavor and are best used fresh, either raw or added at the end of cooking. Tender stems can be eaten like celery. Harvest seeds when mature and brown, but before they drop; check for aphids. Fennel also yields a yellow or brown dye for wool, and fennel oil is used commercially in perfumes, soaps, and liquors. Sugar-coated seeds are used as after-dinner mints in Indian restaurants.

VARIETIES *F. vulgare* '**Rubrum**' (bronze fennel) has beautiful, dark reddish bronze foliage. It makes a striking accent plant in the garden, in addition to its herbal uses. At Cornell Plantations (Zone 5), bronze fennel overwinters reliably, while *F. vulgare* usually doesn't.

F. v. **var.** *azoricum* (Florence fennel or finocchio—sometimes listed as **var.** *dulce*, incorrectly called sweet anise, and sold as anise in supermarkets) has thickened leaf bases that form a bulbous base called the bulb, which is eaten raw or cooked. Florence fennel needs cool weather to develop its bulb, so sow seeds in midsummer for a fall harvest. (Plants grown from a spring sowing may bolt in warm summer weather before forming the bulb.) Plants benefit from frequent fertilization and watering. Cut off flower heads to encourage development of a thicker base. Once the bulb is about egg size, it can be hilled up with soil to blanch. It will be ready to harvest in a few weeks. (CORNELL)

FUMARIA OFFICINALIS (FUMITORY) Slender, climbing stems with small pinkish flowers. Blooms April-October, longer in warm climates.

GALIUM ODORATUM (SWEET WOODRUFF) Low-growing star-shaped leaves with tiny white flowers in late spring. Partial to full shade. Zones 3-9. Not heat-tolerant.

GALIUM VERUM (LADY'S BEDSTRAW) Creeping plant with fine, lacy foliage, small bright yellow flowers in June-September. Full sun or partial shade. Zones 2-8.

GAURA LINDHEIMERI (GAURA) Erect stems with gray-green willowy foliage and panicles of 1-inch white flowers. Loose growth habit. Full sun. Blooms early summer through fall. Zones 6-10. Heat-tolerant.

FUMARIA OFFICINALIS FUMITORY *Fumariaceae (Fumitory family)*

ANNUAL Fumitory is an uncommon herb with slender, weak, climbing stems, native to Europe. Its small pinkish flowers tipped with purple bloom from April to October and through the winter in mild climates. The name is derived from the plant's smokelike appearance, promoted by the silvery gray leaves, when seen from a distance

CULTURE Fumitory grows easily from seed; once established in the garden, it will resow itself each year, although it's not weedy. If you purchase seedlings, choose small ones, as fumitory does not transplant well. Set out or seed in early spring, spacing plants 1 foot apart in full sun or partial shade. Plant where fumitory's climbing habit will not snuff out less vigorous plants. It has a nice effect where its small pink flowers are shown off against dark green foliage.

Fumitory is not fussy about soil; it grows naturally in waste places, and it is not a heavy feeder. Young plants like water; established plants take an average amount. Cut off yellow or dead stems to keep the plants looking good. Be sure to let one plant turn dry and dead at season's end to insure a self-sown supply of new seedlings the following spring.

USES Fumitory was once used medicinally for liver and gall bladder problems and as a laxative and diuretic. (BERKELEY)

GALIUM ODORATUM SWEET WOODRUFF *Rubiaceae (Madder family)*

PERENNIAL Sweet woodruff makes a wonderful ground cover for shady areas, with dark green, pointed leaves growing in whorls and profusions of tiny white flowers in May and June. It is a native of northern and central Europe.

CULTURE Unlike most herbs, sweet woodruff prefers partial or deep shade, with dappled light. It wants a rich, well-drained but moist soil. It propagates best by root division (done almost anytime), as seed is slow to germinate. If purchasing plants, select healthy, dark green specimens with lots of stems. Set plants 1 foot apart, with roots near the soil surface. The plants will quickly spread out, forming a dense mat. Sweet woodruff likes regular applications of a nitrogen-rich fertilizer. Frost protection is not needed, and the plants are disease-resistant. However, if plants dry out, they will burn and scorch; be sure to keep them moist. Cut back old stems in fall or spring before new growth starts.

USES The dried plant gives off a delightful fragrance like freshly mowed hay. Formerly used as a strewing herb and mattress-stuffer, it still is an ingredient in potpourris and a linen-closet freshener. In Germany it is used to transform Rhine wine into May wine. (MATTHAEI)

GALIUM VERUM LADY'S BEDSTRAW *Rubiaceae (Madder family)*

PERENNIAL A pretty herb with creeping stems and fine, lacy foliage, lady's bedstraw is so named because women of all classes once used it to stuff mattresses. It's native to Europe and western Asia and has small, bright, yellow flowers that bloom from June to September.

CULTURE Lady's bedstraw is propagated by root divisions. If the only plant you can find on sale is sad looking, bring it home anyway; it will quickly recover once planted in the ground. You can plant lady's bedstraw almost any time of year; plants placed in spring will grow to good size and flower in the first season. One plant is enough; it will spread, covering the ground around it. Plant in full sun to partial (but not deep) shade in average soil. Lady's bedstraw will tolerate dry but not wet conditions; plants given water during the growing season will look best. Frost protection is not necessary. This plant spreads quickly; avoid planting it with plants that are easily overpowered.

USES The roots of lady's bedstraw yield a red dye; the flowering tops produce a yellow dye. Flowers can be used fresh or dry in arrangements.

Lady's bedstraw is also known as cheese rennet; the plant contains high concentrations of silicic acid, which will cause milk to curdle, and it has been used to make goat cheeses. (BERKELEY)

GAURA LINDHEIMERI WHITE GAURA *Onagraceae (Evening Primrose)*

PERENNIAL Native to Texas through Louisiana, white gaura grows 3-4 feet tall and produces tall flower spikes of white tinged with rose from late June into fall. As the flowers age, the whites give way to pale rose, but all color phases are present on the plant at the same time, creating a lovely effect. Gaura prefers well-drained soil and full sun; it tolerates both heat and high humidity. However, in areas of extreme heat and humidity it may become leggy and need staking. Although it does not overwinter in Zone 5, it grows readily from seed and will bloom the first year. Gaura seed germinates in 14-21 days in warm, humid areas. It can be divided every 2-3 years.

USE Native Americans used related species medicinally and in ceremonies; Navahos used **G. parviflora** as a poultice and also as a fumigant and infusion in their Nightway ceremonies. A Chicano folk remedy for rheumatism included ground **G. coccinea**. (NEBRASKA)

GERANIUM MACULATUM CRANESBILL *Geraniaceae (Geranium family)*

PERENNIAL This beautiful woodland wildflower and herb is one of the earliest bloomers in the garden, beginning in April and continuing through mid May; it sometimes reflowers in the fall. Its foliage is attractive as well. Cranesbill looks best when planted in masses.

CULTURE Cranesbill will flower in shady spots, but will usually be rather leggy; when taken into the sun, it becomes more lush. Set plants 1-1½ feet apart. It will produce without fertilization, but will benefit from a light application of a low-nitrogen fertilizer in early spring. Cranesbill produces a large quantity of seed and freely self-seeds in the garden. Seedlings can be transplanted easily, and seeds can be collected and sown outdoors in the fall or stored in the refrigerator in an air-tight container until the following spring. It is not considered invasive. The root is harvested in the fall and dried for use.

USES Cranesbill contains tannin and was used for its astringent quality by

GROUND COVERS

Ground covers are low-maintenance plants that spread easily over a large area. Many herbs make excellent ground covers; some aromatic herbs, like mint or thyme, have the added advantage of exuding a pleasant scent when crushed underfoot. *Galium odoratum, Asarum europaeum,* and *Epimedium grandiflorum* are good herbal ground covers for shady areas; in sunny spots, try *Arctostaphylos uva-ursi* or *stachys.*

Once established, ground covers require little care. However, at the outset, it is important to provide them with rich, well-tilled soil when planting them. Turn the soil over to a depth of 1-2 feet and add a layer of organic matter. Planting in spring allows the ground cover to become established before winter. Mulching also helps during the establishment period. In subsequent seasons, fertilize with a balanced fertilizer if your soil is not rich.

Plant ground covers in staggered rows, as shown below, to achieve a full, lush look.

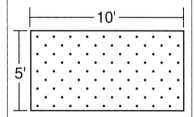

GERANIUM MACULATUM (CRANESBILL) Plant 1½-2 feet tall, with loose habit, deeply divided leaves, and pale to deep pink flowers. Blooms in spring through early summer. Full sun to partial shade. Zones 3-10. Not heat-tolerant.

GINGKO BILOBA (GINGKO) Tree growing to 100 feet tall, with fan-shaped bright green leaves, bearing yellow seed. Full sun to partial shade. Zones 4-8.

GLYCYRRHIZA GLABRA (LICORICE) Erect branching plant, 3-7 feet tall, with divided yellow-green leaves and 3-foot-long spikes of purple or lavender flowers. Blooms in midsummer. Full sun to partial shade. Zones 5-9.

HELIANTHUS ANNUUS (SUNFLOWER) Giant bright yellow flowers with dark seedheads on stems up to 12 feet tall. Smaller varieties also available. Blooms in late summer. Full sun.

Native Americans. It is currently used as an astringent in cases of excessive or abnormal bleeding. The flowers are fragrant and can be used in potpourri. ***G. macrorrhizum,*** another fragrant species, has magenta flower and is useful as a ground cover.

GINKGO BILOBA GINKGO *Ginkgoaceae (Ginkgo family)*

TREE The ginkgo is a "living fossil," the only surviving species of a large order that existed alongside dinosaurs and was long believed to be extinct. Native to China and Japan and closely related to conifers, the ginkgo is a large, picturesque tree that grows up to 100 feet, with attractive fan-shaped and slightly ruffled leaves. It is often planted as a street tree, because it is not fussy about growing conditions and is virtually pest- and disease-free. Mostly male trees are planted; the female trees produce a yellowish fruit that emits a fetid odor after it ripens and drops.

CULTURE Although the ginkgo will grow in most situations, it does best in full sun and very well-drained soil, with moisture supplied throughout the growing season. Purchase well-branched male plants, making sure that the tree is not potbound. Set out in fall or early spring, keeping weeds away from the small seedlings. You probably would not want to plant more than one in an herb garden, since it will shade the surrounding area. You can cut the tree back to keep it small, remove branches to allow more light to the garden, or prune to in the manner of bonsai. The ginkgo is hardy in the North.

USES The seed is considered a delicacy in Japan; it is used in steamed egg custard. Ginkgo is also used in medicines for the respiratory system. Researchers are testing it with elderly people to see if it improves strength and mental acuity.

VARIETIES For interesting variations, cultivar ***'Aurea'*** has yellow leaves and ***'Variegata'***, yellow and green. (BERKELEY)

GLYCYRRHIZA GLABRA LICORICE *Fabacaeae (Pea family)*

PERENNIAL Native to southern and eastern Europe, licorice is not a showy plant, but its divided leaves and 3-foot flower spikes make an attractive pattern in the garden.

CULTURE Licorice is usually grown from sections of root, 6 inches long with 2-3 eyes. Licorice can also be propagated from seed in late winter and ready to plant in spring. Plant in October or February/March, 18 inches apart, with the root 4 inches underground. Licorice needs a deep, rich loam that drains well but remains moist. Plants benefit from regular applications of fertilizer. Keep plants weed-free during the first year. They will not appear vigorous at first; it usually takes 2 years before the plants become robustly mature. They are, however, hardly subject to disease. In the fall, cut back after leaves start to drop, dress with manure, and then mulch heavily to protect from cold winter temperatures. According to some sources, licorice does not like cool weather and even when mulched will not endure severe freezing. However, it has

Competitions are often organized to see who can grow the largest sunflower. The present record is 25 feet tall; the largest blossom ever found was over 32 inches across.

Above: **The large showy blooms of Hibiscus moeschetus, also called mallow rose and wild cotton; other species are more useful herbally.**

been found to be perfectly hardy in Cornell Plantations, Zone 5.

USES Licorice root has been used since ancient times to soothe coughs and other throat and chest complaints; it also benefits disorders of the adrenal and endocrine system; its sweet taste makes otherwise bitter medicinal teas more palatable. It is also used as a distinctive flavoring.

VARIETY The variety **G. echinata** is prostrate rather than erect. (BERKELEY)

HELIANTHUS ANNUUS SUNFLOWER *Asteraceae (Sunflower family)*

ANNUAL The sunflower is a North American native: Native Americans cultivated the plant and found many uses for it, and the ancient sun worshipers of Peru revered it. Sunflowers will grow up to 12 feet tall, with huge yellow flowers borne on rough and hairy stems.

CULTURE As its name suggests, grow sunflower in full sun, in a well-dug and good garden soil; avoid clayey soils. Sow outdoors, in place, once the soil has warmed up, or start earlier indoors in flats and set out once danger of frost has passed. Space seedlings 2 feet apart. The more fertilizer, the bigger and better the growth will be. Extra water also produces more growth; in fact, because sunflower will tolerate high levels of water, it is used in some countries for drying out damp soils. Harvest heads when the seeds are ripe.

USES This robust plant is remarkably useful. Children love the large flowers and tasty seeds; birds flock to your garden to eat the seeds; the flowers attract bees; the seeds are truly delicious and nutritious; the green leaves are useful as animal food; the buds can be boiled and served like artichokes; the plant also yields fiber and has been used medicinally. As a tall, architectural plant, sunflower adds a striking or whimsical effect to any garden area.

VARIETIES Many good varieties of sunflower are available; some are best for seed production and others for ornamental value. (SHIMIZU)

HESPERIS MATRONALIS DAME'S ROCKET *Brassicaceae (Mustard family)*

BIENNIAL Also known as dame's rocket and dame's-violet, sweet rocket is native to the Mediterranean region and western Asia and has become naturalized in parts of North America. An upright, branching plant, it produces showy spikes of sweetly fragrant purple, lavender, or white flowers.

CULTURE Sweet rocket does best in a lightly shaded area, such as a semiwild garden. Plants will self-sow; you can also collect seed and sow outdoors in early spring (or late fall where winters are warm) for flowering the next year. Sweet rocket does not do well in hot, humid weather. If mosaic develops–signaled by mottled and curled leaves–remove and destroy affected plants.

USES Stem tips, young leaves, and tender seedpods can be lightly boiled and eaten as greens, while the flowers add a piquant mustard flavor to fruit dishes and salads. Sweet rocket was traditionally used to scent ladies' chambers; Marie Antoinette requested it while awaiting execution.

HIBISCUS HIBISCUS *Malvaceae (Mallow family)*

ANNUAL AND PERENNIAL The genus *Hibiscus*, sometimes called rose mallow,

HESPERIS MATRONALIS (DAME'S ROCKET) Plant 1-3 feet tall, often shrubby, with many ½-inch purple, lilac, or white flowers arranged in racemes. Blooms in late spring or early summer. Full sun. Zones 3-9.

HIBISCUS SABDARIFFA VAR. ROSELLE (ROSELLE, JAMAICAN SORREL) Plant 4-5 feet tall with red- or yellow-throated flowers. Blooms in summer. Full sun. Zones 8-10.

HIEROCHLOE ODORATA (SWEETGRASS) Low-growing fragrant grass, 10-12 inches tall with ⅛-inch-wide medium green blades. Full sun or partial shade.

HOUTTUYNIA CORDATA 'VARIEGATA' (HOUTTUYNIA) Spreading ground cover, 6 inches to 2 feet tall with heart-shaped dark green leaves edged in red; small white flowers appear in summer. Partial to full shade. Zones 6-10.

HUMULUS LUPULUS (HOPS) Fast-growing tall, twining vine produces male or leafy, pale yellow female flowers. Partial shade to full sun. Can be invasive. Zones 5-10.

HYPERICUM PERFORATUM (ST. JOHN'S WORT) Plant 2 feet tall produces bluish-green 3-inch-long oval leaves with transparent oil glands and yellow flowers. Blooms in summer. Full sun to partial shade. Zones 5-9.

HYSSOPUS OFFICINALIS (HYSSOP) Erect plant 1½-2 feet tall with whorls of ½-inch violet flowers. Blooms in summer. Zones 3-10. Not heat-tolerant.

IMPATIENS BALSAMINA (GARDEN BALSAM) Branching plant up to 2½ feet tall, with oval leaves 6 inches long and white, yellow, or dark red flowers 1-2 inches long; sometimes double. Partial shade.

includes annuals, herbaceous perennials, shrubs, and small trees native to many areas. Hibiscus make showy border or patio plants, with large, striking flowers.

CULTURE Both annual and perennial hibiscus are easy to grow, annuals from seed and perennials form seed or division. Perennial hibiscus are hardy outdoors only in warm regions. Start hibiscus seeds very early indoors for bloom later that summer.

USES Most hibiscus are grown for their showy flowers. *H. sabdariffa* **var. Roselle,** also called Jamaican sorrel, is a strong grower whose calyx is harvested for use in sauces and jellies.

HIEROCHLOE ODORATA SWEETGRASS *Poaceae (Grass family)*

PERENNIAL Also known as Seneca grass, holy grass, and vanilla grass, *H. odorata* is native to Europe and North America. It is a small, low-growing, inconspicuous grass, not especially attractive but valued for its fragrance.

CULTURE Sweetgrass is quite easy to grow, requiring no special care. It does need full sun and prefers moist locations, but it will tolerate a wide range of conditions. It is somewhat invasive, and perhaps best grown in an area where it can spread without overpowering other plants. Start from transplants, taking divisions in spring or fall. Space plants 15-24 inches apart; they may need to be confined. Harvest whole leaves by cutting them off at ground level, and dry in bundles.

USES Sweetgrass's vanillalike odor comes out when leaves and stems are dried. Native Americans used sweetgrass as a perfume and incense and carried it in medicine bundles. Because sweetgrass stems and leaves remain fragrant for years, Native Americans frequently used it to make woven baskets, mats, and boxes. This fragrant grass was once used as a strewing herb in European churches, hence the term holy grass. Today, its essential oils are used for flavoring sweets, beverages, and tobaccos. In Poland, where sweetgrass is known as zubrovka, leaf blades are used to flavor vodka. Dried leaves make a good addition to sachets. (SHIMIZU)

HOUTTUYNIA CORDATA HOUTTUYNIA *Sauraraceae (Lizard's-Tail family)*

PERENNIAL A native of China and Southeast Asia, houttuynia has heart-shaped leaves that are used in Asian cooking. This is a wonderful plant for shady or semishady areas, adding a decorative accent with its beautifully mottled leaves.

CULTURE Grow houttuynia in partial to full shade in any rich, moist soil. Propagate by root division in late fall, or buy nonpotbound plants with many stems and set them out in early spring. Be sure plants have adequate water during the growing season; they will not take hot, dry conditions. Cut plants back hard in the fall when the foliage begins to look unsightly and the plant begins to go dormant. The variegated form is hardy to Zone 5.

USES The flavor of the crushed leaves is pungent, and a little goes a long way in cooking; it is used extensively in Vietnamese cooking. The aroma is similar

The resemblance of its conelike catkins to a grapevine may have first drawn attention to the hop as a plant suitable for making beverages. The ancients used hops in beer; records of the Jews' captivity in Babylon refer to a strong drink made from hops that was said to prevent leprosy. To the ancient Romans the hop was a garden plant: Pliny says the young shoots of hops were eaten as a salad in the spring. Apparently, the hop grew wild among willows and, with its aggressive weedlike growth, had an effect on the willows comparable to a wolf among sheep, so the Romans called it *lupus salictarius*. Linnaeus used this tradition when he gave the plant its scientific name, *Humulus lupulus*. Hops give beer its pleasantly bitter taste, improve its ability to keep well, and give it certain sedative qualities. Pillows stuffed with hops are a traditional cure for insomnia: King George III and Abraham Lincoln used such pillows in the search for much-needed rest.

to the leaves of coriander and can be used as a substitute.

VARIETY The leaves of the variegated variety (also called **'Chameleon'**) are a lovely combination of red, cream, and green. (BERKELEY)

HUMULUS LUPULUS HOPS *Cannabaceae (Hemp family)*

PERENNIAL VINE Hops vines can reach a great length in a single season. *H. lupulus,* the common or European hop, is a native of Europe that is widely naturalized in North America. Hops produce male and female flowers on separate plants. The female flowers have pale yellow catkins with a distinct scent.

CULTURE Hops will grow in full sun to partial shade. It requires deep, rich soil; when planting, be sure the ground is well pulverized, with lots of organic material incorporated. Purchase plants with numerous new leafy shoots rising from the root stalk; propagate by root division. Set out in late fall or early spring, spacing 1-1½ feet apart. The plants require something to clamber on—an armature, wire, string, or post—and they make a useful and attractive screen. Moisture-retaining mulch and fertilizer applied during the growing season are beneficial. Cut down plants to the ground in fall. They are frost-hardy. Spider mites can sometimes affect hops; hose off foliage regularly to avoid this problem. Hops can be very invasive and need to be watched weekly for unwanted sprouts. Be sure to wear long sleeves when working with the plant, because barbs on the stems can irritate the skin.

USES Hops is mostly known for its use in the brewing of beer, although it is also effective as an ornamental in the home garden. Sleeping on a hops-stuffed pillow is said to cure insomnia. The young shoots are also edible.

VARIETY 'Aurea' is a very beautiful golden form that needs partial shade. (SHIMIZU)

HYPERICUM PERFORATUM ST. JOHN'S WORT *Hypericaceae*

PERENNIAL St. John's wort is a plant that seems to epitomize the sun itself. The delicate, dark green foliage is dotted with oil glands; the bright yellow flowers are produced on cymes in the hottest part of the summer, July and August in North Carolina.

CULTURE St. John's wort is a very tough plant and will tolerate any soil type, extreme heat and drought. Even after extreme wilting, the plant will usually revive with watering. Seeds are very small, and germination is spotty. Seeds can be sown in outdoor seedbeds in early winter for spring germination. This plant will reseed very lightly in the garden. Propagate by stem cuttings in early summer. Plant about 1 foot apart. No fertilization is necessary. The entire plant is collected and dried for use.

USES Oil made from St. John's wort is used for bruises and sunburns. More recently, the plant has been tested in the search for treatments for the AIDS virus; although not as promising as first hoped, trials continue. It has also been used as a sedative, a pain reliever, and an antidepressant. It yields yellow and gold dyes. (NORTH CAROLINA)

VARIETY Hypericum frodosum is a small deciduous shrub with similar flowers; it is also called St. John's wort. (NORTH CAROLINA)

HYSSOPUS OFFICINALIS HYSSOP *Lamiaceae (Mint family)*

SUBSHRUB Hyssop is a compact, shrubby evergreen useful in the garden border or as a low hedge. Native to southern Europe and Asia, it is widely naturalized in the United States. Hyssop produces a profusion of fragrant blue flowers on clubby spikes that attract bees and butterflies. The leaves have a strong aroma and flavor.

CULTURE Hyssop prefers full sun and warmth but will accept some light shade. Soil should have a pH of 6.5-7.5 and be well-drained. Start seeds indoors or out in early spring. Set well-rooted seedlings 1½ feet apart. You can also propagate by spring root division or summer stem cuttings. Prune back severely in winter or early spring.

USES In medieval times, hyssop was a common strewing herb, and it has long been used in folk medicine. Dried flowers and leaves are an important potpourri ingredient. Tender leaf tips, used sparingly, add a bitter bite to soups and salads and go well with strong-flavored fish and meat. Hyssop oil is used in perfumes and soaps and to flavor liqueurs. Hyssop makes a good cough medicine and is currently being examined by AIDS researchers.

VARIETIES '**Alba**' has white flowers; '**Rosea**' has pink.

IMPATIENS BALSAMINA GARDEN BALSAM *Balsaminaceae (Balsam)*

ANNUAL Garden balsam is an excellent plant in the shady or semishady border, producing continuously blooming single or double flowers in pink, red, white, purple, or mixed colors from the last spring frost right through autumn. The plant is native to India, China, and the Malay peninsula.

CULTURE The best growing conditions for garden balsam are light shade and a rich, well-drained, moist soil. Purchase full, multibranched plants, or take cuttings in the fall and through the winter to replant out the following spring. You can also start seed indoors in April. Set out seedlings after danger of frost has passed, spacing 1 foot apart. Fertilizing regularly during the growing season will ensure a large crop of flowers. Keep soil moist and weeds away; mulch is helpful. Pinching will keep the plants less leggy and promote branching. Garden balsam is not bothered by disease but may be invaded by aphids.

USES Garden balsam has been used in Chinese medicine.

IRIS X GERMANICA VAR. FLORENTINA ORRIS ROOT *Iridaceae (Iris)*

PERENNIAL The dried rhizomes of Orris root (native to Asia minor, the Balkans, and Italy) have been used by herbalists for many centuries. Fresh, the rhizomes have little odor, but dried, they have a sweet scent of violets. Orris is an attractive iris, with swordlike leaves and violet-scented flowers. It combines well with roses and makes a fine addition to a border.

CULTURE Grow in full sun in deep, rich, well-drained soil. Plant rhizomes in early spring, just below the soil surface, 12-15 inches apart. Or divide rhizomes every few years after flowering in late spring. Orris responds well to general fertilizer and moderate water. Cut back old flowers to prevent seed

SHAKESPEARE GARDENS

William Shakespeare used herbal imagery in his plays so often that many gardeners create gardens consisting only of herbs mentioned in his works. This literary twist can be enhanced with markers citing quotations, adding a new dimension to a walk through the herb garden. Some herbs that Shakespeare mentions:

As sweet as Balm, as soft as air, as gently (*Antony and Cleopatra*)

Though the Camomile the more it is/trodden on the faster it grows,/yet youth, the more it is/wasted the sooner it wears. (*Henry IV*)

There's fennel for you and columbines (*Hamlet*)

Here's flowers for you/Hot Lavender, sweet Mints, Savory, Marjoram (*Winter's Tale*)

I knew a wench married in the afternoon/as she went to the garden for Parsley to stuff a rabbit. (*The Taming of the Shrew*)

Dry up your tears, and stick your Rosemary on this fair corse (*Romeo and Juliet*)

How did she fall a tear, here in this place/I'll set a bank of Rue, sour herb of Grace (*Richard II*)

I know a bank where the wild thyme grows (*Midsummer Night's Dream*)

The Lily, I condemned for your hand,/And buds of Marjoram had stolen thy hair ("Sonnet 99")

formation, which hinders rhizome development. Like other irises, orris is susceptible to borers. It does not require frost protection.

Harvest rhizomes in late autumn. Scrub clean and dry thoroughly, which
may take some time. Or, cut it into chunks while it is still fresh, which is easier than cutting the hardened dry rhizome.

USES Mix small chunks or powder of dried orris roots into potpourri; it acts as
a fixative for the scents of other potpourri ingredients.

ISATIS TINCTORIA WOAD *Brassicaceae (Mustard family)*

BIENNIAL OR SHORT-LIVED PERENNIAL Woad, a native of central and southern
Europe and Asia, was grown commercially for hundreds of years for its leaves,
the source of a blue dye. Julius Caesar mentioned it, writing, "All the Britons
dye their bodies with woad, which produces a blue color, and this give them a
more terrifying appearance in battle." Its production decreased with the
introduction of indigo.

CULTURE Grow woad in full sun in a good, well-drained soil that is moist but
not soggy. Start from fresh seed planted 1/2 inch deep in August, or buy small
plants with lots of healthy green leaves and set them out 6 inches apart in
early spring, allowing plenty of depth for the taproot. Keep plants weed-free
while they are small. Regular fertilizing will produce the best plants. Beware
of snails and slugs, which love the plant's new leaves. Woad is very easy to
grow, and once established it will reseed itself. Frost protection is not required.
Keep in mind when planting woad that its large flowering stalks may engulf
nearby plants if you don't allow enough space.

USES Though no longer commonly used as dye, woad is grown today for the
effect of its large clouds of tiny yellow flowers, which are replaced by flat seed
capsules that turn from green to black. (BERKELEY)

LAURUS NOBILIS BAY *Lauraceae (Laurel family)*

TREE Sweet bay, or bay laurel, is an attractive evergreen tree with shiny and
leathery dark-green leaves. Left to itself, bay will grow to 50 feet; cultivated,
it is most often kept pruned to a standard round-headed form 5-10 feet in
height. Bay is native to the Mediterranean region. Respected poets and schol-
ars of ancient Greece were crowned with wreaths of bay, origin of the term
baccalaureate, "worthy of laurels."

CULTURE Bay is sturdy and easy to grow, even in pots. Because it is slow growing from seed or cuttings (taking up to 6 months to root), start with actively
developing young potted plants. Place in full sun, in sandy to gritty neutral
soil with only small amounts of organic material. Because bay prefers a dryish
soil, avoid mulching, but do provide moderate moisture in summer. Cold
weather will damage or kill bay, so grow in containers in harsh climates, moving to a well-lighted indoor location in winter; at Cornell Plantations, it is
brought inside after the first hard frost. Grow in the largest container you are
comfortable handling, and prune to fit the pot. Although bay is susceptible to
mites, scale, and mealy bugs, it will usually lose these pests when moved out-

IRIS GERMANICA VAR. FLORENTINA (ORRIS) Clumps of double leaves 1½-2½ feet long with very showy, large yellow-bearded white flowers. Blooms in late spring. Full sun. Zones 3-10. Not heat-tolerant.

ISATIS TINCTORIA (WOAD) Produces large blue-green leaves the first year and clusters of yellow flowers the second year. Flowers in May. Full sun. Zones 3-10.

LAURUS NOBILIS (BAY) Small shrub, up to 3 feet tall, with dark glossy evergreen leaves and small greenish flowers. Blooms in May. Full sun. Zones 8-10.

LAVANDULA ANGUSTIFOLIA SSP. ANGUSTIFOLIA 'MUNSTEAD' (ENGLISH LAVENDER) Shrub 2-3 feet tall with arching spikes of lavender flowers. Full sun. Blooms in summer. Zones 5-8.

POTPOURRI

A small bowl of potpourri can bring the pleasures of the herb garden inside. Potpourri is easy to make, and the the herb gardener has the ability to pick and choose the scents that are most pleasing to him or her.

To make potpourri, start with thoroughly dried plants (see pages 198-99 for information on drying). Crumble the flowers, or if they are small, leave them whole; crush leaves or seeds into small pieces. It is important to add a "fixative" ingredient that will keep the scent strong for a much longer time; fixatives include orris root (*Iris* x *germanica*) and sweet flag (*Acorus calamus*). A few drops of essential oils will deepen the fragrance. Mix the combination with your hands and store in a tightly sealed jar for about a month; turn and shake the jar twice a week. This aging process blends the mixture. Then use as needed; the remaining potpourri in the jar will remain strong for months.

Above: Drying flowers.

doors in the summer. Long-lived, a well-tended bay plant can become a family heirloom.

USES The frequent pruning necessary to keep bay to a reasonable size and shape will provide an ample supply of pungent, aromatic leaves for use in cooking, the fresh leaves being much more pungent than the dried ones available commercially.

VARIETIES A golden-leaved variety **'Aurea'** is available. (MATTHAEI)

LAVANDULA ANGUSTIFOLIA SSP. ANGUSTIFOLIA ENGLISH

LAVENDER *Lamiaceae (Mint family)*

SHRUB Lavender has been grown for centuries for its wonderfully fragrant flowers and foliage coupled with its attractive appearance in the garden. This bushy, branching, semievergreen shrub produces showy flowers and silvery gray-green foliage that remains attractive through the winter.

CULTURE Grow lavender in full sun, in a light, sandy, well-drained and alkaline soil. It is tolerant of poor, dry soil. Many cultivars do not breed true to type from seed, so purchase small plants or start from divisions (in spring) or stem cuttings (from spring to late summer). Clip plants back during the first year to keep them from flowering and to encourage lateral branching. Spacing depends on variety and the eventual size you wish the plant to attain; you may plant as close as 12 inches for miniature hedges or up to 4-6 feet apart for spreading. Lavender is also fine for winter pot culture, in the greenhouse or on a sunny windowsill. Water pots infrequently, and maintain nighttime temperatures of 40-50° F., and daytime temperatures 5-10° warmer.

Lavender plants develop a woody base with age and eventually become quite straggly. You can avoid having to replace older plants by pruning in the spring or after flowering to maintain a compact shape. Lavender benefits from a mulch of 1 inch of coarse sand. For maximum fragrance, harvest the flowering stems in early blossom. Hang in small bunches to dry, or spread out on a screen. Pick leaves anytime. Provide plants with winter protection, such as pine boughs, after the ground freezes.

USES Lavender flowers and leaves are widely used in sachets and potpourris. Oil extracted from the leaves scents perfumes, soaps, and toiletries. Cut flowers are a fine visual and aromatic addition to fresh or dried arrangements. It is used as a tonic for afflictions such as nervous headache, stress, and depression.

VARIETIES Among generally available varieties, **'Alba'** has white flowers and **'Jean Davis'** offers pink blooms. **'Munstead'** is a popular dwarf with deep lavender flowers. **'Twickle Purple'** is very fragrant, with soft lavender flowers and broader, more silvery leaves. **'Hidcote'** grows to 12 inches, with deep purple flowers. **'Provence'** bears wonderfully fragrant violet flowers on 2-foot stems and becomes an impressive 3-foot shrub with soft gray foliage.

French lavender **(*L. dentata*)**, also known as fringed or Spanish lavender, has distinctive, roughly toothed leaves and a camphorous aroma. A mature plant can reach several feet in diameter and up to 40 inches in height. North of Zone 9, French lavender must be grown as an indoor pot plant. Prune

Above: Dried flowers can be used in arrangements, or blended for potpourri. *Left:* Flowers prepared for potpourri mixes: blue cornflowers, yellow calendula, rosebuds, blue malva, lemon verbena leaves, lavender, and orris root, which is used as a fixative.

PERFUMES

Humans have always been drawn to flowering plants not just for their many practical applications but also for their beauty and pleasant scents. Such scents could be used to mask unpleasant odors–daily bathing is a relatively recent phenomena–but they also provided a unique pleasure. Flower scents were first developed in Greece, where the use of such perfumes became widespread. The ancient Romans made abundant and extravagant use of perfumes along with various scented oils. Like so many aspects of ancient civilization, the use of perfumes declined drastically during the early Middle Ages, but Crusaders returning from the Holy Land brought back rare Eastern oils and perfumes along with the knowledge of perfumery and other herbal lore. It was at this time that animal substances–primarily musk, ambergris, civet, and castor–were first added as fixatives to perfumes. The Italians became masters of perfume-making, but when Italian perfumers settled in Paris during the early 1500s France became the leader of the industry. The use of personal scents then became fashionable, and both men and women wore an ornamental pomander or pouncet-box, which hung from the waist. By 1900 perfumes and cosmetics were being manufactured on a scientific basis, particularly in France, and today perfume-making is a major industry there.

as needed to keep plants compact and shapely. Note, however, that flowering occurs on stem tips, so too-frequent pruning will delay or prevent blooms. Whiteflies and spider mites can be a problem indoors, as can fungus diseases encouraged by dampness and poor air circulation.

Lavandin (**L. x intermedia**) grosso, or fat spike lavendin, has large gray leaves twice the size of English lavender. A mature plant forms a mound about 16 inches high and 3 feet across, topped by long, thick dark purple flower spikes that bloom later than the English lavenders. Fat spike is also much more hardy than other lavenders and more tolerant of fungus, a big problem in areas where summers are hot and humid. Its flower buds are bigger and better for harvesting. The cultivar **'Dutch'** blooms 2-3 weeks later. (CORNELL)

LEVISTICUM OFFICINALE LOVAGE *Apiaceae (Parsley or Carrot family)*

PERENNIAL Native to the Mediterranean mountains of southern France, Greece, and the Balkans, lovage looks like a giant celery plant and grows 6-7 feet tall.

CULTURE Lovage is easy to grow, but needs a period of winter dormancy. It prefers full sun but will tolerate some shade, and it does best in rich, moist, well-drained soil. Sow seeds in late summer as soon as they ripen and turn brown, or propagate by root division in early spring. Lovage has large, fleshy roots, and it gets bushy as well as very tall, so give it lots of space, about 3 feet all around. A single plant is plenty for one household. Because of its height, lovage is good planted next to a fence or next to smaller herbs to provide shade. Once established, lovage dies to the ground in the winter and comes up quickly and green early in the spring.

To keep this spectacular plant looking good after midsummer, cut off any brown leaves and deadhead the major bloom before it goes to seed. For culinary uses, harvest seed heads when they turn brown (be sure to check them for aphids before using them), pick leaves all summer to use fresh or dry, and dig roots anytime to use fresh and in fall to dry for the winter.

USES The entire plant has a very strong aromatic smell and taste. All parts are edible–seeds, stems, leaves, and root–and impart a rich celery flavor. It is also used to make a liqueur known as lovage cordial. Lovage straws made from the hollow stems are used in bloody marys. (MATTHAEI)

LILIUM BROWNII BROWN'S LILY *Liliaceae (Lily family)*

PERENNIAL Native to China, Brown's lily is a bulbous plant that produces lovely large, tubular white flowers on stems rising 5-6 feet.

CULTURE Brown's lily grows best in full sun to light shade in a moderately rich, well-drained, moist soil. Purchase large, plump bulbs for planting in the fall, 6-8 inches below the soil surface, spacing 6-12 inches apart. Mulch to preserve moisture, and supply water throughout the growing season. After plants have flowered and leaves have begun to yellow and turn brown, cut off stalks at ground level. Add a winter protection after plants go dormant in case of very hard freezes. You may need to protect bulbs from rodents.

USES The roots of Brown's lily are used by Chinese herbalists to treat coughing and insomnia. (BERKELEY)

LAVANDULA DENTATA (FRENCH LAVENDER) Erect shrub up to 3½ feet tall with indented green leaves and light purple flowers. Full sun. Blooms in summer. Zones 9-10; can be used as pot plant north of Zone 9.

LEVISTICUM OFFICINALE (LOVAGE) Plant 4-7 feet tall with large dark green leaves and large, flat clusters of yellow flowers. Blooms in summer. Full sun to light shade. Zones 3-9.

LILIUM BROWNII (BROWN'S LILY) Plant 5-6 feet tall with 1-6 large tubular flowers, with petals up to 6 inches long. Full sun to light shade. Zones 8-10.

LINUM USITATISSIMUM (FLAX) Slender wiry stems, 1-2 feet tall, with bluish green leaves and large panicles of pale blue funnel-shaped flowers. Blooms in late spring through summer. Full sun. Zones 5-10. Not heat-tolerant.

FIBERS

Though the spinning mills of nature run silently, and at no cost, their productivity is tremendous, giving us the material of every fabric that has clothed and sheltered humankind since first our species began. Skins and hides soon proved to be too heavy and clumsy, and their owners were capable of defending them vigorously with tooth and claw. The plant world, however, was far more accommodating, providing us with an abundance of fibers from sources available almost everywhere on earth.

Cotton and flax were among the earliest substances used, having been found throughout remains from ancient Egypt and in both the old and new worlds. Luckily, plants produce both long and short fibers, the long ones usually in the outer portions, such as the stems, whereas the short fibers are more often (but not always) found in the pith.

Versatility is the order of the day in plant fibers, which can be put to use in brooms, mechanical sweepers, upholstery, bowstrings, bags, and sacks (some can transport ore for as long as 10 years), still others are used in rugs, stuffing for railway bearings, life preservers, even strong paper for dwelling walls in Japan. In short, plant fibers present us with a veritable Aladdin's lamp for a multitude of wishes for a better life.

LINUM USITATISSIMUM FLAX *Linaceae (Flax family)*

ANNUAL Flax, also known as linseed, has been used for its fibers since before recorded history and is mentioned in Homer–who refers to sails made of it–and the Bible. Flax is an important economic crop, the source of both linseed oil and seeds and fibers for flax and linen. Probably native to Asia, it has become naturalized in much of North America.

CULTURE Flax is easy to grow from seeds sown directly in the garden in late spring or early summer. It likes full sun to partial shade and well-drained soil. If you have heavy clay soil, start indoors under glass. This plant does not need fertilizer or water until it is ready to flower. Seeds will be ready to harvest in about 100 days; fibers are strongest just after bloom.

USES Until recently, flax was one of the main sources of fabric used in clothing in the United States, including those known as linen and linsey-woolsey. The oil from its seeds is used in paints and linoleum; the seeds are baked in cakes and breads. Seeds are also used in many medications; overdoses cause respiratory distress and paralysis. This plants produces beautiful blue flowers in summer and is often used as an ornamental.

VARIETY *L. perenne,* a perennial species with sky blue, almost translucent flowers, is an absolutely gorgeous plant for a perennial garden. It neeeds well-drained soil and full sun and does not like to be too dry. Fertilize with a weak nitrogen fertilizer in the early spring, just before flowering. (NORTH CAROLINA)

LIPPIA GRAVEOLENS MEXICAN OREGANO *Verbenaceae (Vervain family)*

SHRUB Mexican oregano is an upright shrub native to southern North America and Central America.

CULTURE This shrub requires full sun and moderately fertile, well-drained soil. Because it tolerates only light frost, Mexican oregano must spend the winter indoors in cold zones. Grow as a pot plant, moving it outside and inside with the seasons, pruning and repotting as needed; or plant it out in the garden and dig it up in the fall. Indoors, place it in a moderately sunny spot, in well-drained potting mix, and keep it almost dry. Maintain a minimum temperature of 50° F. Mexican oregano can be grown from seed or from cuttings taken anytime during the growing season. Pinch back to encourage branching. Pick leaves fresh as needed, or dry them for storage.

USES The leaves of Mexican oregano are more pungent than common oregano and are used like that herb in Mexico. (CORNELL)

MALVA SYLVESTRIS MALVA *Malvaceae (Mallow family)*

PERENNIAL Native to Europe and naturalized in North America, mallow has been grown since Roman times for its decorative, medicinal, and flavoring qualities. Malva is an attractive border plant, with its deeply cut kidney-shaped leaves and large, showy purple-pink flowers borne in clusters.

CULTURE Although malva is a perennial, it is often treated as an easy-to-grow summer-blooming annual. Direct-sow seeds in the garden in early spring, in a sunny spot with well-drained, moderately fertile soil. Space plants about 1 foot apart. It self-sows readily.

USES Dried malva flowers and leaves impart a delicate flavor to tea, and the

LIPPIA GRAVEOLENS (MEXICAN OREGANO) Upright shrub produces cream-colored flowers. Full sun. Zones 8-10, grown as pot plant in cooler regions.

MALVA SYLVESTRIS (MALVA) Plant 3-4 feet tall with small kidney-shaped leaves and clusters of pink flowers. Blooms in late summer. Full sun. Zones 5-8.

MANDRAGORA OFFICINARUM (MANDRAKE) 12-inch-long wrinkled leaves with bell-shaped yellow-green flowers in spring. Partial shade. Zones 6-9.

MARRUBIUM VULGARE (HOREHOUND) Plant 2-3 feet tall, with aromatic woolly green leaves and whorls of white flowers in summer. Full sun. Zones 4-9.

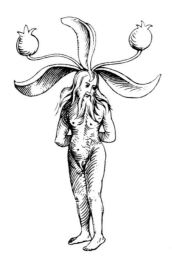

Illustrations of anthropomorphized mandrakes abounded in early herbals. They were often joined by women-drakes, plants that existed only in the imaginations of the illustrators.

dried flowers add color to potpourris. The flat, wrinkled green seed capsules, or "cheeses," along with flowers, make interesting chopped salad ingredients.

MANDRAGORA OFFICINARUM MANDRAKE *Solanaceae (Nightshade)*

PERENNIAL Mystery and lore surround this ancient herb, also known as the love apple. Magical properties were ascribed to it because of the sometimes humanlike form of its branching tuberous roots, and because of its narcotic, hallucinogenic, and anesthetic effects (it contains a number of powerful alkaloids). It is native to the Mediterranean region and the Himalayas.

CULTURE Mandrake requires a warm, sheltered, semishaded location with moist, fairly rich, well-drained soil. It appreciates a mulch to conserve moisture and feeding with compost or well-rotted manure. It is best propagated by root division. Nurseries seldom offer plants, and while seed is occasionally available, it must be sown as soon as it is ripe. Seedling growth is very slow; it may take 3-5 years for a plant to mature, but the plant will then last for many years. Set plants out in late winter, 2 feet apart. Growth begins in late winter, with flowers produced in late winter and early spring. The leaves shrivel by midsummer, and the plant dies back; it's best to mark the plant's location in the garden during this unusually early dormancy period. This plant did not survive the winter at Cornell Plantations.

USES Mandrake is not a showy or ornamental plant, so it is grown today mostly in collections of medicinal plants or of herbs of folklore and magic. (BERKELEY)

MARRUBIUM VULGARE HOREHOUND *Lamiaceae (Mint family)*

PERENNIAL Native to Asia, southern Europe, North Africa, the Canary Islands, and the Azores, horehound has naturalized in North America in dry, sandy spots, wastelands, sheep pastures, vacant lots, and abandoned fields. Horehound is a much-branched, bushy plant with downy white stems and aromatic green leaves with a whitish, woolly coating. The flowers, which appear in dense whorls along the stem during the summer, attract bees.

CULTURE Grow horehound in full sun in poor, dryish, sandy soil. Start from seed sown indoors in a moist seeding mix, covered with a plastic bag and refrigerated 4-8 weeks. You can also divide existing plants in spring or take stem cuttings in late summer. Plants self-sow readily. Thin seedlings to 10 or 20 inches apart. Prune back lanky flower stalks after flowering to maintain a compact, neat appearance. Harvest and use leaves anytime. To retain best flavor for storage, remove leaves from stems and spread out to dry.

USES Horehound is used in cough drops, cough syrup, and medicinal candies. Tea made from its leaves and mixed with honey has a high concentration of mucilage, which soothes a sore throat.

VARIETY *M. incanum* (silver horehound) is an ornamental variety with soft, downy, silvery leaves and stems; it is hardy to Zone 5. It makes an attractive silver accent plant in the garden and is also an effective foil for colorful flowers in pot plantings. (CORNELL)

MATRICARIA RECUTITA CHAMOMILE *Asteraceae (Sunflower family)*

ANNUAL Commonly known as German chamomile this heavy-blooming herb is native to Europe and western Asia. It's attractive in the garden, with delicate foliage and daisylike early spring flowers borne on heads up to 2 feet high.

CULTURE Like perennial chamomile, *M. recutita* likes full sun, any garden soil, and moderate amounts of water; it actually prefers poor soil. It is a reseeding annual and is happiest when allowed to set seed in the garden on its own. You can recognize these seedlings in the spring by their characteristically delicate foliage. Start German chamomile from seed in autumn, or from plants or transplants in early spring; set 8-10 inches apart.

German chamomile looks lovely planted with catnip. It is a short-lived annual, however, and will be gone after it sets seed (which is at the beginning of summer in Berkeley, and later in the summer at U.S. Botanic Garden). You will need to plant something in the empty space after it dies back. It persists longer if flowers are harvested. At Cornell Plantations, a second sowing is planted to fill in after the first one dies back.

USES Flowers and leaves, fresh or dry, make a delicious apple- or pineapple-flavored tea, sweeter and better-tasting than perennial chamomile tea. Chamomile tea is an excellent, gentle sedative and is good for digestion. Leaves and flowers are also good for herbal baths and cosmetics; a rinse made from the leaves is used to brighten blond hair. (SHIMIZU)

MELISSA OFFICINALIS LEMON BALM *Lamiaceae (Mint family)*

PERENNIAL Lemon balm is one of the easiest plants to grow; once established in the garden, it remains. It has the mint family's characteristic four-sided stems, but is far better behaved than most mints. Its fibrous root system spreads quickly, but it is easily torn out in great bunches and will obediently stay within any barricade you erect (though it sometimes does reseed). The whole plant tastes and smells like lemon. This native of southern Europe is now widely naturalized in the United States. Its genus's name, *Melissa*, is Greek for "bee," a reflection of the plant's great attractiveness to honeybees.

CULTURE Start lemon balm from seeds, which germinate slowly and irregularly (seeds have been used successfully at North Carolina Botanical Garden), or more easily by root division in the fall or by cuttings. Lemon balm likes rich soil, plenty of moisture, and full sun, but will put up with much less than the ideal when required. Allow room for the plant to spread. Cut back occasionally to keep the plant neat and prevent seeding, and harvest leaves as needed. The lemon flavor does not last well when the leaves are dried, so use fresh when possible.

The trailing, fragrant stems of lemon balm make it a nice houseplant; you can pot up a few garden plants to enjoy indoors all winter. Plants left in the garden die down to the ground after frost, growing back from the roots each spring.

USES *Melissa* was steeped in wine by the Greeks as a cure for fevers; Arabs chewed it in a gum; Virgil grew balm for his bees; and the French mixed it

SUPERSTITIONS

There is something sinister and threatening about any dense vegetable growth, giving rise to a horde of fears and beliefs that have created a vast body of superstitious folklore. For example, if you wish to become invisible, you have only to go forth barefoot on midsummer's eve at midnight to gather fernseed in its precise moment of ripening. It was also necessary to carry twelve pewter plates for the fernseed would pass through eleven before coming to rest on the twelfth. There only remained the difficulty of seeing it, for it made everything it touched perfectly invisible.

Or perhaps you might wish to attend a witch's Sabbath, in which case you smeared your body with an ointment made mostly from henbane, *Hyoscyamus niger*. Instantly it would transport you to the scene of the revels, where you would hear wild noises and see very strange things. The henbane contained hallucinogens that were absorbed through the skin, producing the effect of flight, noise, and weird visions.

Infertile women often had recourse to mandrake root, *Mandragora officinarum*, to procure offspring. The root also brought freedom from all bodily harm, and great wealth. But unless you disposed of it, at a profit, before you died, you would have a horrible death, and would be claimed by the devil, which explains why its owners were ever induced to part with it.

MINT

Members of the mint family are found throughout the world, but the center of distribution is the Mediterranean region, where these plants form a dominant part of the vegetation. It is not surprising, then, that mint appears in Greek myths. The name *mint* itself comes from Minthe, daughter of Cocytus. Pluto, god of the underworld, was attracted to Minthe, but his wife, Persephone, discovered his unfaithfulness and in a rage transformed the poor girl into the herb. In another myth, Jupiter and Mercury, disguised as mortals, wandered the earth in search of hospitality. The 2 gods went to a thousand homes, both those of the rich and those of the poor, looking for somewhere to rest, but the doors were always bolted and barred against them. At last they came to a hovel, the poorest they had seen, but when they knocked the door was opened wide and a voice called to them to enter. This was the humble home of an old man named Philemon and his wife, Baucis. Although desperately poor, Philemon and Baucis offered the strangers all they had—and when the time came to eat, Baucis wiped over the table with stalks of fresh mint. (It should be mentioned that for their kindness Philemon and Baucis were spared when the gods punished the rest of inhospitable humankind.)

into a perfume called Eau de Melisse des Cannes.

VARIETY The cultivar **'Aurea'** has golden variegated leaves in the spring. (MATTHAEI)

MENTHA MINT *Lamiaceae (Mint family)*

PERENNIAL The mints are a widely variable genus of herbs, most native to or naturalized through parts of Europe. All mints have four-sided stems.

CULTURE Mints will grow under a broad range of conditions but do best in a rich, moist soil in full sun to partial shade. Mints are notorious for their spreading, invasive growth habit. You will have to contain their underground runners with sunken barriers, or plant in underground pots. Mints do not grow true to type from seed, so start from division (best in early spring) or cuttings (in summer). Space 12-18 inches apart, and provide generous quantities of well-rotted manure or compost. After several years, when mint has used up the soil nutrients, divide and refertilize. Prune back after flowering to prevent seed formation, and tip back new growth to encourage branching.

Mints are sometimes troubled by mint rust, which appears as orange spots on the back of leaves. Rust is most likely to infect plants growing in shade. If it strikes, try cutting back the mint and replanting it in a new location.

USES Mints are treasured for their refreshing qualities; their smells and tastes have long been valued for their cooling effect. Both leaves and flowers are often used as a decorative and flavorful garnish in iced drinks and with desserts, salads, and soups. Mints make wonderful teas that are flavorful, soothing to the stomach, and good for congestion and colds.

VARIETIES *M. spicata* (spearmint) is one of the most useful culinary mints, lending itself to tea, mint juleps, jelly, tabouleh, and desserts. It is the source of spearmint oil used for flavoring candies and gum. It grows 18 inches high, with sharply pointed dark green leaves and reddish stems. Spearmint is excellent in a hanging basket or terracotta pot. *M. s.* **'Crispata'** has distinctive rounded leaves, bright green and crinkled, which produce a striking effect in the garden. **Silver mint** is a moderately invasive, flavorful relative of common spearmint that doubles as an ornamental.

M. x piperita (peppermint), valued for its strong and cooling aroma, can be distinguished from spearmint by its taller growth (to about 3 feet) and its darker, purplish stems. A combination of peppermint and spearmint makes one of the best herbal teas. Some of the best of the endless variations of peppermint are **blue balsam mint**, with superb flavor and strong fragrance; **blackstem peppermint**, with strong peppermint flavor and a black stem; **candy mint,** with a flavor reminiscent of peppermint candy; **chocolate mint,** with a slight chocolatey fragrance that's great for desserts; **'Todd Mitchum'**, grown commercially for its uniquely intense peppermint fragrance; and **'Variegata'**, a new bicolor form with ornamental, variegated leaves. *M. x piperata* var. *citrata* (bergamot mint) has a citrusy flavor and aroma.

M. x gracilis (red mint) grows 18 inches high, with shiny red-tinged leaves that have a hint of spearmint fragrance. An excellent culinary mint, it is widely used in southeast Asia with rice or grain salads and fruit desserts.

MARTICARIA RECUTITA (FALSE CHAMOMILE) Plant 2 feet tall with linear leaves and tall yellow daisy-like flowers. Blooms in spring through summer. Full sun. Zones 4-9.

MELISSA OFFICINALIS (LEMON BALM) Plant 2 feet tall plant produces spreading clumps of broad toothed leaves. Full sun to light shade. Zones 4-9.

MENTHA SPICATA (SPEARMINT) Plant 1-2 feet tall produces sharply pointed dark green leaves. Full sun to partial shade. Zones 5-9.

MENTHA x PIPERITA (PEPPERMINT) Plant 3 feet tall with purplish stems, produces 2- to 3-inch-long serrated leaves. Full to partial sun. Zones 5-9.

MENTHA X PIPERITA VAR. CITRATA (BERGAMOT MINT, ORANGE MINT) Plant 3 feet tall, produces large, green leaves, slightly ruffled, with citrus flavor. Full sun to partial shade. Zones 5-9.

MENTHA X PIPERITA 'CHOCOLATE' (CHOCOLATE PEPPERMINT) Plant 3 feet tall produces 1- to 3-inch-long leaves with subtle chocolate flavor. Full sun to partial shade. Zones 5-9

MENTHA AQUATICA VAR. 'CRISPA' (CURLY MINT) Plant 3 feet tall produces small light green leaves and purple flowers. Often grows near water. Full sun to partial shade. Zones 5-10.

MENTHA LONGIFOLIA (HORSEMINT) Plant 1-4 feet tall produces grayish green leaves with white hairs. Full sun to partial shade. Zones 5-10.

M. pulegium (English pennyroyal) is an excellent ground cover, only 6 inches tall, with a creeping growth habit and a pleasing, slightly peppermint scent. The lax stems often root where they touch earth. The dried leaves are an ingredient in herbal flea collars, and the plant is also good in a hanging basket. English pennyroyal is hardy only to Zone 7, and even there it may die out over winter; a covering of pine needles may help. *Hedeoma pulegoides* (American pennyroyal) is a Mint family member native to the central and eastern United States used by Native Americans to repel flies and mosquitoes. A robust annual, 12 inches tall with upright branching, American pennyroyal yields an essential oil valued as a flea repellent. It is quite poisonous and should not be taken internally.

M. requienii (Corsican mint), native to wet, shady areas of the islands of Corsica and Sardinia, needs continuous moisture to grow. It is one of the most beautiful and delicate ground covers imaginable, with tiny, round, bright green leaves that hug the ground and root as they grow. It is also gorgeous grown in a container or as a ground cover in a container with other plants. The leaves give off a wonderful smell of creme de menthe when rubbed. Corsican mint is one of the smallest flowering plants in cultivation, bearing tiny lilac flowers in summer. In hardiness, it is similar to English pennyroyal.

M. suaveolens (apple or woolly mint) has a pleasant apple fragrance and is thickly covered with whitish hairs. *M. suaveolens* '**Variegata**' is pineapple mint, a highly ornamental plant whose green and white leaves look beautiful with Victoria sage and roses and are excellent in container combinations. Young leaves have a pineapple aroma. A form of water mint (*M. aquatica*) known as '**Eau de cologne**' has a fragrance similar to bergamot and perfumes any plant growing near it. **Lime** and **grapefruit** mints also have fruity fragrances—and unclear parentage. (SHIMIZU)

Growing mint in containers controls its tendency to spread throughout the garden.

MESPILUS GERMANICA MEDLAR *Rosaceae (Rose family)*

SMALL TREE A native of Europe, medlar produces large birdlike flowers in the spring and, later, apple-shaped fruits that turn a fine russet color, as do the leaves in the fall. The fruits are edible, but they are very acid and must be eaten when very ripe. Medlar makes a wonderful small specimen tree, resembling a gnarled apple or small cherry, a nice size for a small garden. You can maintain it at a height of 6-8 feet with an extremely small spread, though pruning often reduces number of flowers and fruit. It can also be trained as an espalier.

CULTURE Plant medlar in full sun, in any type of well-drained soil. Purchase a well-branched specimen; medlar tends to flower on its new growth, so the more branches, the more flowers and fruits you will have. Plant in the fall. A fertilizer applied right before leafing out will help the tree get off to a vigorous start as the growing season begins. Water deeply and regularly once every 1-2 weeks; a mulch will help preserve this moisture. Once plants are established they require less water. No frost protection is necessary.

USES Medlar fruit is usually eaten fresh, sometimes used for preserves. (BERKELEY)

Why do garden makers of today so seldom deliberately plan for fragrance? Undoubtedly, gardens of early times were sweeter than ours. . . . Our great-grandmothers prized more highly than any others what they called their posy flowers, moss rose, southernwood, bergamot, marigold, and the like . . . No period has been so unmindful of fragrance in the garden as this in which we are now living. We have juggled the sweet pea into the last word in hues and furbelow, and all but lost its sweetness; we have been careless of the rose's scent . . . We plan meticulously for color harmony and a sequence of bloom, but who goes deliberately about planning for a succession of sweet scents during every week of the growing year?
FROM *THE FRAGRANT GARDEN,* BY LOUISE BEEBE WILDER

MOMORDICA CHARANTIA BALSAM PEAR *Cucurbitaceae (Gourd family)*

ANNUAL VINE This tendril-climbing vine, native to the tropics and naturalized in the southeastern United States, is a fine ornamental, edible landscape plant. It produces deeply lobed leaves, bright yellow flowers, unusual bright orange and warty fruits, and beautiful red seeds. There are 2 types of balsam pear fruits, one that is 12 inches long and another that is shorter and more plump.

CULTURE Given a warm climate, balsam pear is easy to grow, in full sun and average soil. Start from seed, either sown directly in the garden after the soil has warmed up and danger of frost is past or sown indoors 3 weeks before outdoor planting. Space plants 24 inches apart. Balsam pear will not tolerate cold weather.

USES The fruit, which has a bitter taste, is eaten like a vegetable and also used in chutney. There have been recent–unconfirmed–reports that it boosts the immune system. (SHIMIZU)

MONARDA DIDYMA BEEBALM *Lamiaceae (Mint family)*

PERENNIAL Also commonly known as bergamot and Oswego tea, this New World herb was well known to Native Americans as both food and medicine. Its showy, bright red flowers attract bees, hummingbirds, and butterflies and make striking, long-lasting cut blooms.

CULTURE Beebalm can be planted in full sun or partial shade; it prefers a rich, moist soil. Beebalm is best propagated by division, which keeps the cultivars true. Like other mints, beebalm is highly invasive, so divide clumps every 3 years in early spring or in autumn after flowering. Space 2 feet apart, as beebalm spreads rapidly. When harvesting during bloom, cut to the ground to encourage fall flowering. Fertilize during the long blooming season, and keep the plant well watered. Drought encourages powdery mildew, to which beebalm is susceptible; cut back infected leaves. Do not water overhead if infection occurs, as water spreads the fungus. Cut back almost to the ground in the fall, and provide a mulch if winters are cold.

Beebalm is a wonderful plant for low-maintenance situations. Combined with daylilies along the side of house, for example, it can romp freely and bloom after the lilies.

USES Beebalm's aromatic leaves can be used, fresh or dry, in teas, salads, and potpourris; they provide the flavoring for the famous Earl Grey tea. Its flowers are also edible. It is also said to be good for coughs, sore throats, and nausea.

VARIETIES *M. fistulosa* (wild bergamot or horsemint) has pink-lavender flowers and is found naturalized in fields; it can crowd out cultivated varieties. *M. citriodora* (lemon bergamot or lemon mint) is an attractive and unusual annual whose purple pink flowers grow in showy whorls up the flowering stalk. The flowers are beautiful in the garden and as cut flowers and add lovely late-season color. The strongly lemon-scented leaves are excellent in teas or cooking, and the flowers are also edible, in salads or as a garnish. There are many cultivars of *M. didyma* available with different flower colors: **'Cambridge Red'**

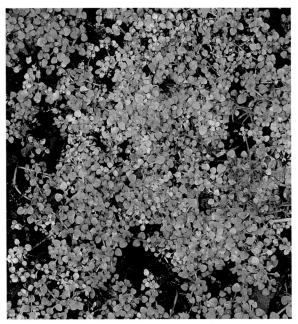

MENTHA PULEGIUM (ENGLISH PENNYROYAL) Plant 12 inches tall with small round to oval dark green leaves on many-branched stems and small bluish flowers in summer. Full sun. Zones 6-10.

MENTHA REQUIENII (CORSICAN MINT) Spreading tiny leaves, not more than 1 inch tall with minute mauve flowers. Excellent ground cover. Full sun to partial shade. Zones 6-9.

MENTHA SUAVEOLENS (APPLE MINT) Plant 3 feet tall with slender erect stems and grayish green rounded leaves. Clusters of mauve flowers appear in summer. Full sun to partial shade. Zones 5-10.

MENTHA SUAVEOLENS 'VARIEGATA' (PINEAPPLE MINT) Plant 1½ feet tall with slender erect stems and grayish green rounded leaves mottled with cream and white. Clusters of mauve flowers appear in summer. Full sun to partial shade. Zones 5-10.

red); **'Adam Red'** (salmon red); **'Mahogany'** (deep red); **'Blue Stocking'** (deep lilac); **'Violet Queen'** (lavender); **'Croftway Pink'** (pink); and **'Snow White'** (white). (CORNELL)

MYRRHIS ODORATA SWEET CICELY *Apiaceae (Parsley or Carrot family)*

PERENNIAL Sweet cicely is found throughout Europe and the British Isles, and while not common it is naturalized in the United States. It has a thick root and bright green, fernlike leaves, borne on branching stems that resemble parsley. Sweet cicely's very small, clustered white flowers bloom in May and June and are followed by dark brown to black seeds.

CULTURE Grow sweet cicely in shady, moist, crumbly soil. Prepare the bed well to accommodate the deep, thick taproot. Seed can be difficult to germinate, although the plant does self-sow (sometimes profusely–the plant seems to need repeated freezing and thawing provided outdoors to break dormancy and germinate freely). Cicely can also be propagated by root cuttings. Start both seeds and roots in the fall. Sweet cicely can be grown everywhere in the United States except along the Gulf Coast and in southern Florida, where the winters are too warm. After flowering, the leaves will turn yellow; if this old foliage is cut back, a new flush of fresh green leaves will soon appear.

USES The sugary leaves of sweet cicely do not dry well, so use them fresh, pick-ing throughout the summer. Harvest seed heads as they turn brown, hang to dry and drop in paper bags. All parts of the plant are edible and taste and smell like anise. Seeds can also be used fresh, in salads or as a garden snack. The flowers retain their anise perfume after drying.

VARIETY Osmorhiza claytonia, a native plant is similar in appearance and growth habit to sweet cicely, and is known as native sweet cicely. (NEW YORK)

MYRTUS COMMUNIS MYRTLE *Myrtaceae (Myrtle family)*

SHRUB Myrtle is a highly aromatic shrub with dense, scented evergreen foliage; fragrant, fluffy white flowers; and peppery blue-black berries. Native to the Mediterranean region, myrtle was featured in ancient Greek and Roman festivals.

CULTURE Grow myrtle in a sheltered, sunny spot and well-drained soil. In warm regions, you can give myrtle a permanent outdoor location in the landscape. In colder climates, you must grow it as a container plant and move it indoors for the winter. Start from seed (soaked for 24 hours before sowing), cuttings, or layering.

USES Myrtle is prized for its aroma and its ability easily to be pruned to the desired form. Where myrtle can be grown outdoors year-round, it makes an excellent hedge or screen. As a container plant, it is attractive for the porch or terrace. (MATTHAEI)

NASHIA INAGUENSIS MOUJEAN TEA *Verbenaceae (Vervain family)*

SHRUB This plant's tiny, fragrant evergreen leaves are covered with fine hairs, yet have a glossy sheen underneath. Eventually the plant develops cream-col-ored flowers, followed by beadlike orange fruit. Its attractive foliage makes it a pretty addition to a mixed pot planting. It is native to the Bahamas.

MESPILUS GERMANICA (MEDLAR) Small tree, grows to 20 feet tall, but can be kept to 6-8 feet. Sometimes thorny or gnarled. Produces 5-inch-long oval toothed leaves, 2-inch white flowers and apple-shaped fruit. Zones 6-9.

MOMORDICA CHARANTIA (BALSAM PEAR) Tendril-climbing vine produces deeply-lobed leaves and warty green or orange fruits with bright red seeds. Full sun. Zones 6-10.

MONARDA DIDYMA (BEEBALM) Plants form large clumps, 2½-5 feet tall, with dark green leaves and clusters of 2-inch-wide flowers. Blooms in summer. Full sun to partial shade. Zones 4-10. Not heat tolerant.

MONARDA FISTULOSA (WILD BERGAMOT) Plant 3-4 feet tall with 3- to 4-inch-long leaves and lavender flowers. Blooms in summer. Full sun to partial shade. Zones 3-10.

CULTURE Moujean tea thrives in full sun and warmth. Propagate from stem cuttings, taken anytime during the growing season (June-September). Pinch back to encourage branching. At Cornell Plantations, a 6-inch cutting planted out after frost grew to 18 inches during a warm growing season; the following year, which was cool and wet, a 6-inch cutting grew to only 8 inches. Dig plants or take cuttings to overwinter inside, or grow moujean tea year-round as a pot plant. Fertilize potted plants once a month with half-strength 20-20-20 fertilizer, or with fish emulsion. Under dry conditions, particularly indoors in winter, misting its foliage is beneficial.

USES The leaves, fresh or dried, add a delicious vanilla flavor to teas. (CORNELL)

NEPETA CATARIA CATNIP *Lamiaceae (Mint family)*

PERENNIAL Catnip is native to Europe but was naturalized here quite early; nearly every garden in U.S. colonial times had some.

CULTURE Catnip is easy to start from seed in early spring and from cuttings and division all summer. Set 18 inches apart, and be prepared for this fast-growing plant to spread rapidly, like all mints. Catnip will grow in partial shade, but the sunnier the spot, the stronger the plant and its minty aroma will be. It likes lime and sandy soil, which must be well drained; like cats, catnip will not tolerate damp feet. Do, however, water during periods of drought. This hardy perennial dies back each fall and reappears, bigger and better, the following spring. Few pests bother it.

Harvest leaves all summer by cutting stems after flower buds form and drying the leaves on the stems. This also acts as pruning, which is necessary to keep the 2- to 3-foot plant from getting leggy. Catnips vary greatly in the amount of aromatic oil they contain. When you find one that is pungent and highly attractive to cats, propagate it by cuttings or divisions; seed will produce variable offspring.

USES Catnip has been used since Biblical times as a tea; it has a calming effect on humans. It's extremely exciting and attractive to cats, who are apt to romp in and tear up the plants (which does not affect their health).

VARIETIES 'Citriodora' is a lemon-scented cultivar. *N. mussinii* 'Blue Wonder' is a catmint with leaves smaller than catnip. It forms a 12- to 18-inch-diameter mound with bright, light blue flowers that last from early spring through summer if deadheaded consistently. (MATTHAEI)

NIGELLA SATIVA BLACK CUMIN *Ranunculaceae (Buttercup family)*

ANNUAL Distinct from cumin (*Cuminum cyminum*, Parsley family) black cumin is native to southwestern Asia and is also known as nutmeg flower, Roman coriander, and, because of its finely divided leaves, fennel flower.

CULTURE Grow black cumin in full sun and light-textured, well-drained soil. Direct-sow seeds in the garden in spring or late autumn. Plants will also self-sow (leave some seedpods unharvested); the resulting seedlings will produce extra early bloom the following summer. Thin plants to 3 or 4 inches apart. The bluish white flowers that bloom in July soon develop into inflated seed-

Nigella is one of many herbs with ornamental blossoms. It is shown below with scented geraniums, nasturtiums, and oregano.

MYRRHIS ODORATA (SWEET CICELY) Bushy plant with fernlike foliage and umbels of small white flowers. Blooms in early summer. Full sun or partial shade. Zones 4-9.

MYRTUS COMMUNIS (MYRTLE) Shrub 5-10 feet tall with aromatic evergreen foliage. Small, creamy white flowers in summer, blue berries in fall. Full sun. Does well in seashore gardens. Zones 7-9.

NASHIA INAGUENSIS (MOUJEAN TEA) Plant 3-4 feet tall produces tiny evergreen leaves, cream-colored flowers, and beadlike orange fruit. Full sun. Zones 8-10.

NEPETA MUSSINII (CATNIP) Loose, spreading plant, 1 foot tall and 1 foot wide, with gray-green foliage and racemes of tiny lavender flowers. Blooms in summer. Full sun. Zones 3-10.

BASIL

Basil comes from the Greek word *basilikon,* "kingly," and the plant has often been given royal treatment. Many ancient peoples considered it sacred; it could be cut only with a gold or silver knife, never with iron. *Ocimum sanctum* (holy basil) is native to India, where it was sacred to Krishna and Vishnu. The Egyptians mixed it with myrrh and incense in offerings to their gods, and it was often scattered over graves. *O. basilicum* (common or sweet basil) has been used in cooking since antiquity and is found in recipes of many Mediterranean lands. Greeks and Romans thought germination was improved if the plant was cursed during sowing; the French expression *semer le basilic,* which means to give abuse, arose from this practice. In Italy, basil was also fed to animals for its reputed aphrodisiac powers and was placed in windows by women awaiting their lovers. Basil was particularly popular in the Ligurian region, famous for its hillsides covered with herb gardens; ships coming into the port of Genoa once met winds fragrant with sweet basil. Liguria is also the homeland of pesto (from an Italian word for "ground-up"), a sauce made of ground basil, olive oil, garlic, pine nuts, and grated cheese.

pods. Harvest the pods in August when they turn brown and the seed has ripened to a velvety black color. Crush the pods open and collect the seeds.

USES When ground, black cumin's spicy seeds are an effective substitute for pepper. They have been used for centuries in Asia, North Africa, and parts of Europe to flavor curries, breads, and cakes. The interesting seedpods are an attractive addition to dried flower arrangements.

VARIETY True cumin, *Cuminum cyminum,* is much more difficult to grow; gardeners in both Washington, D.C., and North Carolina report that they could not produce harvestable seeds despite years of trying. (CORNELL)

OCIMUM BASIL *Lamiaceae (Mint family)*

ANNUAL Basil is one of the most popular of all herbs, for both its wonderful flavor and its lovely form and color. Its sweet, pungent flavor—which comes in many variations—is released when the easily bruised leaves are touched. The compact, bushy plants come in many colors, from bright green to dark purple, although some of the more highly colored versions are used more for their ornamental value than for flavor. Most basils are native to India, Africa, and Asia, where they are grown as perennials.

CULTURE Basils are easy to grow as long as they have full sun, adequate moisture and warmth, and well-composted soil. Basil does not do well if the weather turns cold either by day or by night. Start seeds indoors 6-8 weeks before the last frost, transplanting into the garden once all danger of frost is past and soil is at least 60° F.; some gardeners wait until the soil is 75-85° F. You can also sow seeds directly in the garden. Space plants about 2 feet apart. Pinch back often—easy to do as part of harvesting—to promote new growth and bushiness. To harvest, pick leaves as needed. Keep flowers pinched out so leaves continue to form. If you leave flowers on a few branches, they will go to seed, which you can collect and use the following year. Pot up a few plants to bring inside at the season's end.

USES Basil adds pungency to sauces and soups and enhances the flavor of fresh vegetables and salads. It is indispensable in Italian dishes. Fresh leaves are most pungent, but basil also dries and freezes well. Basil can also be stored in a frozen paste, mixed with oil or vinegar. Store dried basil in tightly sealed containers.

Besides its many culinary uses,.basil is employed by the cosmetic industry in shampoos, perfumes, and other products. It is reputed to bring luster to hair. Its aroma adds depth to sachets and potpourris. It was once considered to have medicinal properties—as a sedative or aid to digestion, but is not currently in use medicinally.

Many gardeners believe that growing basil near tomatoes and peppers makes those vegetables grow faster. Basil is also reputed to repel asparagus beetles.

VARIETIES Sweet basil, *O. basilicum,* grows 2-3 feet tall and is the most commonly grown basil. Dwarf varieties include **'Spicy Globe'** and **'Dwarf Bush Basil'**. *O.*

NIGELLA SATIVA (BLACK CUMIN) Plant 12-18 inches tall with finely divided foliage and blue-purple or white flowers, 1-1½ inches in diameter. Blooms in summer through early fall. Full sun.

OCIMUM BASILICUM 'FINO VERDE' (SWEET BASIL) Bushy 2- foot-tall plant with 4- to 5-inch-long green leaves and white flowers. Blooms in summer. Full sun.

OCIMUM BASILICUM 'PURPURASCENS' (PURPLE BASIL) Bushy 2-foot-tall plant with crinkly, shiny dark purple leaves and lavender flowers. Blooms in summer. Full sun.

OCIMUM BASILICUM 'PURPLE RUFFLES' (PURPLE RUFFLES BASIL) Bushy 2-foot-tall plant with ruffled, shiny dark purple leaves and lavender flowers. Blooms in summer. Full sun.

Above: Cinnamon basil and bush basil.

basilicum **'Crispum'** *(*lettuce-leaf basil) has large, crinkled leaves. **'Dark Opal'** has a rich taste and smooth, vividly purple leaves. **'Purple Ruffles'** is an extremely decorative and flavorful cultivar. **'Citriodorum'** has a strong citrus scent, while **'Fino Verde'** offers a cinnamon taste and scent. Common sweet basil also comes in **'Licorice'**, **'Anise'**, and **'Allspice'**. Miniature or bush basil, *O. basilicum* **'Minimum'**, grows to only 12 inches high.

Tulsi, or sacred or holy basil (*O. sanctum*) with its spicy clove odor, is grown more for ornament than for fresh use. Other ornamental varieties are *O. kilimandscharicum*, camphor basil, an African native that grows to 3-4 feet tall, and *O. gratissimum* tree basil, a shrub with fuzzy leaves that can grow to 8 feet.

ORIGANUM OREGANO *Lamiaceae (Mint family)*

PERENNIAL Oregano is hardier and has a stronger flavor than its close relative, marjoram; it is native to the mountains of the eastern Mediterranean.

CULTURE Oregano grows best in conditions similar to its native habitat. It develops deepest color and strongest fragrance in full sun. Good drainage is essential; add gravel or shale to soil if necessary. Oreganos hybridize readily, so cuttings and divisions are the most reliable propagation methods. Or purchase young plants with strong, healthy leaves and sturdy stems. Set out in fall or early spring, 1-2 feet apart (plants will spread). Water sparingly; fertilizer is not needed. Oregano dislikes muggy, humid conditions and alternate freezing and thawing in winter. Keep weeds away, prune out dead foliage, and cut back leaves in the fall.

Oreganos are wonderful ornamental plants, with showy, colorful flower spikes that last throughout the summer and fall. The spikes dry very quickly for beautiful dried arrangements. Oreganos are a great attraction for bees and butterflies. They blend especially well with thymes, heathers, asters, sages, and winter savory. They make fine container plants and an attractive, fragrant border. Trailing varieties are excellent in rock gardens. Pick fresh leaves as needed for culinary use; leaves also dry easily and can be frozen.

VARIETIES Common oregano or wild marjoram (*Origanum vulgare* **subsp.** *vulgare*) is a vigorous grower, with attractive purple flowers but little flavor. The oregano that is used for cooking is *O. vulgare* subs. *hirtum*, known as Greek oregano; it is often confused with *O. vulgare* subs. *vulgare*. Wild marjoram is a very aggressive plant and has purple flowers, where the true oregano has white flowers and is not aggressive. **'White Anniversary'** has a beautiful rounded leaf, edged with creamy white and a mottled green center. There are also many ornamental oreganos; most are not frost-hardy in Zone 5 and colder. Two types that dry nicely are *O. laevigatum* **'Hopley'**, tallish with dark purple flowers, and *O. rotundifolium* **'Kent Beauty'**, whose large pink bracts remain on the plant after flowering. *O. r.* **'Barbara Tingey'** features pink bracts and purple flowers, and *O.* **x** *hybridum* **'Ray Williams'** is light and airy with elongated purple to lavender bracts and flowers. *O. dictamnus*, dittany of Crete, has thick, hairy, silvery leaves, and attractive lavender flowers; it grows 12 inches high and is used in hanging baskets as an ornamental.

O. basilicum 'Minimum' (bush basil)

O. basilicum 'Green Ruffles'

O. basilicum 'Cinnamon'

O. basilicum 'Citriodorum' (lemon basil)

O. basilicum 'Globe'

O. basilicum 'Spicy Globe'

O. basilicum 'Purple Opal'

O. basilicum 'Well-Sweep Miniature Purple'

O. kilimandscharicum (camphor basil)

O. x *hybridum* 'Ray Williams'

O. rotundifolium 'Kent Beauty',

O. laevigatum 'Hopley'

Ornamental oreganos are not used in cooking; they have little scent or flavor. They are lovely in dried arrangements and make beautiful landscape plants. Although not winter hardy north of Zone 8, they can be used as annuals in colder climates.

O. x *hybridum* 'Santa Cruz'

O. x *hybridum* 'Betty Rollins'

OCIMUM SANCTUM (TULSI, SACRED BASIL, HOLY BASIL) Plant 2 feet tall produces coarse, hairy, gray-green leaves and small pale lavender flowers. Full sun.

ORIGANUM VULGARE (COMMON OREGANO, WILD MARJORAM) Spreading plant 1-2 feet tall produces aromatic leaves and pink and white flowers. Full sun. Zones 5-9.

ORIGANUM VULGARE SUBS. HIRTUM (ITALIAN OREGANO) Plant 1-2 feet tall produces small leaves with true oregano flavor and small flowers in summer. Full sun. Zones 5-9.

ORIGANUM DICTAMNUS (DITTANY OF CRETE) Plant 12 inches tall produces thick, hairy leaves and attractive lavender or pink flowers. Full sun. Zones 8-10.

ORIGANUM MAJORANA MARJORAM *Lamiaceae (Mint family)*

PERENNIAL Marjoram is very closely related to oregano, the main difference being that marjoram is less hardy and has a more distinctively sweet yet more delicate flavor.

CULTURE Marjoram is a small, slow-growing plant that grows only to about 1 foot across. Purchase plants, or take cuttings from overwintered plants, or start new plants from naturally rooted branch tips. At Cornell Plantations it is grown as an annual, started indoors from seed each year. Seeds are sown on the surface of the seeding mix; the flat is covered with a plastic bag and placed under lights. Clumps of 3-4 seedlings are pricked off and transplanted to pots; pinching tops encourages bushiness. Grow in full sun and well-drained soil with a pH of 6.5-7.5. In colder climates, overwinter marjoram indoors or in a cold frame or greenhouse in cool, 40°-50° F. temperatures. When harvesting, cut no more than a third of the top growth at a time, though the plant will sometimes regrow if cut down further. Leaves dry easily.

USES The sweetly fragrant leaves are delightful in dressings and meat and egg dishes and are a good addition to *fines herbes*.

VARIETY 'Aureum' has yellow-green leaves and a spreading growth habit.

PANAX QUINQUEFOLIUS AMERICAN GINSENG *Araliaceae (Aralia)*

PERENNIAL American ginseng is native to central and eastern North America; other species originated in eastern Asia.

CULTURE In the wild, ginseng is found in cool, moist woods, and these conditions must be recreated to grow ginseng successfully in the home garden. Furthermore, buy plants only from nurseries that propagate it and do not collect it from the wild. Plant in shade, in a loose, rich soil, with a heavy mulch of leaves. Ginseng likes cool conditions but a warmish soil temperature. It needs good amounts of water and regular applications of fertilizer. Ginseng can be a difficult plant to come by; look for multistalked plants with strong growth. Start from seed in early spring or from root division in fall or early spring. Plant roots 1 foot apart, with the crown near the soil surface, and add the mulch. Protect the crown by adding more mulch after the plants go dormant in the fall. Keep plants weed-free and do not allow them to dry out. They will be disease-free.

USES Ginseng root has been highly valued, especially by the Chinese, for many centuries for its medicinal properties and as a general body tonic. The name *Panax* comes from the Greek for "panacea," an indication of the numerous powers attributed to ginseng.

PAPAVER SOMNIFERUM OPIUM POPPY *Papaveraceae (Poppy family)*

ANNUAL This well-known poppy originated in southern Europe and western Asia; the word *somniferum* means "to make sleep," and the opium poppy was named for the powerful drug that is made from a similar plant. Its lovely, large flowers, with their papery petals, provide wonderful spring color in borders, cottage gardens, and rock gardens. Even scattered through a vegetable garden, they are beautiful. Choose from among single-, double-, carnation-,

ORIGANUM MAJORANA (MARJORAM) Plant 2½ feet tall produces small leaves and green and white flowers. Full sun. Zones 6-10.

ORIGANUM MAJORANA 'VARIEGATA' (MARJORAM) Plant 2 feet tall produces green leaves edged in white and small white flowers in summer. Full sun. Zones 6-10.

ORIGANUM MARJORANA 'AUREUM' (MARJORAM) Spreading plant 1½ feet tall produces attractive golden leaves in spring that turn green in late summer. Full sun. Zones 3-10.

PANAX QUINQUEFOLIUS (AMERICAN GINSENG) Plant 1½ feet tall produces greenish-white flowers in June and July and red berrylike fruit in late summer. Partial shade. Zone 4.

and peony-flowered varieties. It is illegal to grow them in some areas.

CULTURE The opium poppy enjoys its short life-cycle in most general garden conditions, in full sun. It does not like transplanting, so sow seeds where you intend plants to grow, in fall or spring. They will come back every year from self-sown seedlings; after seeds drop, spread them around and cultivate them into the soil. Thin plants to 6-8 inches apart. You can recognize opium poppy seedlings when they appear in the spring by their blue-gray color. Seedpods mature to golf-ball size. Harvest pods when seeds are ripe; turn the pods upside down, and all the blue-gray seeds will fall out.

Opium poppy is very short-lived: seedlings appear in early spring, flowers bloom in midspring, and plants set seeds in late spring and are usually gone by summer. You will need to overplant, perhaps with scented geraniums, for the summer.

USES The seedpods make an attractive decoration. The addictive and illegal drug opium comes from the sap of a close relative of this plant.

PELARGONIUM SCENTED GERANIUM *Geraniaceae (Geranium family)*

PERENNIAL Scented geraniums, or storksbills, are among the most fragrant of herb plants. The small, colorful (usually a rose shade) flowers are secondary to the aromatic or strongly-scented foliage, which comes in a great variety of forms and shades. Scented geraniums are excellent in the border or along walkways, where you will release their fragrance when you brush against them. They are also fine container and hanging basket plants; use trailing forms for an aromatic ground cover.

CULTURE Give scented geraniums full sun, which releases their scent, and a light, well-drained soil. Purchase the varieties you want, and propagate by stem and root cuttings. When the weather warms up, you can transplant houseplants or set them, pot and all, into the garden. Move whole plants back indoors before fall frost, or take cuttings from them for the next year's flowering plants. Pinch to encourage bushiness.

USES Harvest leaves anytime for fresh or dried use in sachets, potpourris, cold

Scented geraniums thrive in containers, indoors or out. Houseplants enjoy a summer outside; they can be left in their pots or planted in the ground. *Right:* Three of the many varieties of scented geraniums available, arranged in a container. From left to right: 'Peppermint', 'Prince Rupert', and 'Old Scarlet Unique'.

PAPAVER SOMNIFERUM (OPIUM POPPY) Plant 4 feet tall produces showy blossoms in midspring; different varieties have single, double, carnation, or peony forms. Large seedpods follow flowers. Full sun.

PELARGONIUM GRAVEOLENS (ROSE SCENTED GERANIUM) Plant 1-2 feet tall produces semi-heart-shaped foliage and small pink flowers. Full sun. Zones 9-10.

PELARGONIUM QUERCIFOLIUM 'VILLAGE OAK' (VILLAGE OAK SCENTED GERANIUM) Shrubby plant with deeply-lobed leaves produces small pink flowers. Full sun. Zones 9-10.

PELARGONIUM FRAGRANS 'NUTMEG' (NUTMEG SCENTED GERANIUM) Sprawling plant, 1-2 feet tall produces small white flowers. Full sun. Zones 9-10.

Perilla's deep color and and lovely leaf shape make this useful plant a welcome addition to perennial borders as well as herb gardens. *Above:* At the United States Botanical Garden, purple perilla is planted with red cockscomb and silvery dusty miller.

beverages, and teas. The flowers are edible and make an attractive garnish or addition to salads.

VARIETIES A sampling of the numerous scents and varieties: almond (*P. quercifolium*); apple (*P. odoratissimum*); apricot (*P. scabrum*); coconut (*P. grossularioides*); lemon (*P. crispum*); lime (*P. nervosum*); nutmeg (*P. fragrans*); peppermint (*P. tomentosum*); rose (*P. capitatum, P. graveolens*).

PERILLA FRUTESCENS PERILLA *Lamiaceae (Mint family)*

ANNUAL Perilla is a much-branched annual grown for its attractive, colorful foliage, which resembles coleus; it is also known as beefsteak plant and shiso and is native to the area extending from the Himalayas to eastern Asia.

CULTURE Perilla will grow in full sun or partial shade, in a rich, well-drained, but moisture-retentive soil. Start from seed sown outdoors in the fall or chilled for several days and then sown indoors in early spring. Perilla self-sows prolifically. Thin or transplant seedlings as needed, setting about 1 foot apart. Add compost or well-rotted manure to the planting area to encourage quick and vigorous growth. Pinch to encourage bushiness. Harvest leaves as needed for fresh use; perilla is not used dried.

USES This herb has a unique spicy flavor that's popular in Japanese cooking. Leaves are used in salads and tempura and also as a garnish. The flower spikes are added to soups, seedlings spice raw fish, and salted seeds appear in tempura and pickles. Leaves of the purple cultivar yield a beautiful light green dye and impart a lovely red color to pickled fruits and ginger. Oil obtained from the leaves and flowering tops is used in perfumes and as a flavoring, while oil from the seeds is used as a drying agent in paints .

VARIETIES The cultivar **'Atropurpurea'** has deep purple-green leaves. More robust is **'Crispa'**, with wrinkled or crisped leaf margins; one form is bright purple, while another is green, with a lemony-spicy flavor. (Cornell)

PEROVSKIA ATRIPLICIFOLIA RUSSIAN SAGE *Lamiaceae (Mint family)*

SHRUB Despite its common name, Russian sage isn't a sage and isn't exactly Russian. It's a native of Pakistan, the Crimea, and Afghanistan, an association that somehow led to its "Russian" name. It grows up to 4 feet tall and wide, and in August and September it produces a cloud of beautiful purple-blue flowers that float above fragrant and sticky silver green leaves. Russian sage is an extremely valuable landscape plant; it looks great with roses or other perennials.

CULTURE Russian sage is very easy to grow. Purchase bushy plants and set out in spring or early summer, or take cuttings (which root easily in water or vermiculite) in midsummer. Set 2 feet apart at the back of the border, in full or partial sun and average, well-drained soil. Do not crowd or plant in heavy soil. Russian sage is quite hardy and does not need frost protection. Leave it tall in autumn—its gray stems are attractive in winter—then cut back to about 8 inches in spring when plants start leafing out all along the stems. Fertilize at this time too. It will lean toward the light and tend to flop over as it matures;

PELARGONIUM 'SPANISH LAVENDER' (SPANISH LAVENDER SCENTED GERANIUM) Plant 1-2 feet tall produces large hairy leaves and small lavender flowers. Full sun. Zones 9-10.

PERILLA FRUTESCENS 'CRISPA' (PERILLA) Many branched plant, 1-3 feet tall produces ruffled bright green leaves. Full sun.

PERILLA FRUTESCENS 'ATROPURPUREA (PERILLA) Many-branched plant, 1-4 feet tall produces ruffled, deep purple leaves. Full sun. Zones 5-9.

PEROVSKIA ATRIPLICIFOLIA (RUSSIAN SAGE) Many-branched spreading plant 3-5 feet tall produces silvery green leaves and many tiny blue or lavender flowers in summer. Full sun. Zones 5-10.

A floating hedge of Russian sage creates an informal, welcoming entrance.

staking the plants when young will remedy this problem.

USES The plant releases a sagelike odor when touched; it's lovely to use in potpourris and is beautiful dried.

PETROSELINUM CRISPUM PARSLEY *Apiaceae (Parsley or Carrot family)*

BIENNIAL Native to southern Europe and western Asia, over 20 parsley cultivars are now widely grown around the world. Its curled to flat green leaves can be harvested in the first year.

CULTURE Parsley is usually treated as an annual and started fresh from seeds each year. Seeds can be sown outside in the garden after danger of frost is past, or, for an earlier harvest, 8 weeks sooner inside. Seed viability decreases markedly with age, so use fresh seed each year. Parsley can be slow to germinate, taking 3-6 weeks; soaking the seed in warm water overnight before sowing hastens the process. At North Carolina Botanical Garden, gardeners have never had trouble with germination; seeds are sown in early spring for summer harvest and in late summer for fall harvest. Thinned plants should stand 6-8 inches apart; Hamburg parsley needs 8-10 inches for full root development.

Parsley tolerates a fairly wide range of growing conditions, including full sun or partial shade. It prefers moderately rich and moist but well-drained soil. Flat-leafed varieties tolerate dryness better and are more winter-hardy than curled-leaf types. Because parsley develops slowly at first, weed control is important. If heavily harvested, parsley benefits from a sidedressing of compost and some fertilizer during the growing season. Parsley will overwinter, but because it is a biennial it will quickly bolt or go to seed and die during the second summer.

Leaves can be harvested as soon as plants are 6 inches tall, cutting outer leaves back to the crown, but leaving the central growing point undisturbed. To dry parsley, remove leaves from stems and spread out; leaves will turn yellow if hung in bunches. Or freeze chopped parsley or whole sprigs in plastic bags. To grow parsley indoors for winter use, start fresh seed in midsummer; potted plants will need 5 hours of direct light per day.

USES Parsley is a versatile culinary herb, widely used for flavoring and garnishing. It is rich in vitamins, iron, and calcium and also makes an aromatic and appetite-stimulating tea; it also has medicinal uses. Large doses of the essential oil, however, may have toxic effects. Parsley leaves, used as a facial steam, can be beneficial in cases of acne. Dried parsley stems make a green dye. In the garden, parsley repels rose and asparagus beetles.

VARIETIES *P. crispum* var. *crispum* (curly or French parsley) has the popular curled and crisped leaves; it makes an ornamental as well as edible edging plant. **'Extra Curled Dwarf'** is especially curled and compact. The flat leaves of *P. crispum* var. *neapolitanum* (Italian parsley) have a more robust flavor than the curled types. The large flat-leaved **'Gigante'** variety offers a milder, sweeter flavor. *P. crispum* var. *tuberosum* (Turnip-rooted or Hamburg parsley) is grown for its thick, fleshy roots.

'Decora' is another cultivar with an extra-curly leaf that has longer leaves and is not quite as compact as other parsleys. It is more tolerant of hot weather and thrives at North Carolina Botanical Garden, where it is grown as an annual. It likes to have a fairly soft soil so its roots can easily penetrate, and it does well when planted beneath a larger plant, such as lemon grass, that can give it some protection from the sun. After a winter's cold, the young flowering stalks are harvested; they are tender and sweet, a true delicacy. (CORNELL)

PIMPINELLA ANISUM ANISE *Apiacaea (Parsley or Carrot family)*

ANNUAL Native to the Mediterranean, anise has long been treasured for the aromatic licorice flavor of its leaves and seeds.

CULTURE Anise is difficult to grow in the North because it requires a long growing season. Start it early indoors; in warmer areas, direct-seed in spring when danger of frost has passed. Anise does not transplant well, so leave it in pots when transplanting outdoors. Grow in full sun and fertile, well-drained

PETROSELINUM CRISPUM VAR. CRISPUM (FRENCH PARSLEY, CURLY PARSLEY) Plant 1-3 feet tall produces curly dark green or yellow-green leaves. Full sun to partial shade.

PETROSELINUM CRISPUM VAR. NEAPOLITANUM (ITALIAN PARSLEY) Plant 1-3 feet tall produces flat dark green or yellow-green leaves. Full sun to partial shade.

PETROSELINUM CRISPUM VAR. TUBEROSUM (HAMBURG PARSLEY) Plant 1-3 feet tall produces 3- to 5-inch-long parsniplike root. Full sun to partial shade.

PIMPINELLA ANISUM (ANISE) Plant 2 feet tall produces spikes of small white or yellow flowers in summer. Full sun.

Opposite: A great swath of curly parsley forms the center of a striking flowerbed.

SACRED HERBS

Many herbs are associated with religion and ceremony; whether they are still used for this purpose or not, their associations with ritual add a dimension to the herb garden. Some examples:

Laurus nobilis (sweet bay tree) is associated with Saint Lucian and is mentioned in the Bible.

Horseradish and chicory are used at the Passover seder as bitter herbs, commemorating the misery of the Jewish slaves in Egypt.

Geranium robertium (herb Robert) is named after Saint Robert, who halted a plague in England by treating people with the plant.

Viola tricolor (Johnny-jump-up) The three petals of this little flower are said to represent the Father, the Son, and the Holy Ghost.

Angelica is often grown in monasteries because of its connection to the Annunciation, when the Archangel Gabriel appeared to the Virgin Mary.

Iris germanica is also used in the celebration of the feast of the Annunciation.

Lavender is reputed to have been a favorite plant of the Virgin Mary; marigolds were used to decorate the church in her honor.

Costmary, known as Bible leaf, was chewed by worshipers to help them keep awake.

Galium verum (lady's bedstraw) was supposedly used in the manger where Christ was born.

Polemonium (Jacob's ladder) was used to decorate church altars on Ascension Day.

Myrtle leaves are shaken on the Jewish holiday of Sukkoth as part of a ritual.

soil. While you won't get many anise seeds unless you grow a very large number of anise plants, the seeds you do get will be very flavorful and aromatic, and the leaves chopped fresh also yield a milder licorice flavor. Harvest entire plants once the seeds begin to ripen; hang upside down inside a paper bag until all the seeds have ripened and dropped.

USES Seeds flavor desserts and the liqueur anisette. Leaves and seeds add licorice flavor to cheeses, salads, and sauces.

PLATYCODON GRANDIFLORUM BALLOON FLOWER *Campanulaceae*

PERENNIAL Balloon flower's buds swell up into little, round balloon shapes, hence the common name. A native of China and Japan, this is a beautiful plant suitable for perennial gardens and borders, with large, bell- or star-shaped, rich blue, white, or pink flowers; there is a dwarf variety suitable for rock gardens.

CULTURE The best growing conditions for balloon flower are partial shade to full sun in a very rich, well-drained, moist soil. Plants are easily started from seed or root division, in late fall or early spring. Space plants 6-12 inches apart, with rootstock set 4-6 inches below the soil surface. Regular applications of fertilizer during the growing season will keep plants looking their best and increase their flowering. Cut back hard in the fall after flowering, or leave seedpods on plants until they have ripened and dispersed to produce fresh seedlings for the next season.

USES Leaves are used in a cough syrup in Chinese medicine. (BERKELEY)

PLECTRANTHUS AMBOINICUS CUBAN OREGANO *Lamiaceae (Mint)*

PERENNIAL Cuban oregano (not true oregano) is known by a variety of other names: Spanish or French thyme; soup; Mexican or Indian mint; and country borage. It is sometimes sold under the misnomer *Coleus amboinicus*. Native to the tropics, its many stems spread to 3 feet across. Its thick, fleshy leaves—which grow up to 4 inches long—have a distinctive, mild, oreganolike flavor.

CULTURE Cuban oregano is best grown as a pot plant, kept in a greenhouse or indoors on a sunny windowsill in winter. Outdoors, grow in full sun to partial shade. This herb requires warm weather; it stops growing when temperatures drop below 50° F. and turns mushy with even a light frost. Cuban oregano is easily propagated from cuttings, taken anytime. Rather than bring in large plants to overwinter, you can restart with fresh cuttings taken in August. This is a fast grower; it benefits from frequent pinching to keep it full and well-branched. It also needs frequent repotting and fertilizing to maintain healthy green leaves. Give potted plants a slow-release fertilizer plus monthly half-strength booster feedings.

USES Use leaves fresh; they are too thick and fleshy to dry. These leaves are a favorite in Jamaican and other tropical cuisines. In India, where the herb is known as Suganda, the leaves are dipped in batter and fried.

VARIETIES The form **'Variegata'** has white-margined leaves that produce an

PLATYCODON GRANDIFLORUM (BALLOON FLOWER) Plant 1½-2½ feet tall with gray-green pointed leaves and 2-inch 5-pointed flowers in summer. Full sun to partial shade. Zones 3-10.

PLECTRANTHUS AMBOINICUS (CUBAN OREGANO) Plant 2-3 feet tall produces spreading roots, up to 3 feet wide, and thick, fleshy green leaves edged in creamy white, up to 4 inches long. Full sun.

POGOSTEMON CABLIN (PATCHOULI) Plant 2 feet tall and wide with shiny medium green, slightly scalloped leaves. Full sun. Zones 9-10.

POLEMONIUM CAERULEUM (JACOB'S LADDER) Plant 2-3 feet tall produces feathery leaflets, arranged like the rungs of a ladder, and lavender-blue flowers. Flowers in early spring through summer. Partial to full shade. Zones 3-9.

attractive ornamental effect hanging over the edge of mixed pot and box plantings outdoors. (CORNELL)

POGOSTEMON CABLIN PATCHOULI *Lamiaceae (Mint family)*

PERENNIAL A tropical plant native to the East Indies, patchouli is grown for the distinctive odor of its foliage—rich, deep, spicy, and earthy. It is cultivated mainly in the Philippines, Indonesia, and the Seychelles.

CULTURE Patchouli is extremely tender, with no frost tolerance. It will grow well in warm regions or as a container plant, in full sun and any good garden soil. At the North Carolina Botanical Garden, it is grown in partial shade because strong sun produced sunburned leaves. Start from rooted cuttings, taken anytime; when purchasing plants, look for well-branched specimens. Set out after all chance of frost has passed, spacing 12-18 inches apart. Harvest leaves 2 or 3 times a year.

USES Patchouli's fragrant dried leaves are used in incense blends and, in India, to protect carpets and fine woven goods from moths. A perfume oil is distilled from the leaves.

VARIETIES *P. heyneanus*, known as Java patchouli and grown in India and Malaya, is very similar to *P. cablin* in appearance and use, but its oil is said to be inferior. It is also more demanding and easily sucumbs if allowed to dry out. (SHIMIZU)

POLEMONIUM CAERULEUM JACOB'S LADDER *Polemoniaceae (Phlox)*

PERENNIAL Also known as Greek valerian and charity, Jacob's ladder is native to Europe and Asia and has long been popular in cottage gardens and borders for its feathery leaves and bright, lavender-blue flowers produced from late spring into summer. It got its common name from the ladderlike arrangement of its leaves on its stem.

CULTURE Jacob's ladder grows easily in any good garden soil but does best in a rich loam. It prefers a semishaded position and moderate moisture. Start from seed in the fall, or from root division in fall or early spring. Set plants 1 foot apart, and mulch for moisture retention. Jacob's ladder does not require additional fertilizer, frost protection, or pruning.

USES Jacob's ladder was traditionally taken in wine for medicinal purposes. At Cornell Plantations it is included among the bee herbs as a rich source of nectar and pollen.

VARIETIES *P. caeruleum* grows to 2 or 3 feet. The species **P. reptans** grows to only 6-12 inches and is well-suited for the front of the border or the rock garden. (BERKELEY)

POLIOMINTHA LONGIFLORA MEXICAN OREGANO *Lamiaceae (Mint)*

SHRUB This attractive shrub has small glossy green leaves and bears long lavender flowers in late summer.

CULTURE Mexican oregano does best in full sun. Although it can stand a frost, it is not hardy north of Zone 8, but can be grown as an indoor pot plant in cold-

POLIOMINTHA LONGIFLORA (MEXICAN OREGANO) Small shrub produces evergreen glossy leaves, ½ inch long, and long lavender flowers in late summer. Full sun. Zones 8-10.

POLYGONUM ODORATUM (VIETNAMESE CORIANDER) Plant 1-2 feet tall with arching stems produces 1- to 2-inch leaves. Partial to full shade. Zones 9-10.

PORTULACA OLERACEAE (PURSLANE) Prostrate spreading plant, 3 inches tall, 12 inches wide, produces succulent spoon-shaped leaves on thick, fleshy stems. Invasive. Full sun.

POTERIUM SANGUISORBA (SALAD BURNET) Plant 12 inches tall produces deep blue-green leaves on wispy bending stems and rose-colored flowers in June through August. Foliage color is retained through winter. Full sun to light shade. Zones 4-9.

EARLY AMERICAN HERBS

The first settlers who came to this country brought with them both a love of gardening and the tools and seeds to enable them to grow their own food in the new world. Gardening magazines and seed catalogs were among the first publications printed in this country, and many leading statesmen–notably George Washington and Thomas Jefferson–were actively involved in agriculture.

Most colonial homes included a kitchen garden in which plants were grown for food and other household uses; the products of this garden were an important part of the settlers' life. Almost all of these gardens included herbs that were used as potherbs, for tea, and as medicines. Among the herbs grown in 18th-century gardens:

Anise: used in salads, baked in cakes and breads

Basil: used as a flavoring for cooked vegetables

Burnet: used to flavor ale

Camomile: used for tea and as an insect repellent

Dill: used in some of the earliest gardens in America for flavoring and pickling

Horehound: used in a syrup as a cough medicine

Hyssop: used in soups, stews, and salads, and as a remedy for bronchitis and cattarh

Lavender: used for its scent

Lovage: used as flavoring for cakes, candy, and sometimes meats

Marjoram: used with stuffed game

Mints: used as flavoring

Purslane: used as a potherb

Sage: used as a stuffing ingredient

Savory: both summer and winter, used as flavoring

Tarragon: used in cooking

er regions and taken outdoors in spring after the danger of frost has passed. In the fall it should be pruned back, repotted, and brought inside. Or, take stem cuttings in August and keep them indoors overwinter. If planted in spring, these cuttings grow 10-12 inches tall during the first growing season. Stem cuttings can be taken at any time during the growing season for propagation purposes.

USES Mexican oregano is used in Mexico for its oreganolike flavor. (CORNELL)

POLYGONUM ODORATUM VIETNAMESE CORIANDER *Polygonaceae (Buckwheat family)*

PERENNIAL Also known as Vietnamese mint and rau ram, this herb has jointed stems and resembles its relatives smartweed and knotweed.

CULTURE Vietnamese coriander prefers semishade and lots of water. It will not overwinter outdoors in Zone 5. Start new plants from cuttings every year (taken in late summer), as the mature plants get tough. Stem cuttings root readily in a jar of water and quickly grow to fill a pot. Set out in the garden during the frost-free months. Pick leaves as needed for fresh use. Be sure to water during dry weather. A Vietnamese coriander plant that shriveled up over a particularly hot, dry weekend at Cornell Plantations quickly put out lush new growth when cut back completely to the ground and kept well watered.

USES Popular in Vietnamese cooking, it has a flavor similar to coriander leaves and can be used where a fresh cilantrolike flavor is desired. (CORNELL)

PORTULACA PURSLANE *Portulacaceae (Purslane family)*

ANNUAL Also known as pussley, purslane is a native of Europe first introduced into America by colonists as a food source and now naturalized widely in the United States and southern Canada. It's a fleshy, low-growing, highly branched plant that is a common and persistent garden weed.

CULTURE Purslane grows well in any decent garden soil in a sunny location. Sow seed in place in the garden, or leave some plants in a corner of the garden after weeding others out. Purslane is tolerant of dryness.

USES Tender young stem tips and greens are meaty and juicy to eat either raw or cooked.

VARIETIES *P. oleracea* **var. *sativa*** is the common wild or kitchen-garden purslane. ***P. grandiflora,*** known as rose-moss or simply portulaca, is the familiar garden flower that flourishes even in poor, dry, sandy soils. (CORNELL)

POTERIUM SANGUISORBA SALAD BURNET *Rosaceae (Rose family)*

PERENNIAL Salad burnet is a decorative garden or houseplant. Its attractive foliage is deep blue-green, deeply cut on the edges as if with pinking shears, and its thimble-shaped, rose-colored flowers bloom from June through August. It is one of the first herbs to start growing in the spring, and it retains green foliage through the winter. The wispy, bending stems stay close to the ground, so burnet makes a fine edging plant or ground cover. It's native to the Mediterranean region and later adapted to Asia and Britain.

CULTURE This delicate-looking, fernlike plant is easy to grow. It is adaptable to a variety of soils, although it does need good drainage; excessive moisture will cause crown rot. It will grow in full sun or partial shade, requires no frost protection or extra fertilizing or water, is not susceptible to disease, and thrives on neglect. It does not like to be transplanted as a mature plant, however, because of its long taproot. If purchasing plants, buy small, young seedlings. The plant readily self-sows; if transplanting "volunteers" (self-sown seedlings) do so when they are still small. Space 8-12 inches apart. Snip leaves when young and tender and use fresh; drying destroys the flavor. Burnet thrives through winter at the North Carolina Botanical Garden, and is hardy at the Matthaei Botanical Gardens in Michigan, though the leaves die back.

USES Salad burnet has the aroma and flavor of cucumber; it's a great garnish for soups and drinks and a tasty addition to salads and salad dressings. (MATTHAEI)

PRUNELLA GRANDIFLORA SELF-HEAL *Lamiaceae (Mint family)*

PERENNIAL Self-heal, also known as heal-all, gained its name for its use as a self-administered cure for many ills. Native to Eurasia, it is now widely naturalized in North America.

CULTURE Self-heal is a small, low, weedy plant that will grow in sunny to fully shady conditions. It will outcompete nearby plants, so it's best grown as a ground cover in the shade under shrubs. Any soil (except hard and dry) will do; plants will be especially vigorous in moist soil. Purchase healthy plants with many stems and leaves. Once established, plants will seed themselves, and seedlings transplant easily if kept moist. Set out plants in early spring or fall, 1 foot apart; they will quickly fill in. Keep old flowers cut off to encourage production. Plants die out in the middle as they get older; cut them back hard, or take rooted sections and start over. Self-heal needs no frost protection.

USES Self-heal was once used as a domestic remedy for sore throats and other minor ailments. It also yields fiber dyes in shades ranging from soft yellow to brilliant gold.

VARIETIES Although **P. vulgaris** is the most common self-heal, *P. grandiflora* has much larger and showier purple or violet flowers. **P. laciniata** has creamy white, occasionally violet-tinged flowers, and deeply cut leaves. (BERKELEY)

PULMONARIA OFFICINALIS LUNGWORT *Boraginaceae (Borage family)*

PERENNIAL A native of Europe and Asia, lungwort is closely related to the forget-me-not.

CULTURE Lungwort is best suited to light shade, moist soil, and cool to moderate temperatures. Start by division or seed, preferably in the fall to assure early spring bloom. Stem cuttings taken in late summer are also usually

Above: The early American garden at the National Herb Garden at the National Arboretum in Washington, D.C., includes herbs used by settlers, including purslane, burdock, lovage, salad burnet, and hyssop.

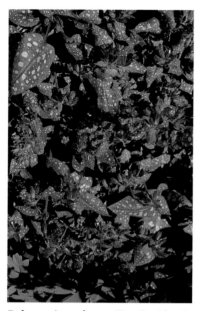

Pulmonaria saccharata 'Roy Davidson' bears small pink and blue flowers in late spring.

successful. Space plants 2 feet apart and mulch for moisture retention. Pruning is not necessary, but you can cut back old leaves in late summer. Lungwort does not require fertilizer or frost protection.

USES Because of an imagined resemblance of its leaves to lungs, this hardy perennial was traditionally used to treat pulmonary ailments; it was later learned that the herb actually damaged lung tissue. Today lungwort is grown for its decorative, mottled leaves, which make a good year-round ground cover, and its early spring flowers.

VARIETIES *P. officinalis* has large white- or silver-spotted leaves; its flowers open pink and change to blue. Its clumps grow to 1½ feet wide. **P. saccharata** (Bethlehem sage) has white-spotted leaves and white or reddish violet flowers; the variety **'Roy Davidson'** has gray-blue leaves with silvery splotches; its flowers turn from clear blue to light pink. **P. angustifolia** has dark blue flowers and **P. montana** has violet flowers and bright green leaves.

PULSATILLA VULGARIS PASQUE FLOWER *Ranunculaceae (Buttercup)*

PERENNIAL This very beautiful, early-flowering herb was given its common name (*pasque* is Old French for Easter) because it flowers near Easter, and it was once used to color Easter eggs. It is native to northern and central Europe and western Asia. Grow it close to a front walk or in a rock garden to enjoy its low flowers up close. It has been renamed *Anemone pulsatilla*.

CULTURE Pasque flower will do well in any well-drained, dryish soil in full sun. Start from firm, thick rootstock, planted in the fall, with the top of the rootstock at the soil surface. Or start from seed, sowing as soon as the seed head ripens, placing seedlings in their permanent place in the spring. Set 8-12 inches apart in informal massings. Seedlings will bloom in 2 years. Apply fertilizer at the beginning of the growing season, and peat or leaf mold in the fall. Keep young plants weed-free so they can develop a good rootstock. Cut off old leaves in the spring. Pasque flower is highly disease-resistant, but the rootstock will rot in wet conditions. Winter frost protection is not needed.

USES Caution: Pasque flower contains a poison that causes skin irritation and violent convulsions. It is used in some homeopathic remedies. Grow only to enjoy its lovely purple bell-shaped flowers in early spring, and keep children away from plantings.

VARIETY There is also a white-flowered form, **'Alba'.**

PUNICA GRANATUM POMEGRANATE *Punicaceae (Pomegranate family)*

SMALL TREE Pomegranate is a round, shrubby tree that grows 6-10 feet high. Native to tropical and subtropical Asia, pomegranate is frost-tender and will grow only in warmer climates—it is hardy only to the warmer parts of Zone 7.

CULTURE Grow pomegranate in full sun. It will do best in a moist, well-drained, fertile soil, but once established will tolerate a poorer soil. When purchasing pomegranate to grow as a shrub, look for well-branched plants.

PRUNELLA GRANDIFLORA (SELF-HEAL) Low-growing plant 1-1½ feet tall produces showy purple or violet flowers. Full sun to full shade, any soil type. Zones 4-9.

PULMONARIA OFFICINALIS (LUNGWORT) Plant growing in clumps 1 foot tall and 1½ feet wide produces large white- or silver-spotted leaves and blue flowers that turn pink after opening. Full sun to partial shade. Zones 3-10. Not heat-tolerant.

PULSATILLA VULGARIS (PASQUE FLOWER) Plant 1 foot tall produces ferny leaves and purple campanulate flowers; entire plant is covered with silky hair. Full sun. Zones 6-9. Not heat-tolerant.

PUNICA GRANATUM (POMEGRANATE) Round shrubby tree 6-10 feet tall produces bright orange, red, or purple flowers and edible orange-red fruit. Full sun. Zones 7-10.

HAZARDOUS HERBS

Several herbs (and other plants) once used in cooking—or for the preparation of medicines—are no longer considered safe; indeed, some are often listed as poisonous. Remember that some plants are poisonous only at certain stages of growth, sometimes only part of the plant is unsafe, and some plants are always poisonous and poisonous in every part. Plants that are unsafe to humans don't necessarily harm animals: birds can eat berries that are poisonous to humans. Small children are at greatest danger, and if you use any of these plants in your garden you should remember to keep children away from them and to pick up and discard fallen leaves and berries. The following list is not inclusive; your local nursery or botanical society will have more information.

Arnica (*Arnica montana*)
Autumn crocus (*Colchicum autumnale*)
Belladonna (*Atropa belladonna*)
Bittersweet (*Solanum dulcamara*)
Black cohosh (*Cimicifuga racemosa*)
Bloodroot (*Sanguinaria canadensis*)
Blue flag (*Iris versicolor*)
Broom (*Cytisus scoparius*)
Castor Bean (*Ricinus communis*)
Cherry laurel (*Prunus laurocerasus*)
Comfrey (*Symphytum officinale*)
Foxglove (*Digitalis purpurea*)
Henbane (*Hyoscyamus niger*)
Horsechestnut (*Aesculus hippocastanum*)

Right: Oleander is lovely to look at, but highly poisonous; in the poison garden in New York City's Cloisters.

For a tree, look for one main trunk topped by a good branching pattern. Plant out in fall or early spring; one specimen should be sufficient. Water regularly when first planted, then cut back on watering once the tree or shrub is established. Prune to keep the plant in the shape you prefer. Over a period of 7 years, a specimen died back only once over the winter at the North Carolina Botanical Garden, but came back vigorously from the roots.

USES Pomegranate is grown for its bright, orange red or purplish flowers and its large juicy edible red fruit. (BERKELEY)

PYCNANTHEMUM MUTICUM MOUNTAIN MINT *Lamiaceae (Mint family)*

PERENNIAL Mountain mint, native to the eastern United States, is an attractive, upright garden plant with soft, silvery flower bracts and pale, whitish pink flowers.

CULTURE Mountain mint will grow in full sun or partial shade, in average, well-drained soil. Start from seed anytime. Plants self-sow readily and are also easily divided. Space 12-15 inches apart. It takes about 3 years for a small plant to become a sizable, many-stemmed clump. Pick leaves as needed, and use fresh or dried.

USES Mountain mint leaves have a fresh minty scent and are used like spearmint; they make an especially good hot or iced tea. The lovely flower bracts are a good addition to dried flower arrangements. Native Americans used the flower buds to tenderize deer meat.

VARIETIES Other species, all with a fresh, minty scent and flavor, include **P. pilosum**, which produces showy off-white flowers late in the season; **P.**

tenuifolium, whose fine, narrow leaves are delicately textured; and **P. montanum**, with leafy bracts that take on a rosy-purple tint as the season progresses. (CORNELL)

REHMANNIA GLUTINOSA CHINESE FOXGLOVE *Gesneriaceae (Gesneria)*

PERENNIAL An uncommon but very beautiful plant, Chinese foxglove (which is native to China) produces tubular flowers with a darker, brightly colored lip, resembling foxglove, borne on 1-foot stems above a rosette of sticky-hairy tubular leaves. The showy flowers add color and interest in the late spring to early summer garden, while the foliage adds beauty to the fall garden, as the normally green leaves flush to pink and dark red with the arrival of cold weather.

CULTURE Chinese foxglove grows best in full sun to partial shade in a moist, well-drained, rich soil; avoid extremely dry and hard or very wet and mucky soil. Purchase plants with well-formed rosettes of leaves, or start from seed or root division. Sow seed or set out plants in late fall or early spring; take root divisions in spring. Space plants 6 inches apart and add a mulch to conserve moisture. Plants do not need frost protection at Berkeley Botanical Garden, where they survived 15° F. weather for several days and seemed to reseed themselves. It is grown as an annual in cooler zones, but under frost-free conditions can be treated as a biennial. To keep Chinese foxglove looking its best, keep old flower stalks and old leaves pulled off. However, if you want fresh seedlings, leave old flowers on plants until the seed has ripened and dropped.

USES Chinese foxglove roots ares used medicinally. (BERKELEY)

RICINUS COMMUNIS CASTOR BEAN *Euphorbiaceae (Spurge family)*

SHRUB Castor bean is a large to "gigantic" herb with striking foliage native to tropical Africa, where it may grow to a 40 foot tree. Outside the tropics and other warm regions it is grown as an annual and reaches only about 12 feet. Because it grows tall quickly, castor bean is often used as a temporary screen or background, filling in before slower-growing shrubs take its place.

CULTURE Because castor bean is extremely sensitive to frost, seed must be started indoors in early spring in cooler climates, or outdoors only in warm ground. Space plants 3-4 feet apart in full sun. Castor bean is adaptable to most soils; adding fertilizer will give brighter color and faster growth. At North Carolina Botanical Garden, castor bean reseeds itself; transplants are usually not vigorous. Plants like lots of water, which mulching will help conserve. Do not pinch or tip-prune castor bean; this may kill the plant. While spider mites may be a problem on indoor seedlings, they usually disappear when the plants are set outdoors.

USES Caution: the prickly reddish seed pods of castor bean contain beautiful gold, silver, and black seeds. These temptingly attractive seeds are quite poisonous, so you must be sure to keep them away from children and unknowing adults–3 seeds are sufficient to kill an adult. The plant is the

(Hazardous Herbs, continued)

Jalap (*Ipomoea purga*)
Jimson weed (*Datura stramonium*)
Lily of the valley (*Convallaria majalis*)
Lobelia (*Lobelia*)
Mandrake (*Mandragora officinarum*)
Mayapple (*Podophyllum peltatum*)
Mistletoe (*Phoradendron flavescens; Viscum album*)
Mountain laurel (*Kalmia latifolia*)
Pennyroyal (*Hedeoma pulegioides*)
Peony (*Paeonia*)
Poison hemlock (*Conium maculatum*)
Rue (*Ruta graveolens*)
Sassafras (*Sassafras albidum*)
Senna (*Cassia senna*)
Wild senna (*Cassia marilandica*)
Shave grass (*Equisetum hyemale*)
Sweet flag (*Acorus calamus*)
Sweet woodruff (*Asperula*)
Tansy (*Tanacetum vulgare* or *Chrysanthemum vulgare*)
Tonka bean (*Dipteryx odorata*)
Virginia snakeroot (*Aristolochia serpentaria*)
Wahoo (*Euonymus atropurpureus*)
Wintergreen (*Gaultheria procumbens*)
Wormwood (*Artemisia absinthium*)

PYCNANTHEMUM MUTICUM (MOUNTAIN MINT) Upright plant produces silvery flower bracts and small pale pink flowers; after 3 years, it becomes a many-stemmed clump. Full sun, partial shade. Zones 5-9.

REHMANNIA GLUTINOSA (CHINESE FOXGLOVE) Plant 10 inches tall produces tubular flowers on 1-foot stems and green leaves that turn pink or red in autumn. Full sun or partial shade. Zones 8-10.

RICINIS COMMUNIS (CASTOR BEAN) Fast-growing plant often reaches 12 feet tall (40 feet in the tropics) and produces large, striking leaves and seedpods containing beautiful but very poisonous black, silver, and gold seeds. Full sun. Frost-tender.

ROSA CHINENSIS 'SLATER'S CRIMSON' (CHINA ROSE) Nearly thornless canes produce long pointed leaves and single, double, or semidouble flowers. Full sun. Zones 5-8.

source of the purgative castor oil.

VARIETIES Castor bean comes in a variety of forms, with foliage of differing size and color. The varieties **'Carmencita'** and **'Dwarf Red Spire'** have attractive red foliage. Since mixed seed is usually all that's available commercially, save your your own seed from the year's most highly colored plants.

ROSA RUGOSA RUGOSA ROSE *Rosaceae (Rose family)*

SHRUB Roses, native to the Northern Hemisphere, have prickly and thorny stems, leathery leaves, and showy single or double flowers in pink, white, or yellow.

CULTURE Grow rugosa roses in full sun in a rich, well-drained soil. Purchase healthy, well-branched plants, or propagate by cuttings or division. Plant in early spring before active growth begins, spaced 2-3 feet apart. Keep plants well watered, but never soggy; a deep watering once a week is beneficial during establishment, or in dry areas. Rugosa roses are very hardy and do not need winter protection. They are relatively disease resistant, but may be susceptible to mildew or blackspot in moist, overcast conditions. Fertilizing once at the beginning of the growing season is sufficient, but regular applications of fertilizer will encourage continued flowering.

USES The aromatic petals from roses, produced from late spring throughout the summer into the first frost, dry beautifully for potpourris and sachets. They are also used fresh in salads and as garnishes. Petals can be candied to

At the United States Botanical Garden, a rose bush is surrounded with germander and ornamental sage.

ROSA RUGOSA 'FRAU DAGMAR HARTOPP' (RUGOSA ROSE) Shrub 3-5 feet tall produces pink flowers and very large hips. Full sun. Zones 4-8.

ROSMARINUS OFFICINALIS 'MISS JESSUP' (ROSEMARY) Upright plant 4-6 feet tall produces gray-green foliage and pink flowers. Full sun. Zones 7-10.

ROSMARINUS OFFICINALIS 'PINKIE' (ROSEMARY) Upright plant 4-6 feet tall produces gray-green foliage and pink flowers. Full sun. Zones 7-10.

ROSMARINUS OFFICINALIS 'TUSCAN BLUE' (ROSEMARY) Upright plant 8-10 feet tall produces large-leaved green foliage and blue flowers. Full sun. Zones 7-10.

decorate cakes and are used to make jellies and rosewater, an ingredient in some East Indian and Arabic dishes. Rose hips, which are very high in vitamin C, are used for tea and jam.

VARIETIES *R. rugosa* is a species rose from Japan, very fragrant, easy to grow, hardy, and resistant to disease. The pink or white flowers of rugosa roses are normally single, although some double forms are known. They are followed by round, bright red hips about the size of small tomatoes, full of vitamin C and prized for tea and jelly; the double rugosa forms do not form hips. Rugosas are renowned for their ability to endure extreme conditions that would doom many other plants. The variety **'Frau Dagmar Hartopp'** produces especially large, showy hips and flowers of a nice, deep pink. As its name implies, *R. chinensis* is native to China. Its flowers are pink through red, single or double. (BERKELEY)

ROSMARINUS OFFICINALIS ROSEMARY *Lamiaceae (Mint family)*

SHRUB Rosemary—its name is based on Latin words meaning "dew of the sea"—is native to the rocky Mediterranean region. It has small light-blue flowers and narrow, pine-needle-like evergreen leaves that carry a strong, sweet, piney scent and impart a distinctive flavor to foods.

CULTURE Rosemary is an outstanding perennial for permanent landscape use in areas where winters are mild enough. Older plants develop a handsome, gnarled appearance; prostrate forms drape gracefully over low walls, dwarfs make fine ground covers, and uprights serve as handsome hedges. Grow in full sun in light, fairly dry, well-drained soil. Feeding and excess water create rank growth and woodiness and eventual death. Propagate by stem cuttings taken in August and rooted for fall planting, or by layering; some gardeners find cuttings taken anytime of the year are successful. Control growth when plants are small by frequent tip-pinching. In northern areas, rosemary must be wintered indoors. To succeed with container-grown rosemary, aim for perfect drainage and no waterlogged soil; pot in a very coarse mixture and water sparsely during the winter. Provide plenty of sun and choose compact varieties. Contrary to popular belief, rosemary is not an easy plant to grow indoors; it needs high humidity to prevent leaf drop and has the best chance for success if kept in a greenhouse or misted regularly. In the South (Zone 7) rosemary will survive winter if protected from wind and placed near a source of warmth like a house or brickwork.

USES The aromatic leaves of rosemary are used as a seasoning, and the oil is used in perfume and medicine. It is used in herbal baths, rinses, and shampoos, and medicinally to relieve tension and calm indigestion.

VARIETIES The variety **'Prostratus'** (dwarf or creeping rosemary) is an excellent fast-growing ground cover, 2 feet high with a 4- to 8-foot spread. **'Collingwood Ingram'** grows 2-3 feet high with graceful curved branches that spread to 4 feet or more. **'Tuscan Blue'** has rigid, upright branches up to 6 feet high and dark blue flowers. **'Arp'** and **'Hardy Hill'** are considered hardy, but 'Arp' has not overwintered at Cornell Plantations (Zone 5).

ROSEMARY
This popular culinary herb has had an important role in legend and religion throughout the world. Ancient Greeks used it to adorn virgins before sacrificing them; they also believed it improved memory, and wore it while studying. Romans made hedges of it; Pliny suggested it as a substitute for boxwood in areas where sea spray might damage the box. In North Africa it was used as a border for roses in formal gardens. Rosemary is also connected to Christianity; it supposedly changed from white to blue when Mary hung her cloak on it while fleeing Herod's soldiers. The famous monastery gardens of Europe always included rosemary, which was used in cooking and as medicine. It was believed to cure depression, headaches, muscle spasms, and stomach ailments; as a bonus, it was said to repel the black plague. Even as recently as World War II, rosemary branches were burned to kill germs. Few of rosemary's medicinal properties are relied on today, though the herb does contain some beneficial oils. Rosemary is spoken of fondly throughout literature as a symbol of remembrance and love, and was often used in wedding ceremonies. Sir Thomas More wrote in *Utopia*, "I let it run all over my garden walls, not onlie because my bees love it, but because 'tis the herb sacred to remembrance, and therefore to friendship."

RUMEX (SORREL) Plant 1½ feet tall with long leaves and spreading roots. Full sun to partial shade. Zones 5-9.

RUTA GRAVEOLENS 'BLUE MOUND' (RUE) Plant 3 feet tall with lacy blue-green leaves and showy yellow flowers from mid-summer to fall. Full sun. Zones 4-9.

SALVIA CLEVELANDII (CLEVELAND SAGE) Plant 3 feet tall produces small blue-green leaves and blue flowers in midsummer. Full sun. Zones 8-10.

SALVIA DORISIANA (FRUIT SALAD SAGE) Plant up to 3 feet tall produces large leaves and shocking pink flowers in winter (when grown indoors). Full sun. Zone 10.

RUMEX SORREL *Polygonaceae (Buckwheat family)*

PERENNIAL Sorrel as a garden herb encompasses both *R. scutatus*, French sorrel, and *R. acetosa*, garden sorrel. It is native to Europe and now grows as a weed there and in the United States. Sorrel is a low-growing plant with long, shield-shaped leaves.

CULTURE Sorrel is easy to grow from seed, sown in spring in a sunny location with moist, rich soil; French sorrel needs drier conditions. Space seedlings 1 foot apart. Provide protection from wind for the brittle leaves. You must contain sorrel's spreading roots so it does not become a weed. Divide plants every 2-5 years. A circle of wood ash discourage slugs. Harvest before leaves become fully mature.

USES The fleshy, bittersweet leaves are prized by the French in salads and soups. The lemony tang of sorrel is also excellent in egg dishes and combined with spinach. Contains oxalic acid, which some people must avoid.

VARIETIES The broad, bright green leaves of **R. scutatus** are ornamental as well as useful in the garden. **R. acetosa** is a larger plant, with narrower, arrow-shaped leaves. **R. crispus** is yellow or curled dock, whose young leaves are also used to flavor salads and steamed greens. (MINNESOTA)

RUTA GRAVEOLENS RUE *Rutaceae (Rue family)*

SUBSHRUB This Mediterranean native is also known as herb o' grace, because Roman Catholic priests once used rue branches to sprinkle holy water. Rue is a lovely garden plant, with lacy gray-green or blue-green leaves and many erect, showy yellow flowers that bloom from midsummer to fall.

CULTURE Rue prefers full sun and an average, well-drained soil; it will tolerate partial shade and poor soil. Moist soil produces the most intensely blue leaves. Start seeds indoors and transplant to garden after danger of frost is past. Propagate by division in late spring, or by root or tip cuttings. At Cornell Plantations (Zone 5) it must be severely pruned in the spring to remove winter-damaged stems; some plants do not survive the winter. Cuttings can be taken in August to provide replacements in the spring. Note: handling rue plants can cause skin irritation due to a photochemical reaction with plant oils.

USES Caution: Pregnant women should not eat rue; more than a small amount taken internally is toxic to anyone. In the past, very small amounts of bitter, crushed rue leaves were added to salad dressings and sandwiches, but this is a risky idea. The foliage and dried seedpods are lovely in cut arrangements, and dried leaves are a fine addition to wreaths.

VARIETIES **'Blue Mound'** is extra-compact. **'Jackman's Blue'**, also dwarf, offers the bluest foliage. The foliage of **'Variegata'** has creamy white edges. (MATTHAEI)

SALVIA SAGE *Lamiaceae (Mint family)*

PERENNIAL AND ANNUAL The sages are a large group of shrubby Mint family members, long grown for medicinal purposes and now prized in the garden for their foliage and flowers, as well as for their flavor.

Rosemary trained on stakes will, after many years, form a sturdy bush that can be sheared and shaped. Start with a single cutting and train onto a stake; cut off tips to promote branching.

Above: Salvia leucantha (Mexican bush sage) spreads along a pathway; this species is a very useful landscape plant, but is not used in cooking.

CULTURE Sages grow best in full sun and well-drained soil. Start from seed, from 4-inch stem cuttings taken in July or August, or by layering (cover scraggly growth with soil in spring, leaving tips of growth protruding). Space plants 18-24 inches apart. Prune severely in the spring, cutting back to 3-4 inches, to keep plants from getting scraggly. Give hardier varieties winter protection, like a layer of pine boughs. In some areas, particularly in the South, sage is susceptible to wilt, root rot (especially in soggy soil), slugs, spider mites, and spittle bugs. Yellowing leaves are an indication that roots need more space. After 5-7 years, plants will have become so woody and ragged-looking that they will have to be replaced. At North Carolina Botanical Garden, root rot often claims sage, so it is started annually from fresh cuttings.

Harvest sage leaves anytime for fresh use. To dry, remove leaves from stems and spread on cloth or paper. Do not harvest too much in late summer or early fall; this will encourage new growth that won't be hardened off when winter arrives.

USES Sage is popular for seasoning stuffings and cheese and egg dishes and is also good with rich, fatty meats such as sausage and duck. It makes a flavorful tea (good for sore throats, colds, and flu), yields an oil used in soaps, perfumes, and cosmetics, and produces a natural dye in shades of yellow, buff, and gray-green; when used in hair rinses, it sometimes darkens hair. The foliage dries well for wreaths and arrangements. As a companion plant in the vegetable garden, it is said to repel cabbage moths and carrot flies.

VARIETIES S. officinalis (common garden sage) is native to the Mediterranean region; it grows about 2 feet high and is hardy to Zone 4 or 5. It produces grayish green leaves and tubular whorls of purple flowers. A range of cultivars is available. **'Purpurea'** has purple foliage in a compact growth habit. **'Holt's Mammoth'** has larger, rounder leaves and grows to 3 feet across. **'Nana'** has smaller, narrower leaves, while **'Berggarten'** has very large gray-blue or silvery leaves and a broad, robust, low growth habit. **'Albiflora'** produces spikes of white flowers; **'Rubriflora'**, pink. **'Icterina'**, with a dwarf habit, has variegated green and gold leaves; **'Tricolor'** has leaves of cream, purple, and green; both are less hardy than other types of *S. officinalis*.

The foliage of **S. elegans** (pineapple sage) adds a fresh pineapple scent to drinks, chicken, cheese, fruit salad, and jams and jellies; dried, the leaves lend this scent to potpourris. The sweet flowers are a good garnish and addition to salads and drinks. Pineapple sage is a perennial but is hardy only to Zone 7, so it must be overwintered indoors in most areas. It makes a fine houseplant, as it produces spikes of brilliant red flowers. The cultivar **'Frieda Dixon'** has salmon-colored flowers. Prune after bloom to keep the plant compact and shapely.

S. clevelandii (Cleveland sage, also known as blue sage) is an aromatic shrub that grows to 3 feet tall and produces royal blue flower spikes. It is hardy only to Zone 8 and must be brought indoors for the winter; in the greenhouse it is prone to mildew and attacks by whiteflies. The foliage is very sweetly fra-

SALVIA FARINACEA 'VICTORIA' (ORNAMENTAL SAGE) Plant 18 inches tall produces pointed green leaves and spikes of showy deep purple flowers. Full sun.

SALVIA OFFICINALIS 'HOLT'S MAMMOTH' (HOLT'S MAMMOTH SAGE) Plant 1-2 feet tall with large round gray leaves. Full sun. Zones 4-8.

SALVIA OFFICINALIS 'PURPUREA' (PURPLE SAGE) Plant 1-2 feet tall produces purple and green leaves and showy purple flowers. Full sun. Zones 7-8.

SALVIA OFFICINALIS 'TRICOLOR' (TRICOLOR SAGE) Plant 2-3 feet tall produces leaves in variegated colors of purple, cream, and green. Full sun. Zones 7-8.

SALVIA SCLAREA (CLARY SAGE) Plant up to 5 feet tall produces rosettes of coarse leaves and spikes of pale blue, lilac, or white flowers with showy pink or purple bracts. Full sun. Zones 5-9.

SAMBUCUS CANADENSIS (ELDER) Shrub 8-12 feet tall (some species grow taller) produces clusters of white flowers followed by red or black berries. Partial shade. Zones 3-8.

SANTOLINA CHAMAECYPARISSUS (SANTOLINA) Low woody shrub produces feathery gray foliage and small yellow button flowers in early summer. Full sun. Zones 6-8.

SATUREJA HORTENSIS (SUMMER SAVORY) Plant 1-2 feet tall produces gray-green or bronze-green foliage on many-branched stems, and small white or pale pink flowers in midsummer through fall. Full sun.

grant, is a good substitute for common garden sage in cooking, and is especially good in potpourris.

S. dorisiana (fruit salad sage) is a much-branched, tender perennial that grows up to 3 feet (less when pot-grown), with large leaves and shocking pink flowers produced indoors in winter. The foliage has a mixed-fruit flavor, good in fruit salads and for tea, or rubbed on fish or beef before cooking. The flowers are sweet flavored and make a pretty garnish or addition to salads.

S. sclarea (clary sage) was traditionally used as an eyewash, hence its name of clear eye, shortened to clary. Hardy to Zone 5, clary sage grows to 5 feet tall. It's a biennial or perennial that produces a basal rosette of coarse leaves the first year from seed and spikes of pale blue lilac or white flowers, with showy purple or pink bracts, the second year. Clary sage tolerates a pH range of 4.8-7.5 and self-sows readily. It makes a showy ornamental for the back of the border. Use leaves like common garden sage; they are also often eaten as fritters or added to omelets. The flowers make a pretty garnish, and the plant yields the essential oil muscatel, used in cosmetics, perfumes, soaps, and lotions. (CORNELL)

SAMBUCUS CANADENSIS ELDER *Caprifoliaceae (Honeysuckle family)*

SHRUB *Sambucus* is a member of a widely distributed genus of smooth-stemmed shrubs with showy clusters of white flowers followed by prominent clusters of black or red berries. *S. canadensis* is the native American elder, with flower clusters up to 10 inches wide and heavy clusters of purplish-black berries.

CULTURE In the wild, elder is found in low ground, wet areas, and borders of fields. Grown around the home, it's hardy and not fussy about location, but does best in rich, moist soil and some shade. Elder can be propagated by cuttings in fall, or by seed. *S. canadensis* is easily propagated by the suckers that it freely produces.

USES Over the centuries, all parts of the elder have had many medicinal uses; the hollowed-out stems have served as musical instruments, and the plant has been used to ward off evil spirits and witches. Today, it's grown as a handsome ornamental shrub; for its berries, rich in vitamin C and prized for jams and wine; and for its flowers, which can be used as fritters, in salads, or for tea. Elder flower water is used to soothe and tone sensitive skin.

VARIETIES Cultivated varieties offered by nurseries produce much larger fruit than wild plants. These include **'Adams No. 1'**, which blossoms in May and ripens berries around August 1, and **'Johns'**, slightly less productive than 'Adams' but with larger fruit clusters and berries, ripening about mid August. You must plant one of each for proper pollination and large crops of fruit. They start bearing 1 or 2 years after planting. (MATTHAEI)

SANTOLINA CHAMAECYPARISSUS SANTOLINA *Asteraceae (Sunflower)*

SHRUB Also known as lavender cotton, santolina is a low, woody shrub with aromatic feathery gray foliage. Small yellow buttons of flowers appear in midsummer. Santolina has a fine fragrance and spreads gracefully. It's excellent for

VIEWPOINT

PLANT COMBINATIONS

I tried several combinations this year that were very successful: deep blue rue, purple perilla, and green-leaved *Salvia lyrata*; two native plants, *Pycnanthemum muticum* and *Lobelia syphilitica*; *Nicotiana sylvestris* (6 feet tall) with a 2-foot-tall ornamental pepper with tiny purple fruit, and low-growing *Marrubium incanum*. And I've always liked to plant roses with thymes.
DIANE MISKE,
CORNELL PLANTATIONS

I try to create layers of plants when I combine them. The lowest level might be creeping lemon thyme; the next one a contrasting, taller plant like blue rue; and the tallest level could be golden feverfew. Contrast is created with size, shape, texture, and color: feathery bronze fennel with more solid madonna lilies; tall, large-leaved castor bean with low-growing lace-leaf marigold. I like striking and unusual color combinations, like deep purple perilla with red celosia, softened with a silver dusty miller.
HOLLY SHIMIZU, UNITED STATES BOTANICAL GARDEN

My favorite combinations usually involve contrast–blues next to grays or yellows. One of the combinations I like best is fernleaf tansy grown with *Lysmachia numillaria* and *Santolina virida*.
LISA CADEY, THE NEW YORK BOTANICAL GARDEN

I love gray and silver-leaved plants with blue-gray herbs. Sometimes startling combinations are great–one of my favorites is *Origanum vulgare* 'Aureum' with *Salvia officinalis* 'Purpurea'; the chartreuse with the purple is quite striking.
JERRY PARSONS, UNIVERSITY OF CALIFORNIA BOTANICAL GARDEN

I love the way garlic chives look with gasplant (*Dictamnus albus*).
PATRICIA HOPKINSON, MATTHAEI BOTANICAL GARDEN

SATUREJA MONTANA (WINTER SAVORY) Plant 6-12 inches tall spreads up to 2 feet wide and produces stiff, glossy leaves and small white or lavender flowers. Full sun. Zones 5-9.

SATUREJA VIMINEA (JAMAICAN MINT BUSH) Woody shrub up to 6 feet tall produces bright green leaves. Full sun. Zones 9-10.

SCROPHULARIA NODOSA (FIGWORT) Plant 1-2 feet tall produces variegated green and creamy yellow foliage. Full sun or partial shade. Zones 6-9.

SENECIO AUREUS (LIFEROOT) Produces heart-shaped basal leaves and golden yellow flowers borne in flat-topped clusters. Full sun. Zones 5-9.

borders. At Matthaei Botanical Garden, santolina is planted with germander in the center knot. Its small leaves keep their neat appearance when sheared.

CULTURE Santolina grows best in conditions similar to its native Mediterranean hillsides. Give it full sun and well-drained, not overly rich soil. Propagation is best from cuttings. If buying plants, look for full specimens with good new growth. Spacing of plants depends on use; in the knot at Matthaei, it is planted 4-5 inches apart and pruned in early summer to cut out the woody parts, and again in early July and mid August to maintain its compact shape. Be sure to keep oxalis out of the santolina growing area. This plant has no problems with disease or pests. Unusually cold winter weather may kill santolina, so a protective mulch is a good precaution.

USES Santolina dries well for potpourris or wreaths. Harvest branches for drying in late spring or early summer. For an interesting contrast with *S. chamaecyparissus*, plant the species **S. viridis**, which has dark green leaves; this variety is resistant to fungal disease, but is not as hardy as *S. chamaecyparissus*. (MATTHAEI)

Above: Green-leaved *Santolina viridis* contrasts beautifully with silvery-gray *S. chamaecyparissus.*

SATUREJA HORTENSIS SUMMER SAVORY *Lamiaceae (Mint family)*

ANNUAL Summer savory, native to the Mediterranean region, has gray-green or bronzy green foliage borne on much-branched stems.

CULTURE Grow summer savory in full sun and good garden soil, in warm to hot temperatures. Start from seed sown directly in the garden after the last spring frost; set seedlings 10 inches apart. As plants grow, pinch back tips often to encourage branching and discourage flowering. If stems get too long, they will flop over. (At Cornell Plantations, summer savory seedlings are planted 6 inches apart so that they can support one another; soil is hilled up around plants to keep stems from flopping.) If you let flower heads develop and mature, plants will reseed heavily. Although summer savory is sensitive to frost, it has usually declined by late September, so fall frosts are of little concern. It requires no extra fertilizing. Summer savory makes a good container and border plant.

USES Use the narrow leaves fresh, frozen, or dried. These aromatic, peppery leaves are excellent in soups and stews and combine so well with green beans that the plant is sometimes called the bean herb.

SATUREJA MONTANA WINTER SAVORY *Lamiaceae (Mint family)*

SHRUB Winter savory originated in the Mediterranean. It's somewhat shorter than summer savory, its annual relative, and its evergreen leaves are stiffer and more aromatic, with a stronger peppery thyme flavor. They can be harvested fresh all year.

CULTURE Grow winter savory in full sun, in warm to hot temperatures. Give it a sandy, well-drained soil, adding gravel or lava rock if necessary to ensure good drainage. Water sparingly. Winter savory is best started from cuttings, layering, or division. Set plants out anytime, 8-10 inches apart. Fertilizer,

NATIVE AMERICANS AND HERBS

The inhabitants of this continent came to know the medicinal qualities of the plants around them; the plants they gathered can be put together to create a very particular kind of garden. Such a garden would include the maidenhair fern (*Adiantum pedatum*), which some Native American tribes used as an emetic; black cohosh (*Cimifuga racemosa*), used to treat a variety of ailments and as an antidote to snakebite; American pennyroyal (*Hedeoma pulegioides*), used as a treatment for colic and colds; horse mint (*Monarda punctata*), used as a hot infusion to induce sweating in the treatment of colds (a practice soon adopted by the first European settlers); and white hellebore (*Veratrum album*), used to treat wounds. Tribes taught European settlers the properties of local herbs, and in 1672 John Josselyn published *The Physical and Chymurgical Remedies wherewith the Natives constantly use to Cure their Distempers, Wounds and Sores.* A medicine man named Joe Pye is said to have shown settlers how to cure typhus using a species of hemp agrimony (*Eupatorium purpureum*), today known as joe-pye weed. Native Americans also used herbs for flavorings, such as mint (*Mentha canadensis*) and wild ginger (*Asarum canadense*), and they used beebalm (*Monarda didyma*) to make a hot drink that came to be known as Oswego tea and was popular with early colonists. Native Americans also used plants to make dyes: the Navajos used the bark of Osage orange (*Maclura pomifera*) to make a yellow dye; bloodroot (*Sanguinaria canadensis*) was used to make a red dye for warpaint.

mulch, and frost protection are unnecessary. Prune back in fall or early spring.

Winter savory's low-growing habit makes it a fine ground cover or edging plant. It is excellent in a rock garden, cascading over a wall.

VARIETIES *S. montana pigmea* is a fully prostrate form of the species. *S. montana* **subs.** *illyrica* is creeping savory. (MATTHAEI)

SATUREJA VIMINEA JAMAICAN MINT BUSH *Lamiaceae (Mint family)*

PERENNIAL Jamaican (or Costa Rican) mint bush, sometimes sold as *Micromeria viminea,* has small, bright green leaves with a strong peppermint aroma and flavor.

CULTURE This herb is a woody shrub that can grow up to 6 feet tall. To control its size, grow as a pot plant, or plant out in the garden during the growing season and then dig it up in the fall, prune it back, and pot it to overwinter in the greenhouse or on a sunny indoor windowsill. Plants treated this way will grow 1½-2 feet tall in a season. Fertilize pot plants once a month with a half-strength 20-20-20 fertilizer, or with fish emulsion. Grow in full sun, and prune as necessary to keep a well-branched, compact shape. Propagate from 3- to 4-inch stem cuttings taken in spring or summer; pinch these back as they grow to encourage branching. Plants produce white flowers in winter.

USES Mint bushes are popular in Jamaica for teas and to relieve indigestion. (CORNELL)

SCROPHULARIA NODOSA FIGWORT *Scrophulariaceae (Figwort family)*

PERENNIAL Found growing wild in damp woods and wastelands throughout the Northern Hemisphere, figwort is native to Europe and temperate Asia.

CULTURE Figwort will grow in sun or partial shade, and it needs damp soil; avoid hard clay. Grow from seed in the fall, or from divisions of the rhizome in the spring. If purchasing plants, choose small, leafy ones; they will grow quickly. Plant rhizomes near soil surface, spacing 12-18 inches apart. Once established, figwort will seed itself so freely it can become a weed. Cutting off the flower stalks will keep this problem in check. The plant is disease-free. It goes dormant in the fall; cut to the ground and protect the rhizome over the winter with a layer of mulch.

USES The name *Scrophularia* derives from the early belief that because figworts are characterized by deep-throated flowers, they would cure such throat ailments as scrofula.

VARIETY The variety *S. n. variegata* is nonweedy, with lovely variegated foliage of green and creamy yellow. It shows to best advantage in half shade and lights up dark corners of the garden. (BERKELEY)

SENECIO AUREUS LIFEROOT *Asteraceae (Sunflower family)*

PERENNIAL Also known as squaw-weed and golden ragwort, liferoot has heart-shaped basal leaves and lance-shaped cut leaves on the flowering stems. Traditionally used for female disorders, liferoot is now grown for its golden yellow flowers, borne in flat-topped clusters from early spring through July.

SESAMUM INDICUM (SESAME) Plant 3 feet tall with leaves 5 inches long and pale pink flowers and red, black, brown, or creamy white seeds. Full sun. Zones 8-10.

SOLIDAGO ODORA (SWEET GOLDENROD) Plant up to 5 feet tall produces long narrow leaves and showy yellow flower spikes. Full sun. Zones 3-10.

STACHYS OFFICINALIS (BETONY) Plant 3 feet tall produces spikes of purple flowers above leaves arranged in rosettes. Full sun or partial shade. Zones 4-9.

SUCCISA PRATENSIS (DEVIL'S BIT) Plant 3 feet tall with oddly-shaped roots, narrow leaves, and purple flowers in long spikes. Blooms in July through November. Zones 5-9.

SYMPHYTUM OFFICINALE (COMFREY) Plant 3-4 feet tall forms 3-foot mound when mature and produces large fuzzy leaves and small pink or blue flowers. Full sun or partial shade. Zones 5-9.

TAGETES FILIFOLIA (IRISH LACE MARIGOLD) Many-branched plant up to 1 foot tall produces fine-textured foliage and small white flowers in late summer. Full sun. Zones 9-10.

TAGETES LUCIDA (SWEET-SCENTED MARIGOLD) Plant 2 feet tall produces bright orange yellow blooms; flowers more profusely and longer in warmer climates. Full sun. Zones 9-10.

TANACETUM VULGARE (TANSY) Plant 2-4 feet tall produces ferny foliage and clusters of bright yellow buttonlike flowers. Full sun or partial shade. Zones 4-9.

Liferoot is extremely hardy and can be invasive. Cutting back flowering stalks before seeds drop keeps it from spreading. It likes moist soils and dappled shade to full sun.

SESAMUM INDICUM SESAME *Pedaliaceae (Pedalium family)*

ANNUAL Sesame is grown for its nutty, oily, and nutritious seeds, which may be red, brown, black, or creamy white. It is native to the tropics and now naturalized from Florida to Texas. It is most attractive when planted in masses.
CULTURE Sesame is happiest in its native tropics and will grow only in warm climates. It requires full sun and rich, moist soil, and is grown as an annual from seed each year. Start seeds indoors in midspring and transplant 12 inches apart after all chance of frost is past and the soil is warmed. The seedpods will not develop without adequate moisture, so water during dry periods. Harvest seeds as soon as they ripen, as the pods brown before they burst. Each plant produces only 1 tablespoon of seed, often none in cool climates.

Sesame can be an attractive garden annual, with its upright, tall growth, shiny green leaves, and bell-shaped flowers similar to foxglove. It blends well into a vegetable garden and makes an attractive border.
USES Toasted sesame seeds are used for breads, vegetables, and salads. An oil derived from the seeds is used in cooking. (SHIMIZU)

SOLIDAGO ODORA SWEET GOLDENROD *Asteraceae (Sunflower family)*

PERENNIAL Goldenrod is native to the eastern and southeastern United States, and its bright yellow flowers are a common sight in many parts of North America. Sweet goldenrod is valued in the garden for both its leaves and its flowers. The showy yellow flower spikes are produced over a long blooming period, from August to frost, and are lovely in the garden and in both fresh and dried flower arrangements. Contrary to popular belief, goldenrod pollen is not airborne and does not cause hayfever.
CULTURE Sweet goldenrod is very cold-hardy. It grows readily in full sun and poor, sandy soil. In rich soil it tends to grow lanky and flop over. Plants are easily propagated by division. Seed has slow and erratic germination; sow in fall or spring. Space plants 12-15 inches apart.
USES The long, narrow, anise-scented leaves are brewed fresh or dried for a cooling, anise- or licorice-flavored tea. Flowers and leaves produce green and gold dyes with excellent colorfastness; valued by Native Americans. (CORNELL)

STACHYS OFFICINALIS BETONY *Lamiaceae (Mint family)*

PERENNIAL Betony's purple flowers are borne on spikes above a rosette of leaves over a long blooming period. This low-care herb, native to Europe, is a very attractive landscape plant either in a formal garden or naturalized.
CULTURE Betony will grow in full sun or partial shade, in any good garden loam. Avoid dry, heavy soil. Grow from seed, or divide established plants every 4-5 years, starting in early spring or autumn. (At North Carolina Botanical Garden, seeds sprout only sporadically, and divisions work best.)

EXOTIC SPICES

The marketplaces of ancient Rome were full of herbs and spices from the East: pepper and cinnamon, saffon, sesame, and cloves, ginger, sugar, cardamon, and a host of others. Most of these spices were produced in the East Indies, in tropical Asia, and were carried by caravan across China and India to ports on the Mediterranean Sea or the Persian Gulf and from there to the marketplaces of Athens, Rome, and other cities–where they were sold at exorbitant prices. With the fall of Rome, this contact with the East ended, for exploration and commerce came to a halt during the Dark Ages, and the availability of herbs and spices diminished to near extinction. Merchants of Venice, Genoa, and Pisa still sold such exotic products, but they bought them from middlemen at ports in the eastern Mediterranean: the routes inland were blocked by Muslims. For about a decade, at the height of the Mongol empires, the way was clear again; this is when Marco Polo made his famous journey, and he returned to Venice with tales of Eastern treasures–spices, silks, perfumes, drugs, and jewels. But the Mongols were expelled from China, and the route closed again. Later, large numbers of Crusaders returning from the Holy Land brought home a taste for Eastern luxuries. The route to the East was closed even more firmly in 1453 when Constantinope fell to the Muslims. Europeans began thinking about ways to bypass the old trade routes–and all the middlemen involved—to buy direcly from the producers in the fabled Spice Islands. This quest for spices led to an unexpected discovery: the New World

Space 12-18 inches apart. Water while young plants are establishing themselves and during dry spells. Keep old flowers cut off. Stem cuttings taken in summer root well. Betony does not need frost protection.

USES During the Middle Ages betony was grown in monastery gardens and was believed to ward off a host of evils, including dropsy, headaches, shortness of breath, convulsions, serpent bites, and mad dogs.

Betony was the subject of a prayer by Antonius Musas, "Betony, you who were discovered first by Asclepius or by Chiron the centaur, hear my prayer. I implore you, herb of strength, by Him who ordered your creation and ordered that you should be useful for a multitude of remedies. Kindly help in making these seven and forty remedies." Since it protected against evil spirits, people wore it around their necks as charms, and it was planted in graveyards. Today, betony is grown as an ornamental; it is particularly useful as an edging plant.

VARIETIES *S. officinalis* **'Alba'** produces white flowers. *S. lanata* (lamb's-ears) has dense, woolly, silver-white leaves and whorls of small purple flowers; it's grown mostly in beds and edgings for its foliage. *S. lantana* 'Silver Carpet' doesn't flower and its foliage remains fresher-looking than *S. lantana.* (SHIMIZU)

SUCCISA PRATENSIS DEVIL'S BIT *Dipsacaceae (Teasel family)*

PERENNIAL Devil's bit is a member of the Teasel family, a group of herbs with dense, spiky flower heads. It is native to Europe and is now found growing wild in open meadows and on heaths. According to legend, the devil found the plant growing in Paradise. Recognizing that it could do a lot of good for the human race, the devil tried to destroy it by biting away a large portion of the root. The plant continued to flourish in spite of the odd bitten-away shape of its root. Today, devil's bit is grown for its purple flowers, borne from July to November, providing color and interest when not much else is blooming and creating a light, airy feeling with its long flower spikes.

CULTURE Devil's bit is not fussy; it will grow in full sun to partial shade, in average soil, with moderate water, and it's disease-free. It is easily grown from seed, gathered and sown when seeds ripen. Set seedlings 2-3 feet apart. Plants

An edging is often the finishing touch in the garden, providing a separation, a demarcation, or a softening touch. *Top:* Stachys lines a pathway. *Right:* A border of lavender rings a rosebush.

will grow into moderate mounds 2 feet across, with flower stalks 3-4 feet tall. They carpet the ground, keeping weeds down. Cut plants to the ground in early winter, or in spring before new growth starts. (BERKELEY)

SYMPHYTUM OFFICINALE COMFREY *Boraginaceae (Borage family)*
PERENNIAL Comfrey, an ornamental plant with large fuzzy leaves and small pink or blue flowers, is native to Asia and has naturalized in Europe and the United States.

CULTURE Grow comfrey from root cuttings or divisions, planting on cleanly cultivated ground in good soil. The mature plant will form a 3-foot mound, so space roots accordingly. Take great care in choosing where to plant comfrey; when moved, it will leave a trace of root behind from which a new plant will grow. However, it will not spread or multiply unless the roots are disturbed. Comfrey will grow in full sun or partial shade, and it likes moisture. This is one of the first herbs to green in the spring, and it is not touched by early frost. Like other members of the Borage family, comfrey wears its flower stem in a question mark. Keep these stalks cut in order to encourage leaf growth.

USES Because comfrey leaves have a high mineral content, they make an excellent liquid fertilizer for garden and houseplants (allow leaves to decompose in a container of water). Comfrey is also a fine addition to the compost pile; use only well-wilted leaves, however, so they do not take root in your compost.

In olden times, comfrey was used to hasten the mending of broken bones, earning it the names boneset and knitbone. Comfrey leaves were added to salads and cooked in soups and stews and comfrey tea was believed healthful. Comfrey is now considered a carcinogen and internal use is not recommended. It can be used as an external poultice for cuts, wounds, and sprains. (MATTHAEI)

TAGETES LUCIDA SWEET-SCENTED MARIGOLD *Asteraceae (Sunflower)*
PERENNIAL Sweet-scented marigold, also known as Mexican marigold, Mexican tarragon, pericon, and sweet mace, is often cultivated as an annual in colder zones. It is native to Mexico and Guatemala.

This plant's small size makes it a good choice for the front of the garden bed. At Berkeley Gardens, *T. lucida* is a full, showy flower with orangish yellow blooms from December through January. At Cornell Plantations, however, it flowers only sparsely late in the season or, in some years, not at all; in North Carolina, it flowers in October, just before frost kills it back.

CULTURE Grow sweet-scented marigold in full sun in average, well-drained, moist soil. Start seed indoors in early spring and plant out after danger of frost is past. In areas where *T. lucida* can be grown as a perennial, you can propagate by taking divisions after plants have gone dormant in late winter. Space plants about 1 foot apart. Fertilizer applied throughout the growing season will produce many vegetative shoots and keep the plants looking good. Pick foliage as needed for fresh use. If you are growing sweet-scented marigold as a perennial, cut plants back to the ground after flowering. In areas where *T. lucida* will not overwinter dependably, you can pot up some plants and grow

[The marigold] is actually an American native, and really not native to any other place on earth. It is grown in great profusion in every one of the 50 states. . . . One of the outstanding characteristics of the marigold is its robustness and rugged character. If there is any flower that can resist the onslaught of the insect world better than the marigold, I would not know what it was. I grow thousands of them for my own delight and the delight of my neighbors, and I know what this flower will do. I class it, therefore, with the American eagle when it comes to a symbol of our country that manifests stamina; and when it comes to beauty I can think of nothing greater or more inspring than a field of blooming marigolds tossing their heads in the sunshine and giving a glow to the entire landscape.
SENATOR EVERETT DIRKSON, THE CONGRESSIONAL RECORD, 1969 (NOMINATING THE MARIGOLD AS NATIONAL FLOWER)

Above: Tagates lucida with oregano.

them indoors on a sunny windowsill or take stem cuttings in August to over-winter inside.
USES In its native Mexico, this is a popular culinary herb, Its foliage has a very sweet anise scent and flavor and can be used in place of tarragon.
VARIETY *T. filifolia* (Irish lace marigold) also has a sweet anise flavor and finely textured foliage. In areas where it blooms, it produces small white flowers late in the season.

TANACETUM VULGARE TANSY *Asteraceae (Sunflower family)*
PERENNIAL Tansy, a native of Europe, was one of the first plants brought to North America by European settlers; even before the Revolution it had escaped colonial gardens and was showing up along roadsides. It is now naturalized in fields and meadows of the northern United States. It is grown today for its large, handsome, aromatic, fernlike foliage and clusters of bright yellow buttonlike flowers.
CULTURE Propagate tansy from seed or by root division. Space plants 1-4 feet apart. Cutting back keeps the plants from becoming leggy, and planting against a wall or fence provides some protection and support for the potentially floppy foliage. Tansy is also handsome naturalized, or as a backdrop for other plants. It thrives in sun or part shade and sandy or clay (not wet) soil. It is invasive, spreading by underground rhizomes; if you mix tansy with other garden perennials, contain it with an underground strip of edging.
USES Tansy leaves, strewn in the house or used in sachets, are supposed to repel ants and moths. Tansy flowers dried as everlastings are truly lovely and are also excellent in potpourris. They maintain their rich golden color well and do not crumble or break apart like so many more delicate flowers. (Tansy's generic name, *Tanacetum*, is from the Greek word *athanasia*, "immortality"; in times past, coffins were filled with tansy to preserve corpses precisely because the flowers don't wilt when dried.) Pick blossoms just after opening fully, on long stems, and hang upside down to dry. Leaves are also effective in dry arrangements. Caution: Do not use tansy as a tea, food, or medicine; it can be toxic.
VARIETY *T. v. crispum* (fernleaf or curly tansy) is highly ornamental and less rampant, growing to only 18 inches, but flowers less freely than *T. vulgare*. (SHIMIZU)

TEUCRIUM CHAMAEDRYS GERMANDER *Lamiaceae (Mint family)*
SUBSHRUB Germander is a low-growing herb, widely naturalized in Europe and North America, that has been used for centuries in ornamental knot gardens. Germander has attractive foliage that can be clipped or allowed to spread as a ground cover, edging, border, or hedge.
CULTURE Germander will grow in full sun to partial (not excessive) shade. Any average soil will do, but a sandy, peaty soil is best, and it must be well-drained. Propagate from cuttings, which may take 2-3 months to root; seed is slow to germinate. Germander is quite pest- and disease-resistant.
USES Germander was once used medicinally to treat gout and rheumatism.
VARIETIES The species *T. chamaedrys* (wall germander) has dark green, glossy

TEUCRIUM CHAMAEDRYS (WALL GERMANDER) Compact, low-growing plant produces dark green glossy foliage and lavender blooms (unless clipped as a hedge or edging). Full sun to light shade. Zones 5-9.

THYMUS HERBA-BARONA (CARAWAY THYME) Prostrate sprawling plant 3-6 inches tall produces small glossy dark green leaves and lavender flowers. Full sun to partial shade. Zones 5-9.

THYMUS 'ARGENTEUS' (SILVER THYME) Shrubby plant 10 inches tall produces gray-green leaves banded in silvery white. Full sun to partial shade. Zones 5-9.

THYMUS X CITRIODORUS 'AUREUS' (GOLDEN THYME) Plant 6-15 inches tall produces glossy yellow and green leaves and small white or pale lilac flowers. Full sun to partial shade. Zones 5-9.

THYME

Thyme grows wild on hillsides in Greece–indeed throughout Mediterranean Europe and even as far as the British Isles–so it was well known to the ancients. Around 3000 B.C. the Sumerians were using it as a medicinal ingredient, and the Egyptians included it among the herbs and spices used in mummification. The Greeks used thyme as a temple incense (the name *thyme* comes from a Greek word meaning "to fumigate"), and both they and the Romans praised its healing virtues and considered it useful in the treatment or prevention of a wide range of maladies, including, inevitably, snakebite (evidently not uncommon in their bare-legged, outdoor world). Thyme's fragrance was thought to awaken the senses, including those amorous: as an aphrodisiac it was enthusiastically strewn around banquet halls. During the Middle Ages thyme was considered a symbol of courage, and knights rode into battle wearing scarves on which their ladies had embroidered sprigs of the herb. Thyme is also connected to the world of dreams and fairies: "I know a bank where the wild thyme grows," says Oberon, king of the fairies, in Shakespeare's *A Midsummer Night's Dream*. Thyme, bees, and honey go together, and wild thyme honey has long been appreciated. Wild thyme (*T. serpyllum*, also known as creeping thyme or mother-of-thyme) is an Old World evergreen naturalized in North America and popular as a ground cover, edging, and rock plant. Common thyme (*T. vulgaris*) is the thyme used as a seasoning herb and is cultivated mainly in Spain and France.

foliage and a neat, compact growth habit. It will grow to 1-1½ feet as a low hedge (space these plants 1 foot apart), or it can be cut back for a low edging or knot (space 4 inches). It combines and shears well with santolina in a formal knot garden; be sure to keep oxalis out. Prune 3 times (late spring, early July, and mid August) to maintain its neat appearance in a knot. If not clipped, it produces lavender-pink blooms from July to September. In an unusually severe winter, some plants may die.

VARIETIES *T. scorodonia 'Crispa'* has attractive bright green crinkled leaves. *T. fruticans* has silver stems and leaves and is an attractive pot plant. (MATTHAEI)

THYMUS THYME *Lamiaceae (Mint family)*

PERENNIAL *Thymus* is a genus of over 400 species of aromatic hardy and non-hardy perennials with very small, very fragrant leaves and twiggy stems, native to the Mediterranean region. Thymes have long been cultivated for their neat, attractive appearance in the rock garden, border, containers, herb garden, and dry walls. Creeping varieties are excellent as ground covers or to fill in between paving stones. Bees love thymes.

CULTURE All thymes require full sun and fairly dry, light, well-drained soil. A soil that is too rich prompts excess growth that makes plants susceptible to disease and winterkill. Start from purchased plants or root division in spring, or propagate by cuttings. Keep thymes well cut back during the growing season so they don't become woody. Divide or replace older plants once they develop an open center. Fungus diseases may be a problem in the humid South. In cold climates, thyme needs winter protection in the form of a mulch or overwintering in a greenhouse or cold frame. It grows well indoors on a sunny windowsill. In cold regions, do not harvest late in the growing season, for doing so can encourage young, succulent growth that would not have a chance to harden off and would die when frost hit. Elsewhere, harvest leaves anytime and use fresh, hang in bunches to dry, or dry stripped leaves on trays.

USES Thyme is a major culinary herb with an intense aroma used in a multitude of dishes, fresh or dried. Leaves and flowers add fragrance to potpourris and sachets, while lemon thyme in particular makes a fine tea.

VARIETIES *T. vulgaris*, common thyme, is the kitchen staple herb and includes English, French, and German winter types; all are small, upright shrubs. Lemon thyme, *T. x citriodorus*, is an upright plant with richly lemon-scented leaves. Both lemon and common thymes have silver and gold cultivars, **'Argenteus'** and **'Aureus'**. The leaves of caraway thyme, *T. herba-barona*, have a caraway scent. Mother-of-thyme or creeping thyme, *T. praecox* **subsp.** *arcticus* or *T. serpyllum*, forms a thick, ground-filling mat. Woolly thyme, *T. pseudolanuginosus*, has densely hairy leaves and grows well between paving stones. These thymes are usually hardy in Zone 5, but gardeners at Cornell cover T. vulgaris and T. x citriodorus with a protective layer of pine boughs because some plants die die in severe winters. (MATTHAEI)

THYMUS PRAECOX (CREEPING THYME) Low-growing plant forms a dense groundcover 4 inches tall with tiny dark green leaves and, with some varieties, tiny pink flowers. Full sun or partial shade. Zones 5-9.

TRACHELIUM CAERULEUM (THROATWORT) Plant 2-4 feet tall produces a profusion of tiny blue-purple flowers in large heads. Full sun to partial shade. Zones 8-10.

TRACHYSPERMUM COPTICUM (AJOWAN) Plant 1-3½ feet tall produces finely divided leaves and umbels of white flowers. Full sun.

TROPAEOLUM MAJUS (NASTURTIUM) Plant 1 foot tall, 2 feet wide (sometimes growing as a vine up to 6 feet long), produces brightly colored red, orange, or yellow flowers. Full sun.

Thymus vulgaris (Common thyme)

Thymus x *citriodorus* (Lemon thyme)

Thymus x *citriodorus* 'Orange Blossom' (Orange blossom thyme)

Thymus glabrescens

Thymus mastichina

Thymus praecox subsp. arcticus (Mother-of-thyme)

Thymus pseudolanuginosus (Woolly thyme)

Thymus serpyllum (Wild thyme)

Thymus serpyllum (closeup)

TRACHELIUM CAERULEUM THROATWORT *Campanulaceae (Bellflower)*

PERENNIAL A native to Europe, throatwort produces small, inconspicuous blue-purple flowers that nevertheless make the plant extremely showy because they are borne in profuse quantities on large, flat heads.

CULTURE Throatwort will grow in full sun to partial shade in any rich, moist, well-drained soil. Propagate by cuttings or root divisions, or purchase young, nonwoody plants. Throatwort can also be grown from seed; if started indoors early it will flower the first year. Set out in the spring about 1-1½ feet apart. To maintain the best appearance, mulch, fertilize regularly, and keep plants well watered. When throatwort is finished flowering, cut it back to the ground to encourage new growth. Plants will tolerate light frost, but they are not hardy in the North–they are grown as annuals at the United States Botanic Garden.

USES Throatwort got its name from it its ability to soothe sore throats. (BERKELEY)

TRACHYSPERMUM COPTICUM AJOWAN *Apiaceae (Parsley family)*

ANNUAL This leafy plant is native to India and Egypt and produces umbels of white flowers and finely divided leaves.

CULTURE Ajowan grows best in full sun and needs well-drained soil. It is grown from seeds started indoors and planted in the garden when the soil is warm. It can also be sown directly in the garden. Space seeds or transplants 12-18 inches apart.

USES Ajowan's seeds have a spicy, sweet flavor, somewhat similar to thyme. It is used for flavoring. (CORNELL)

Above: Throatwort looks nice planted along a bank of steps at the University of California Botanical Garden at Berkeley.

TROPAEOLUM MAJUS NASTURTIUM *Tropaeolaceae (Nasturtium family)*

ANNUAL Also called Indian cress, nasturtium is a native of South America. Both climbing and dwarf bush varieties are available, with double or single flowers.

CULTURE Nasturtiums are one of the easiest annuals to grow. Simply supply full sun and well-drained soil. Too-rich soil will result in lush foliage but few flowers. Direct-seed outdoors after danger of frost. Supply trellises or strings for climbing varieties; bushy types are fine for the border and all sorts of containers and can also be grown indoors in bright light and cool temperatures. Aphids can be troublesome. Keep flowering stems trimmed to ground level to maintain neat plants.

USES Nasturtium flowers and leaves add color and a delicious peppery taste to salads. Pickled buds and seeds substitute for capers.

VARIETIES *T. m. nanum* 'Tom Thumb' is a dwarf hybrid, with long, trailing runners and double flowers. *T. minus* is a naturally dwarf form.

TULBAGHIA VIOLACEAE SOCIETY GARLIC *Liliaceae (Lily family)*

PERENNIAL Native to South Africa, society garlic produces umbels of fragrant lilac-colored flowers in early summer and continues to bloom periodically throughout the summer.

CULTURE Grow society garlic in full sun. Where it cannot overwinter outside,

Above: A lovely landscape plant, society garlic has a milder flavor than true garlic; it doesn't leave a tell-tale aroma on the breath.

grow it as a pot plant, or plant it out and then, at the end of the growing season, cut it back to the base, dig it up, and bring it inside. Water sparingly during the winter. When the plant resumes growth in February, water more freely and begin to fertilize regularly. Propagate by division or from seed sown when it ripens on the plant or in the spring.

USES The mild, garlic-onion-scented and -flavored leaves of this herb are used in place of garlic, for a subtler flavor and to avoid garlic breath–hence the name society garlic.

VARIETIES The flat, thin leaves of the form **'Variegata'** are cream-striped. (CORNELL)

VALERIANA OFFICINALIS VALERIAN *Valerianaceae (Valerian family)*

PERENNIAL Also known as garden heliotrope, valerian is an old-time garden favorite native to Europe and Asia, now naturalized locally in northern North America. It's a tall, spreading plant that grows to 5 feet. Valerian is appreciated for its cut leaves and attractive clusters of very fragrant flowers, produced from early summer and suitable for cutting.

CULTURE Valerian grows best in semishade (but will also grow in full sun) and slightly moist soil; avoid too much sun or very dry or soggy soil conditions. Its finger-thin rhizome root system has a creeping habit, which you may need to contain. Propagate from root division. Set out plants 2 feet apart in early spring when growth begins; they will spread. Mulch to maintain the moist soil valerian prefers. Additional fertilizer and frost protection are not necessary.

USES The dried rhizome has a pungent aroma that's used to scent linen and in potpourris, though some people find the scent offensive. The drug valerian, derived from the dried rhizome, was traditionally used to treat problems of the nervous system; it is still used in some parts of England and the United States. It is a sedative useful in a wide range of problems.

VARIETIES *V. officinalis* bears pinkish-lavender or -white flowers and grows to 4 feet; the variety **'Alba'** bears white flowers; **'Rubra'**, red; and **'Coccinea'**, deep red.

VERBASCUM THAPSUS GREAT MULLEIN *Scrophulariaceae (Figwort)*

BIENNIAL Native to Europe and temperate Asia, many species of mullein are now found naturalized in North America, growing readily in sunny fields and roadsides. It is grown ornamentally, for its attractive woolly foliage and dramatically tall flower spikes.

CULTURE Mullein grows easily in full sun and a well-drained, dryish soil. It will not tolerate cold, soggy soil, especially during the winter months. If purchasing seedlings, look for healthy, many-leafed ones. Because mullein is a biennial, if you purchase a plant in flower, it will die after the flowering. Mullein is easy to start from seed, sown in the fall or spring, covered lightly with soil. Put down more seed than you think you will need, as germination is patchy; thin seedlings to 2 or 2½ feet. Keep weeds away until the large leaves shade them out. Mullein doesn't need any special applications of fertilizer or frost protection over the winter. Flower stalks appear in summer; leave them on plants until seed is formed and released to ensure a fresh batch of seedlings for

TULBAGHIA VIOLACAEA (SOCIETY GARLIC) Plant 2½ feet tall produces 1-foot-long pointed leaves and bright lilac flowers. Blooms throughout summer. Full sun. Zones 5-9.

VALERIANA OFFICINALIS (VALERIAN) Spreading plant grows to 5 feet tall and produces a cluster of pink or white flowers in summer. Partial shade. Zones 4-9.

VERBASCUM THAPSUS (GREAT MULLEIN) Plant 6 feet tall produces woolly leaves up to 1 foot long and tall, dramatic flower spikes. Full sun. Zones 3-8.

VERNONIA FASCICULATA (WESTERN IRONWEED) Plant 2-5 feet tall produces deep red-violet circular flowers in late summer and early fall. Full sun. Zones 4-9.

the following season.

The gray fuzzy leaves of mullein look wonderful with dark green and yellow-tinged plants. Remember, however, that the flower stalk can grow up to 8 feet in height; consider this when selecting a location for your mullein plants. Collect leaves in midsummer and dry; collect flowers when in bloom and dry or infuse in oil.

USES The large stalks of mullein were oiled and used for funeral torches in early times. It has been used medicinally since ancient times; it is still used in some parts of England for skin problems, earaches, and respiratory ailments.

VERNONIA FASCICULATA WESTERN IRONWEED Asteraceae (Sunflower)

PERENNIAL Western ironweed is prized by gardeners for its deep red-violet flowers, enjoyed during the growing season and in dried everlasting bouquets. Growing 2-5 feet tall, western ironweed flowers at the ends of short branches near the top of the plant. It prefers full sun in moist or low areas with good drainage and no standing water. It is considered a wet prairie plant and competes easily with grasses like joe-pye weed. (Nebraska)

VETIVERIA ZIZUNIOIDES VETIVER Gramineae (Grass family)

PERENNIAL Vetiver is found in tropical and subtropical plains throughout northern India, Bangladesh, and Burma (Myanmar). It is a large, erect, sod-forming grass but has no running rhizomes. Vetiver is a grand, tall source of texture and fragrance for the garden; at Berkeley Botanic Garden, it is grown as a waterplant at the edge of a pond. The original, undomesticated species from north India sets fertile seed. The cultivated type, V. zizunioides, from south India, does not flower or set seed. Vetiver is highly valued for erosion control in warm parts of the world; it will grow in all types of conditions.

CULTURE Vetiver requires full sun and likes heat; it will not tolerate temperatures below -12° F. While vetiver is not fussy about soil type, richer soil will produce more luxuriant growth. Vetiver will also tolerate drought, but the more water it gets, the more it grows. Plant from divisions in mid- to late spring. Space 2-3 feet apart; plants will be large by summer's end. Weeds will not grow in this strong grass, and no significant pests bother it. Harvest roots in late autumn, and wash thoroughly before using.

USES The wonderful spicy smell of the roots is excellent in potpourris as well as for weaving; they are used in India to weave pleasant-smelling mats. Oil from the roots is used in many expensive perfumes. (Shimizu)

VIOLA ODORATA VIOLET Violaceae (Violet family)

PERENNIAL Much-beloved through the ages, the violet is admired for the fragrance and beauty of its flowers and its heart-shaped leaves. Violets are native to Europe, and they make a lovely border plant, ground cover, or naturalized edging for a woodland.

CULTURE Violets prefer fairly rich, loamy soil that is evenly moist and partially shaded. Set out young plants (purchased from a nursery or taken by

Edible flowers are colorful, nutritious, and delicious additions to salads. Among popular edible flowers are nasturtiums (shown below), violets, scented geraniums, calendula, and borage. Make sure that the flowers you choose are safe–many are highly–or slightly–toxic.

VETIVERIA ZIZUNIOIDES (VETIVER) Large, erect, sod-forming grass, up to 8 feet tall. Full sun. Zones 6-10.

VIOLA ODORATA (VIOLET) Low-growing plant 4-6 inches tall produces brightly colored flowers in combinations of violet, pink, yellow, and white. Partial shade. Zones 5-8.

WASABIA JAPONICA (WASABI) Tall leafy plant produces large bright green leaves and enlarged root. Full sun to partial shade; plant near flowing water. Zones 5-8.

ZINGIBER OFFICINALE (GINGER) Tall bushy plant with large medium green leaves and thick knobby rhizomes. Sometimes produces flowers if grown in greenhouse. Light shade. Zone 10.

runner division) in spring; they will spread freely by runners. A mulch of compost or leaf mold is beneficial.

USES Violets—both leaves and flowers—can be added to salads, jellies, and drinks. Violet flowers make wonderful candied decorations.

WASABIA JAPONICA WASABI *Brassicaceae (Mustard family)*

PERENNIAL Also known as Japanese horseradish, wasabi is native to the wet banks of cool mountain streams and springs in Japan. It's botanically closely related to nasturtiums.

CULTURE Wasabi requires the very specific growing conditions of its native habitat, including a cool climate, shade, and gently flowing spring water whose temperature does not fluctuate much during the year. Wasabi will grow successfully when these unique conditions are created artificially. In Japan, soils for wasabi are quartz or basalt, occasionally volcanic. To grow, set out seedlings in September to November 12 inches apart. Add a slow-release 12-12-12 fertilizer. Mulch with straw to protect from summer heat, and with straw, plastic sheets, or cheesecloth for frost damage protection. Do not let mulch inhibit water flow. The best average minimum winter temperature for wasabi is 30° F. In Japan, wasabi is bothered by a diverse range of pests and fungal and bacterial pathogens. Harvest wasabi root from April to November.

USES Wasabi's enlarged root, or stem, is prized as a traditional condiment in Japan for its hot taste and tangy flavor. Grate it fresh and eat with raw fish (sushi or sashimi) or add to soy sauce. Leaves and petioles can be pickled. [23]

ZINGIBER OFFICINALE GINGER *Zingiberaceae (Ginger family)*

PERENNIAL Ginger is native to southeast Asia and is widely cultivated in tropical areas. This tall, bushy herb is grown from a thick, knobby rhizome that's used fresh or powdered for its piquant flavor.

CULTURE While ginger is hardy outdoors only in tropical and subtropical climates (temperatures below 50° F. can stunt it), it can easily be grown in pots indoors. Purchase fresh ginger root at a food market in late winter, choosing fat tubers with numerous buds. Plant whole, or break into pieces. First, soak in warm water overnight; then plant about 2 inches deep in a rich, humus-rich compost; about 3 tubers to a 14-inch pot is good spacing. Temperatures of 75°-85° F. are needed to sprout the dormant tubers. Water lightly at first, then more heavily as growth commences. (But keep the plant dry during its winter dormancy.) Ginger prefers light shade, not hot direct sun. When planted in a rich compost, ginger needs little fertilizer. If grown in a greenhouse, it may bloom and produce an exotic and interesting flower that looks somewhat like a miniature pineapple.

USES To use, dig up new young sprouts that appear in front of the mature plant. The roots of these sprouts will be fresh and flavorful. Store in the refrigerator for up to 3 weeks, or freeze. (Matthaei)

MORE PLANTS FOR THE HERB GARDEN

As you have seen in the previous pages, there is a vast range of choices for the herb gardener, whether he or she is specializing in one particular facet or simply creating a spot of beauty and interest. Space precluded listing every conceivable herb with a full entry. Here are some other plants our horticulturists wanted to mention.

ACINOS THYMOIDES (BASIL THYME) This hardy creeping plant has mildly aromatic leaves that can be used like thyme. Hardy to Zone 4, it does well in dry locations with full sun.

AGRIMONIA EUPATORIA (AGRIMONY) This leafy green perennial herb has small yellow flowers; it grows best in light shade and dryish soil. It is used in teas and gargles to relieve sore throats.

AJUGA REPTANS (BUGLEWEED) A popular perennial groundcover for shady spots, bugleweed was used to treat tuberculosis. Its roots produce a black dye.

ARCTIUM LAPPA (BURDOCK) This easily-grown, and quite invasive plant was used as a blood purifier as far back as Shakespeare's time; it is now used as a root vegetable, it has a taste that combines potatoes and celery.

ARMORACIA RUSTICANA (HORSERADISH) A perennial often grown as an annual, the sharp-tasting horseradish root is used in many folk remedies, and is grated or pickled as a condiment for use with fish, beef, and sauces.

ARNICA MONTANA (ARNICA) Arnica flowers are used in ointments and liniments to ease body aches and sore muscles. This perennial herb requires sandy soil and full sun.

BERBERIS VULGARIS (BARBERRY) Barberries thrive in rich well-drained soil in full sun to partial shade. In the past, the berries were made into teas used to alleviate respiratory symptoms. Barberry makes a good edging shrub in a knot garden.

BETULA (BIRCH) The leaves of the tall birch tree were used in teas by Native Americans to ease a host of symptoms, including gout, abdominal and menstrual cramps, and headaches.

CALLUNA VULGARIS (HEATHER) An ornamental groundcover often used on barren, acidic soils, heather have been used medicinally for their mild anti-inflammatory and sedative properties.

CANNABIS SATIVA (HEMP) It is illegal to grow this plant without a permit; it is the source of a tough fiber used to produce ropes, and the illegal drug marijuana.

CAPSELLA BURSA-PASTORIS (SHEPHERD'S PURSE) This easy-to-grow plant is sometimes considered a weed; its mustard-flavored leaves can be added to salads, and the whole plant can be used in wreath-making if cut in its seed stage.

CATHARANTHUS ROSEUS (MADAGASCAR PERIWINKLE) This plant produces showy magenta flowers; it is perennial in Zone 10, but can be grown as an annual further north. It contains strong chemical properties and is currently being researched as a cancer drug; it is too powerful a drug to be used in home cures.

CAULLOPHYLLUM THALICTROIDES (BLUE COHOSH) A decorative plant that does well in shade, blue cohosh has been used treat female ailments by Native Americans,

Catharanthus roseus

Chelidonium majus

who passed the information on to early settlers. The plant is now considered unsafe.

CEANOTHUS AMERICANUS (NEW JERSEY TEA) Early settlers in the United States made a tea from this deciduous shrub, which is hardy in Zone 5 and grows in full sun to partial shade.

CENTAUREA CYANUS (CORNFLOWER) A popular annual flower, often found growing wild–and even considered a weed–cornflower adds color to potpourriand can be used to make tea. It has weak medicinal properties, and is also used in bath and cosmetic preparations.

CHELIDONIUM MAJUS (CELANDINE) This perennial herb produces a bright yellow flower; its stems, when broken, emit a milky sap that stains and burns the skin. Celandine was used in folk remedies to relieve abdominal distress, and is currently being tested as a cancer drug.

CONRADINA VERTICILLATA (CUMBERLAND ROSEMARY) The leaves of this plant can be used as a substitute for rosemary; the plant, which is easy to grow and tolerates drought, heat, and humidity, is also ornamental, producing lovely pink or lavender flowers.

CUNILLA ORIGANOIDES (AMERICAN DITTANY) A low-growing, many-branched perennial with wiry purple stms and small dark leaves, this plant was a folk remedy for colds, fevers, headaches, and snakebites. It grows well in cracks and crevices in well-drained or dry soil in full sun or dappled shade.

CYTISUS (BROOM) The branches of this shrub produced crude but useful brooms; the plant itself is toxic and should not be taken internally. It is very ornamental, and tolerates poor soil.

CINNAMOMUM ZEYLANICUM (CINNAMON) The popular spice is derived from the bark of a small evergreen tree that will grow in some parts of the American South.

DATURA STRAMONIUM (JIMSONWEED) Jimsonweed has a foul odor, and is toxic and possibly hallucinogenic. It does however, have an interesting history–it was used in witchcraft–and large, showy flowers. Keep it away from areas where children play.

DICTAMNUS ALBUS (GASPLANT) This lovely perennial plant has diuretic and laxative properties; it is toxic if taken in large quantities.

EQUISETUM HYEMALE (HORSETAIL) This rough plant can be used as pot scrubber; it is also used in folk remedies, though its usefulness has not been proven and it is toxic if taken in large doses. It is very coldhardy and grows in full sun or partial shade.

EUPATORIUM PERFOLIATUM (BONESET) A perennial plant that grows best in full sun and rich, moist soil, boneset was a popular remedy for fevers (including the "breakbone" fever), coughs, and colds.

EUPATORIUM PURPUREUM (JOE PYE WEED) Native Americans used this plant as a cure for typhus. A showy but somewhat invasive perennial with large purple flowerheads, it was named for Joe Pye, the medicine man who taught early settlers how to use it.

EUPHRASIA OFFICINALIS (EYEBRIGHT) At one time thought to alleviate eye fatigue and other eye diseases, this plant is not considered safe today.

INULA HELENIUM (ELECAMPANE) This tall, yellow-flowered perennial is often used as an ornamental; a hardy plant, it grows in most soils and in full to light shade. Elecampane has been used in many parts of the world to remedy respiratory problems.

EUCALYPTUS GLOBULUS (EUCALYPTUS) This aromatic plant has silvery branches of blue-gray leaves that are used in potpourris and air fresheners; extracts of the plant are used in cough medicines and cough drops to ease respiratory problems. This plant will only grow in warm climates, and does not tolerate frost.

GAULTHERIA PROCUMBENS (WINTERGREEN) Used as a flavoring and in liniments, this woody perennial is hardy to Zone 4 and grows in most soil types in partial shade.

GENTIANA LUTEA (GENTIAN) This bitter-tasting but ornamental perennial herb has been used a stimulant. It should only be taken in small doses, and never by pregnant women.

GEUM RIVALE (WATER AVENS) has antiseptic and astringent properties, and is also used for gastric disorders.

HAMAMELIS VIRGINIANA (WITCH HAZEL) The popular astringent is also a popular shrub; its small yellow flowers are often the only color in the winter landscape.

HELICHRYSUM PETIOLATUM (CURRY PLANT) This spreading, vining plant has curry-scented foliage; it is not used in cooking curry dishes.

HELIOTROPUM ARBORESCENS (HELIOTROPE, CHERRY PIE) This tall perennial is hardy only in zones 9-10; it is used as an annual in other areas. A popular ornamental with clusters of small purple flowers (some cultivars have white flowers), it is used in perfumes.

HYDRASTIS CANADENSIS (GOLDENSEAL) Used for many ailments by Native Americans, goldenseal has been called "one of the most wonderful remedies in the entire herb kingdom"; this claim has not been proven, and the plant is considered unsafe for internal consumption by many experts. It is difficult to cultivate.

ILEX VOMITORIA 'NANA' (DWARF YAUPON HOLLY) This dwarf holly grows slowly, and is excellent for use in a knot garden. Natives Americans used it to make "The Black Drink" used for ceremonial and ritualistic purposes.

ILLICUM PARVIFLORUM (STAR ANISE) This tender perennial, hardy only to Zone 7, has creamy yellow flowers and fragrant foliage. It is related to the plant used in Chinese cooking

INDIGOFERA TINCTORIA (INDIGO) Once the most important dye plant in cultivation, indigo requires a very warm climate and full sun.

JUNIPERUS COMMUNIS (JUNIPER) An oil from the berries of juniper shrubs and trees is used in making gin, as well as in many effective medications. Juniper berries are also useful in marinades and stews. These shrubs grow in full sun in all climate zones and most soils.

LAMIUM MACULATUM (SPOTTED NETTLED) Teas made from the flowers of this perennial herb are purported to act as a tonic. The young leaves can be eaten like spinach.

Heliotropium arborescens 'Alba'

Leonourus cardiaca

LEONURUS CARDIACA (MOTHERWORT) An easy-to-grow herb often found in waste places, motherwort has mild sedative and antispasmadic qualities. It can also be dangerous.

MAGNOLIA VIRGINIANA (SWEET BAY) The fragrant leaves of this small tree are sometimes used for flavoring.

MAHONIA AQUIFOLIUM (OREGON GRAPE) An ornamental shrub with shiny green foliage, Oregon Grape is used to treat skin disorders. It is harmful to some people.

MYRICA PENSYLVANICA (BAYBERRY) This small shrub grows well in poor soil, and produces the wax used in making bayberry candles.

MYRISTICUS FRAGRANS (NUTMEG) This tree, which has dark, glossy leaves resembling rhododendron, requires a hot moist climate. Its fleshy fruit splits in half to expose a membrane which, when dried, becomes the spice mace. The mace is wrapped around a shell that, in turn encloses a seed which, when dried and ground becomes the popular spice nutmeg.

OENANTHA STOLONIFERA (VIETNAMESE CELERY) is a leafy biennial plant that grows in warm climates and has leaves with a celery-like taste.

PASSIFLORA INCARNATA (PASSIONFLOWER) Usually grown for its large blooms, which appear on vines, passionflower has been used as a sedative. It grows best in partial shade in rich, moist, well-drained soil.

PHYTOLOCCA AMERICANA (POKEWEED) This very hardy native herb was used by Native American to treat tumors, as a salve, and as a rheumatism cure. Its fruits produce a red, brown, or pink fabric dye.

PLANTAGO MAJOR (PLANTAIN) Widely used as a laxative, this perennial herb produces long leaves and leafless flowering stems. It grows best in dry soil.

PODOPHYLLUM PELTATUM (MAYAPPLE) A popular ornamental with single white flowers, mayapple has been used as a laxative and diuretic. It has toxic properties that have resulted in birth deformites and fatalities.

PRIMULA VULGARIS (COWSLIP) Often found growing wild in Europe, this ornamental, sweet-scented flower has expectorant, diuretic, and antispasmodic properties. The flowers can be used in a mildly sedative tea, or as candied decorations.

RUBBIA TINCTORUM (MADDER) This popular dye plant (it produces orange, red, and garnet colors) needs full sun; it is hardy up to Zone 8.

SALIX (WILLOW) The bark of the willow tree is the source of one of our most potent drugs, the aspirin.

SAPORONIA OFFICINALIS (SOAPWORT) This hardy perennial tolerates poor soil as long as it is well-drained, and full sun or light shade. It has been used to make soap, and well as for medicines (though it is now believed to toxic and is only used externally).

SASSAFRASS ALBIDUM (SASSAFRASS) Hardy to Zone 5 in any garden soil, sassafras has been used to flavor teas and soft drinks, but is now a suspected carinogen.

SILYBUM MARIANUM (MILK THISTLE) This annual or biennial herb produces a thistle-like flower; preparations from its fruits are used by the pharmaceutical industry in medications for gall bladder and liver diseases.

SMYRNIUM (ALEXANDER) Once a major medicinal herb, this biennial has a celery taste; it grows best in shade.

SYZYGIUM AROMATICUM (CLOVES) This plant, the source of an exotic spice, requires tropical conditions.

TANACETUM COCCINEUM (PYRETHUM) This popular ornamental produces a powerful natural insecticide.

TARXACUM OFFICINALE (DANDELION) The dandelion, often considered an invasive pest, has many herbal uses. It is used by herbalists in Europe to treat diabetes and blood deficiencies, and also is the base of the popular dandelion wine.

TAXUS (YEW) Compounds in this popular coniferous shrub have been found to be effective in the treatment of breast cancer.

TRIGONELLA FOENUM-GRAECUM (FENUGREEK) Seeds of this annual herb are used in pickling brines and marinades, as well as in folk cures for diseases ranging from diabetes to rickets. It was an ingredient in tonic medicines (including Lydia Pinkham's) in the nineteenth century. It needs full sun and rich soil.

URTICA DIOICA (STINGING NETTLE) This coldhardy plant, which is covered with small sharp hairs, thrives in rich moist soil and in full sun or partial shade. It has been used in teas as a remedy for asthma.

VERBENA OFFICINALIS (VERVAIN) An ancient herb used by Druids, Egyptians, Persians, and British herbalists for a vast range of ailments, vervain is no longer considered to have healing properties. It is grown as an ornamental for its small purple flowers.

VERONICA OFFICINALIS (SPEEDWELL) A perennial herb with small white or lilac flowers, often grown as an ornamental, speedwell has been used for herbal medicines for stomach and kidney disorders. It also makes a pleasant tea.

VISCUM ALBUM (MISTLETOE) The popular New Year's plant grows wild through-out America. It appears in many Greek and Roman myths, was used in Druid ceremonies, and is reputed to have been used to make Christ's cross.

Herbs come in a wide range of shapes, sizes, and colors that can be combined in exquisite patterns.

The variety and lore of herbs have fired your interest, and you've decided you're definitely going to become an herb grower. Where do you go from here?

GARDEN TYPES

First, decide what you want your herb garden or garden area to do for you. Are you mainly interested in growing herbs to use in cooking? Do you want to create a fragrance garden? or a garden that will make a visual impact in terms of texture and shape? Perhaps you want to attract a variety of butterflies to your backyard, or grow herbs that have a special meaning in folklore and ancient beliefs. You might prefer herbs as accent plants in existing locations. The purpose of your herb growing will influence the site, size, and appearance of your herb garden area.

Next, consider the type of garden you want. Are you a casual, relaxed gardener? An informal kitchen or cottage garden may work best for you. Is your house accentuated by formal plantings? A traditional knot garden might then be your choice for herb growing, provided you're willing and able to keep it well clipped and shaped. Perhaps you prefer natural-looking low-maintenance gardens. A meadow or woodland garden could be the answer.

With purpose and garden type in mind, survey possible sites for your herb-growing area. Many gardens seem to evolve from the site. Your first consideration should be sun—most herbs need at least 6 hours of sun a day. Remember that shade will encroach as nearby trees grow; allow for a buffer zone. If you're planning to grow mostly culinary herbs, you'll want your garden to be convenient to your kitchen so you'll be able to easily pop out for sprigs of herbs while you're cooking. If you're growing in a very dry area, you'll want to consider access to water when siting your garden. Also, be aware of slope—many people who put in a long, narrow garden are surprised to see the fruits of their labor wash away in the first heavy rainstorm. A very sloped site will have to be leveled out, terraced, or broken up into smaller individual areas.

Right: Before you start planting, sketch your garden in scale; note all permanent structures, areas of shade and sun, water sources. Then fill in plants.

Previous pages: In the display garden at Catnip Acres, an herb farm in Connecticut, herbs of different color, form, height, and texture are combined. The garden includes lavender, santolina, lambs' ears, and wormwood.

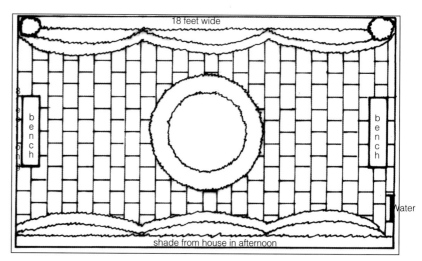

PLANNING ON PAPER

Now you're ready to draw up an actual plan on paper. If you're starting from scratch, start small. Plan to create one perfect little garden spot, perhaps a half-circle border of cooking herbs accompanied by a few pots of tender perennials. If you start too big, you may find you can't keep up, and you'll get very discouraged at the resulting plot of scraggly herbs and rampant weeds.

Use a tape measure to figure the exact dimensions of your garden area, and draw these to scale on graph paper. Fill in any existing structures that will remain in the garden—an interesting boulder, a stockade fence that will serve as a backdrop for a long border of herbs, a tree. If it's a large garden, allow for working and access paths, remembering that as edging plants fill out they will encroach on the pathways. The main walking and wheelbarrow path should be 4 feet wide; smaller access paths can be 2 feet wide, or could be made of 2-foot-wide stepping stones. Structural edgings for garden beds are a good idea. They give the garden a more defined look and keep invading grass and people out but your improved garden soil in. A good choice for herb garden edging is naturally rot-resistant wood like cedar or locust; bricks or rocks are other possibilities.

Once you've penciled in on your garden plan the space taken up by pathways and edging materials, you can lay out the growing beds and figure out just how much growing space you actually have. Finally, you're ready to decide what to plant. Make a wish list of herbs you think you'd like to grow. Next to each, note whether it's an annual or perennial, how much space it

When choosing plants, pay attention to growth habit. Placing taller plants behind shorter ones is an obvious necessity; in the photo above, catnip (*Nepeta mussinii*), beebalm (*Monarda didyma*), and inula form a pleasing vertical mass; their strong lines are broken by a simple bench. Consider how wide the plants will grow as well; a mass of lavender in the picture on the left contrasts well with tall, spikey angelica and feathery elderberry.

ELEMENTS OF DESIGN

Proper use of scale and proportion is essential to good design. Scale is defined as the relationship of a design element or group of elements to the balance of the landscape, i.e., trees to building, statues to garden, etc. Proportion is the harmonious relationship of object sizes in a designed landscape. Proportional harmony results from ideal size relationships between objects in the landscape. As an element of garden design, harmony is the consistent recurrence of form, line, shape, texture, and color in the landscape. These elements are also used to create rhythm or movement in a garden—the physical movement of the viewer as he or she walks through the garden, and the journey of the eye as well. The latter movement is created by repetition of colors, forms, and textures.

needs, and what growing requirements it has. Use this information to figure out how many of these wished-for herbs you can actually fit into the available space. In a small garden, especially a small culinary one, plan on only 1 plant of each herb type. In larger gardens, plan on 3-5 of each herb type; groupings of plants give more visual impact and create a unified effect. As a rule of thumb, plan on 3-9 square feet for 1 perennial herb and 1-3 square feet for each annual herb.

Place your perennials on your plan first; they will form the backbone of your design. Leave space between the perennials for annuals like basil and parsley. This allows room for the perennials to fill in as they become established; you'll find you may need fewer and fewer annuals each year. For economy's sake, you can buy only one plant of those herbs that are readily propagated, like monardas (bee balm), chives, and mints. In other cases, like lavender, you'll have to buy as many plants as you plan eventually to have. When planning, beware of invasive, aggressive plants like wormwood, lemon balm, and tansy; you might prefer to put these in an area of their own. Do your homework, and choose the best cultivars available of each herb. Some lavenders, for example, are larger plants with bigger blooms than others. Russian tarragon may be cheaper to buy than French tarragon, but it's much less flavorful and will try to take over the garden. We've listed some superior cultivars in Chapter 2, but talk to other gardeners in your area as well as horticulturists at your local botanic garden or nursery; they will know which cultivars are particularly suited to your area.

While planning your garden on paper is helpful in steering you toward what you want, remember that your written plan is only a guideline. Expect that you'll want to change some parts of the plan when you start to actually

Once you get to know your herbs, you will be able to combine the textures of their foliage, branches, and flowers; your garden will be lovely not only for the brief period of blossom, but for the entire season. *Right:* Tall spikes of veronica combine with santolina and thyme. *Opposite:* In a more dramatic display, great sweeps of marigolds and petunias surround mounds of hyssop, yarrow, and thyme.

Transitions–ranging from simple entry gates to elaborate fences or trellises–let visitors know that they should stop and look. Focal points are elements that hold your attention. They can be used as points of reference or as a way of pulling you into another part of the garden. The way that the focal point is placed within the composition will determine its success or failure. A focal point should create a sense of anticipation, such as a statue that pulls you down a path because there is a sense that there is something waiting to be discovered.

Many garden designers liken landscape design to musical composition in that both require carefully planned organization of elements–notes in a musical composition, plants in a garden. Their sequence and repetition convey a theme that governs the organization of elements, where some dominate and others support.

BY HOLLY SHIMIZU

plant your garden. Maybe you planned on just 3 sages, but now that the 3 plants are in place, you see the area would look better with 5; go out and buy 2 more sage plants. Use your plan as a reference point; if the tall pink bloomer you'd penciled in isn't available, look through your herb books and catalogs and choose a similar substitute. You won't really know what you want to grow, or where, until you know from experience what each herb looks like, how they all look together, and how they grow in your area. Remember that you can always rearrange your herbs (they won't mind), and you probably will, often. An ever-changing variety is one of the aspects that make herb gardening so interesting.

COLOR, TEXTURE, SHAPE

In deciding what to place where in your herb garden, try to achieve a contrast of foliage texture and color, avoiding a monotonous all-green look. Keep in mind that visual interest in an herb garden comes from the foliage; the flowers are only a little bonus of occasional color. Arrange herbs in patterns of contrasting shades of green and gray interspersed with silvery plants like santolina and wormwood and variegated, golden, or purple cultivars like purple basil and golden or tricolor sage. For splashes of color, add fast-growing edible

Although beautiful gardens can be created in shadings of foliage colors, gardeners looking for more brilliant hues will not be disappointed. *Right:* Garlic chives and dianthus provide purple and magenta blossoms. *Below:* Deep purple basil and perilla are as colorful as a nearby bed of tulips.

annuals like Johnny-jump-up, calendula, and nasturtium, or put a few dianthus in among your scented geraniums.

Vary the shapes and sizes of adjoining herbs for additional interest in your garden. Contrast the soft gray-green mound of a sage with the tall purple spikiness of the Japanese cooking herb shisho (also known as perilla). Pull a taller but open plant like catnip toward the front of the garden to break up the front-to-back progression of ascending height. Put a small-leafed herb next to a plant with broad leaves. Don't be afraid to cut a plant back to adjust its size and time of bloom. If your monarda is too tall, chop it back by half—it will bloom later and lower.

You may want to define your herb garden by planting edgings. Good choices for this purpose include creeping thyme, lady's mantle, betony, rock soapwort, and Greek or golden oregano. Lemon gem marigolds create a charming edging effect, an airy soft mass of green dotted with little yellow buttons.

With all their versatility, herbs don't have to be confined to their own garden area. You can mix them in with existing plantings, which can be especially helpful if you're just starting out with herbs. You can get to know the herbs before you decide which ones to grow in a large, separate garden area, and since you probably already have some existing planted areas, you're spared the not inconsiderable work of digging up a whole new garden. Be innovative! Put herbs everywhere in your landscape. Nest some scented geraniums around your mailbox. Screen out unsightly parts of your yard with a hedge of tall herbs like angelica, lovage, or bronze fennel. Plant shade-loving lady's mantle instead of the usual impatiens around the base of trees. Line your drive with lavender instead of boxwood and be rewarded with wafts of wonderful

scent as you go to and from your car. Grow mint near the pool to liven up
iced drinks, and cooking herbs to pluck on the spot near the grill area. If
you're planning to put in a tree or shrub, choose one with an herbal use, like
witch hazel. Let hops grow over your arbor or shed.

PLANNING FOR YEAR-ROUND INTEREST

To keep interest in your herb garden year-round, plan for good structure and
texture even when most plants are dormant. Use attractive materials for
paths, mulches, or edgings, and select edging plants that maintain winter
interest, like boxwood, barberry, rue, and winterberry. Plant shrubs and trees
with interesting texture, bark, or branching characteristics, and winter berries
or blooms. Include herbs in your garden plan that bloom in the fall, like
pineapple and Mexican sage and saffron crocus.

In cold climates, you will have to continue your winter herb gardening
indoors. Plan for this by growing spicy fragrant types that you can arrange
attractively in your house at the end of the outdoor growing season–scented
geranium, rosemary, patchouli, cardamom, jasmine. Start some fresh annual
seedlings in late summer or early September specifically for indoor windowsill
growing, like basil, cilantro, and dill. Your older annuals in the garden will be
too big and sprawling to continue growing successfully indoors. Do, however,
dig up large specimens of your tender perennials, like bay and rosemary, and
bring them indoors 2 weeks before the heating system starts up, to acclimate
them gradually to the hot and dry indoor conditions. Take cuttings of your
full-grown garden scented geraniums to create compact indoor plants for the
winter. Group your indoor herbs together–they'll help keep each other moist.
Putting them on a tray with moist pebbles helps, too. You want to keep the
air around the herbs moist; if you keep their soil wet, they'll drown.

GARDEN PLANS

We've given you a lot of design ideas in the preceding pages. To help you
visualize some ways to put these possibilities into concrete form, the following
pages offer you some actual herb gardens, in both photographs and diagrams.

Above: A collection of thymes is
arranged in a series of stone planters.
Left: The knot garden at The New
York Botanical Garden under cover of
snow.

Knot gardens are not for everyone, but are perfect for those who enjoy a bit of formal geometry in their garden. For these gardens, it is absolutely necessary to start with a plan. First decide on a shape—it can be a series of elaborate interlocking loops or just a few circles—and then choose plants. It is critical to select plants that you can depend upon to thrive; if one plant in your seamless knot dies, the entire section will have to be replaced (unless you've taken the precaution of keeping a similar plant in reserve). As in all other gardens, many successful knots take advantage of contrasting colors, textures, and leaf shapes. But some of the most simple knots, using only one or two species, work beautifully, too, valued for classic design that showcases healthy plants.

Other elements in the knot garden include edgings (paving stones, as shown in the photograph on the left, can be lovely) and mulches (which range from simple white stones to cocoa hulls to varicolored gravels).

Planning a knot garden allows indulgence; caring for one does not. A knot must be meticulously pruned and maintained or its shape and attractiveness will be lost. Again, make sure you can count on your plants; water them as needed, tend themccarefully, and provide them with protection over winter.

For more photographs of and information about knot gardens, see pages 48, 49, and 51.

EDGING PLANTS FOR KNOT GARDENS

Berberis (barberry), which has red and purple-leaved cultivars, such as 'Crimson Pygmy', which is very compact.

Buxus sempervirens **'Suffriticosa'** (boxwood), also known as edging box, is one of the most popular edgings for knot gardens.

Ilex vomitoria (Yaupon holly) works better than most other edging shrubs in the South.

Lavandula angustifolia (English lavender) grows about 1 foot tall and produces spikes of purple flowers in summer. It may need winter protection.

Teucrium chamaedrys (germander) is a traditional knot garden element.

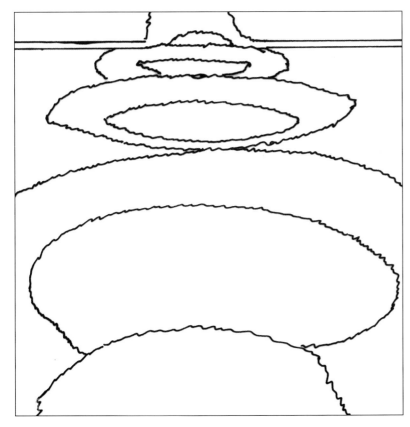

design guide

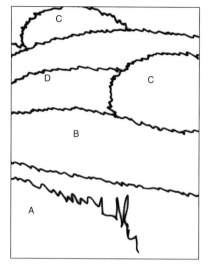

A=Iris
B=Thyme
C=Santolina
D=Germander

At the University of California Botanical Garden, a border of thyme is the background for mounds of santolina and germander; a stand of iris foliage lines the other side of the pathway. When the thyme is in flower, its small pink blossoms create a foil for the deeper color of the germander flowers. The rounded, fluffy santolina presents a different geometric form. In early the spring, before the thyme and germander bloom, *Iris* x *germanica* var. *florentina* is a mass of large white flowers with deep yellow markings.

The herb garden at Well-Sweep Herb Farm in Port Murray, New Jersey, contains hundreds of types of herbs, including culinary, ornamental, medicinal, and fragrance herbs; the owners introduce dozens—sometimes over one hundred—new herbs each year. Their display garden is organized into sections, called parterres, grouping many varieties of each herb around an antique sundial. A pathway is edged with a wide swath of stachys; its neutral silver-gray foliage complements the other sections of the garden as they burst into flower.

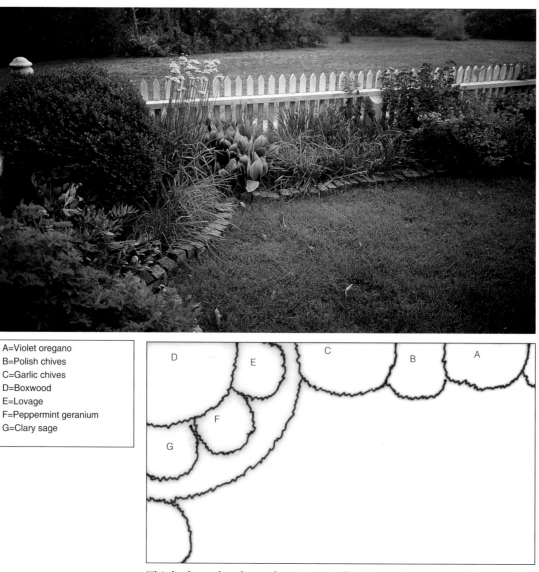

A=Violet oregano
B=Polish chives
C=Garlic chives
D=Boxwood
E=Lovage
F=Peppermint geranium
G=Clary sage

This herb garden, located on Cape Cod in Massachusetts, contains a wealth of culinary and ornamental herbs. Over many years, the gardener has accumulated a collection of particularly flavorful or ornamental favorites, including lemon thyme, nutmeg geranium, polish chives, and broadleaf sage; she has integrated many different shapes and textures into a pleasantly informal pattern. Carefully pruned boxwoods provide structure to this garden, which is edged with a simple border of bricks. A traditional picket fence adds to its charm.

A steeply sloped site in an area with poor soil is a challenge to even the most experienced landscaper. This area was transformed into a lovely herb garden using two sophisticated methods. The sloping area was terraced to create several level planting surfaces; and raised beds were installed to circumvent the poor soil.

Raised beds are made by mounding soil and enclosing it with some sort of boundary. A raised bed allows a gardener to choose his or her own soil, and to amend it as necessary. In southern areas, raised beds can provide much better drainage than natural soil. Some gardeners believe that a raised bed interrupts the natural flow of the garden; they are sometimes difficult to integrate into the garden.

VIEWPOINT

SOIL TESTS

We recommend soil tests for all types of gardens; it's the only way of knowing just what your garden needs. Soil tests should be done every few years.
AMY GREVING, DR. DONALD STEINEGGER, UNIVERSITY OF NEBRASKA

We don't do soil tests regularly here; we would think it was necessary only if we encountered an unexplainable problem. Soil tests are somewhat expensive and are not necessary so long as the garden is doing well.
DIANE MISKE, CORNELL PLANTATIONS

It's always a good idea to have a soil test done before you start a new garden, or before you make considerable changes in an existing one. It's better to find out what your soil needs before your plants are in it than after they start dying.
LISA CADEY, THE NEW YORK BOTANICAL GARDEN

Soil tests are only one way of monitoring garden soil, and it is not a method that I focus on. An experienced gardener learns to understand his or her soil, and to maintain it over a long period. Many inexperienced gardeners rely on additives rather than improving the structure of the soil.
HOLLY SHIMIZU, UNITED STATES BOTANICAL GARDEN

Preceding pages: A stone-enclosed raised bed at the Robison York State Herb Garden, Cornell Plantations.

CHOOSING AND IMPROVING THE SITE

Herbs are among the easiest plants to grow, but they cannot be grown without preparation and care. Most of the plants in our herb gardens are not native to North America; many originated in the Mediterranean region, an area with a much different climate and topography. It is best to choose a site that will welcome them and to improve it as much as possible.

The most important requirements for growing herbs are sunshine, protection from the elements, and well-drained, moderately fertile soil. Good drainage is often more important than richness and fertility; in some cases, herbs actually do better in poor soil than in very rich soil, which can encourage the growth of weedy foliage at the expense of flowers and fruit.

When considering sites for your garden, observe all possible areas over a period of time. Note how much sun each site receives and whether it is direct sunlight, sunlight that is filtered through trees and fences, or if the sunlight is totally blocked by buildings or dense tree foliage; note whether conditions change at different times of the day. If you can find a site that includes all three types–full sun, partial sun, and shade–you will have the greatest flexibility, since there are herbs that thrive in each condition.

SOIL Although you cannot change the type of sunlight your garden receives (without altering major structures), you can change the composition of your soil. Soil improvements can be made for the short run with the addition of chemical fertilizers; but serious gardeners are able to manage their soil to attain peak production over a long period of time.

There are three basic types of soil: clay, sand, and loam. Clay soil has very little space between its particles; clay soil is often very rich in nutrients, but water and nutrients have trouble traveling through clay soil to the roots of the plant. Sandy soil transports material easily, but it can't hold nutrients and water for very long. The best mix of the two is loam, which is light but rich; this type of soil is often called "friable," which means it is easily pulverized.

To identify exactly what the soil in your garden needs requires a soil test. A small–but representative–amount of garden soil is analyzed for nutrient deficiencies and excesses. To get an accurate reading for your entire garden area, take small amounts from several different spots in your garden, mixing them to make a total of about ½ cup of soil. The acidity or alkalinity–pH–of the soil can be measured with a simple home kit. A full analysis can be done by a county extension service, an agricultural university, or perhaps even a local garden center. The analysis will generally be accompanied by recommendations for needed nutrients and their application rates.

There are many ways to maintain good soil; simply adding a lot of chemical fertilizer is not one of them. It takes experience to understand what your soil needs and to provide it. Some basic principles:

1. Match the crop to the soil; planting the wrong crop can result in not only a crop failure, but also damage to the soil.

2. Use organic matter generously; planting cover crops and adding compost and other fertilizers will keep your soil rich in organic matter.

3. Rotate crops so that soil can replenish materials used by a particular plant.

4. Keep a layer of topsoil in place.

5. Adjust soil that is too acidic with lime only when indicated by a soil test.

6. Use fertilizers that add missing ingredients, including trace elements, only when you have reason to suspect that they are necessary.

If you manage your soil properly, it will increase in fertility after several years of cultivation and provide the best possible home for your plants.

SITE IMPROVEMENT Whether you are establishing an elaborate knot garden or just planting a few herbs for the kitchen, your plants will be healthier if you take the time to improve the ground in which you put them. The first step in preparing a garden site is a general cleanup, the removal of rocks, sticks, stumps, or other debris. Once the area is relatively clean, lay out the boundaries of your site using string, garden hose, or spray paint.

If the site is a grassy area, skin the turf off using a shovel or spade. Take the top 2 inches off–grass and roots–and knock the soil loose from the roots. Don't throw away the turf–use it to start a compost pile. If the area is covered with brush or weeds, mow first and then skin off the vegetation. Once you have bare ground, you're ready to begin improving the soil for a productive garden.

Before planting, it is critical that you grade the planting area properly. This will determine how the water moves and, if done correctly, can prevent puddling. Insure that the planting site is free of turf and weeds. The soil should be loose and well-drained, with moderate fertility and ready access to water for irrigation.

PREPARING THE SOIL Loosen the soil to a depth of 4-6 inches. If there is tender vegetation growing on the site, turn it into the top part of the soil. Pull out any woody stems.Wait at least 2 weeks after tilling to allow the tilled plants to decompose and again turn the soil under to a depth of 4-6 inches to ensure the breaking up of dead plants and to further loosen the soil.

After the second tilling, apply soil amendments such as fertilizer, lime, compost, or sand. Till once again, this time to a depth of 8-10 inches with a tiller, or 12-18 inches by hand with a spading fork.

Double digging is a process by which two spadesful of dirt are lifted and loosened. It is time-consuming, back-breaking, and really not necessary for

To determine whether your drainage is adequate, dig a hole large enough to hold a gallon pot. Fill the hole with water, and see how long it takes to drain. There are several ways to correct poor drainage:

1. Add sand and organic matter to the soil. Sand plus clay results in cement; but sand, clay, and organic matter will give you friable soil.

2. Use raised beds, which always provide better drainage and also allow you to mix better soil from elsewhere into your site.

3. Insert a drainage pipe. These pipes, usually plastic, can be purchased at most garden supply or hardware stores and move water to a place where it will do less harm.

4. If your problem is serious, or if you think it is worth the investment, talk to a professional landscaper about inserting a drainage system, such as tile, gravel beds, or more elaborate drainage ditches.

Left: Tilling the soil; break up all clods of earth.

Above: A healthy plant, with solid green foliage, upright, undamaged leaves, and a sturdy root system. Before buying a plant, remove it from its pot to make sure it is not root-bound.

an herb garden. If you are starting a major garden and wish for high yields, consider looking into this process.

WHAT TO LOOK FOR WHEN CHOOSING HERBS

The most important aspect of choosing herbs for your garden is to select plants that are vigorous and healthy. Holly Shimizu has judged flower shows where plants in groups are represented by various growers; she easily recognizes the great growers because their plants have a healthy, robust appearance. The plants have received enough but not too much fertilizer; they show strong growth that has not been forced in a hot greenhouse or stressed as a result of inappropriate conditions; their color is rich green with no sign of yellowing.

Another significant consideration in choosing herbs is to understand your own conditions and to buy only plants that will thrive in those conditions. For example, if you have extremely sandy, dry conditions, then you would not consider buying sweet flag since it requires moist soil.

As plants go, herbs do not have a particularly long shelf life. Therefore, you should be sure to purchase plants at the correct stage of growth and in good health. If they are too young, they will be weak and easily killed. If they are too old, often they have experienced a great deal of stress (such as too much or too little water) from which they may never recover. Here is what to look for.

• Plants should be well established in their pots, in appropriately sized containers, and have an overall appearance of vigor.

• Plants should be established beyond the seedling stage and have developed into good, sturdy individuals—a minimum pot size of 3 inches is recommended.

• If the plant is a rooted cutting, it should have been pinched when young, which creates bushy and full growth, with more than a single stem.

• Plants that are repotted divisions should have been given ample time to establish themselves in the container.

• Foliage should be turgid (full, slightly swollen) and solid green.

• Leaves should be upright and undamaged.

• No infestation or damage by insects or disease should be evident. Pick the plant up for a close inspection. Mottled leaves could be a sign of mites. Yellowish stripes or stunted or distorted shapes could be signs of virus. You do not want any plant that has little white flies hovering around it. If you add herbs with insect or disease problems to your garden, these unwanted guests could spread to the soil or to other plants. However, if a plant you want to buy is infested, you will probably be able to eliminate the problem by washing it in a strong stream of water. Be sure to get a discount, and be sure that the problem is gone before you set the plant near any others.

• A potted plant should have a sturdy root system. This is harder to check, but some buyers knock the plant out of the pot to be sure a healthy root system has been established. Often the top growth is an indicator of a healthy root system.

• Many yellow leaves at the base of a plant are often an indication that the plant is pot-bound. After an extended period of time in a pot, a plant can lose its vigor, often because it has used up the available nutrition in the container If replanted with care, and if the root system is spread out at planting time, a pot-bound plant may recover. (This problem is much more severe with woody plants because their roots are sometimes impossible to redirect, and if they continue to grow in a circular pattern, they will eventually choke themselves.)

• Many roots growing out of the bottom of the pot is another indication that the plant is pot-bound. A few roots is no problem, but many roots out the bottom is not a good sign.

PROPAGATION

STARTING FROM SEED Many herbs can be started from seed. Not only is it cheaper to start your own plants from seeds, it also makes a much wider selection available to you. There are many containers suitable for holding seeds started indoors under lights. Some of the best include small, 2- to 3-inch pots or a 3-inch-deep corrugated fiberboard or plastic tray. The potting mixture should be lightweight and sterile to prevent seedlings from damping off and to avoid weed seeds. Several "soilless" mixtures are available commercially, containing perdite, sand, and peat moss.

OTHER METHODS Plants can also be started by root and stem cuttings, layering, and in some cases division. Herbs that can be divided include yarrow, orris root, chives, oregano–and others that spread throughout your garden. To divide, dig under the entire plant and lift out clumps of roots. Separate the roots into two parts with your hands–or with a sharp knife if they are densely matted–and replant each division. Division serves two purposes: it produces new stock for planting and keeps the existing plants healthy.

PLANTING

Gather together all the herbs you will be able to plant in one day and set them out in the proposed locations, being sure that each plant fits the

Above: The seedling stage. Once they reach this size, seedlings should be repotted into individual pots so that they have plenty of room to grow.

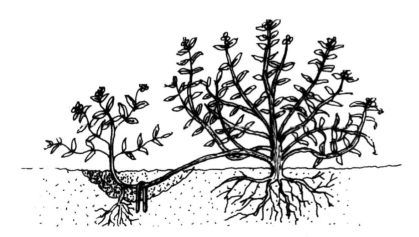

Left: To propagate by layering, strip the leaves from a flexible branch and bury it, without cutting from the main plant, with its top sticking out. Keep it well watered. Once the new plant begins to grow, indicating root formation, it can be cut from the mother plant and replanted elsewhere. Plants that are recommended for layering include marjoram, winter savory, sage, and lavender; don't try it with plants that tend to be invasive.

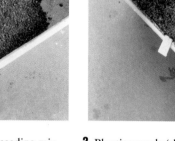

1. Fill seed flats with seeding mix. The potting mixture should be lightweight and sterile to avoid weed seeds.

2. Planting seeds (these are 'Forest Green' parsley). Most seeds should be spaced about 2 inches apart. Be sure to mark the flat with the name of the herb and the date it was sown.

3. Cover the seeds with a layer of soil, about 2-3 times the diameter of the seed. Some seeds (such as dill or lemon balm) need light to germinate and should be pressed into the soil but not covered.

4. Mist the seed flats and put them in a spot where they receive light and where temperature remains between 65-70° F. Most seedlings do very well if left under lights; they grow best when they get 12-15 hours of light per day.

5. When the first true leaves appear, transplant seedlings to individual pots. Cut out the entire block of soil, or very gently lift the seedling and transplant.

1. Choose a healthy plant (this one is *Salvia officinalis*); take cuttings from shoots that are not woody and not in flower. With a sharp knife or clippers, make a cut; cuttings should be 3-4 inches long. Cut just below a node, where leaves join the stem; roots form more readily at nodes.
2. Strip off leaves from the bottom of the stem.

3. Insert the cut end of the cutting into a rooting hormone; these preparations are available in most nurseries and garden centers; ask for one that is recommended for herbs.

4. Stick the cutting into a rooting medium; perlite is the recommended choice. Water gently.

5. Cuttings need humidity and moisture. At Cornell Plantations, they are placed on a mist table. You can also create a good environment by placing the pot or flat in a plastic bag and tying the top; insert sticks in the pot to keep the plastic from touching the cuttings. Cuttings should be placed in an area where there is bright light, but not in direct sunlight. When cuttings begin to grow (an indication that rooting is taking place), remove the plastic bags. Continue to water for a few days.

COMPOST

In forests and prairies, swamps and backyards, an amazing process is continuously taking place. Plant parts and animal leavings rot or decompose with the help of fungi, bacteria, and other microorganisms. Earthworms and an assortment of insects do their part digesting and mixing the plant and animal matter together. The result is a marvelous, rich, and crumbly layer of organic matter we call compost.

BENEFITS OF COMPOST Compost encourages the growth of earthworms and other beneficial organisms whose activities help plants grow strong and healthy. It provides nutrients and improves the soil. Wet clay soils drain better and sandy soils hold more moisture if amended with compost.

HOW TO MAKE COMPOST A compost pile keeps organic matter handy for garden use and, as an added advantage, keeps the material from filling up overburdened landfills. To make your own compost, start with a layer of chopped leaves, grass clippings, and kitchen waste like banana peels, eggshells, old lettuce leaves, apple cores, coffee grounds, and whatever else is available. Keep adding materials until you have a 6-inch layer, then cover it with a 3- to 6-inch layer of soil, manure, or finished compost.

Alternate 6-inch layers of organic matter and 2- to 3-inch layers of soil or manure until the pile is about 3 feet tall. A pile that is 3 feet tall by 3 feet square will generate enough heat during decomposition to sterilize the compost. This makes it useful as potting soil, topdressing for lawns, or soil-improving additives.

COMPOST CARE Keep your compost pile in a semishaded area to keep it from drying out too much. But if your compost pile is near a tree, turn it frequently to make sure tree roots don't grow into it. Make an indentation in the top of the pile to hold water and sprinkle the pile with a garden hose when it looks dry. Keep the compost moist, but not wet. Beneficial organisms cannot survive in soggy conditions.

USING COMPOST When your compost is ready, it can be mixed into the soil before planting, or applied to the surface of the soil as a soil-enriching mulch.

QUICK COMPOST If you need compost in a hurry, speed up the process by turning the pile with a pitchfork once a week for a month. Mixing the compost allows oxygen into the center of the pile, where it encourages the growth of bacteria and fungi. A pile that is turned regularly will become finished compost in 4-8 months.

MAKING A COMPOST BIN As illustrated below, many elaborate compost bins are sold. Some of these have devices for turning the compost and for removing it from the bin. Although these store-bought bins don't do the compost pile any harm, they are really not necessary. An enclosure made from chicken wire or from 5 wood pallets (one on the bottom, and four wired together for the sides) does the job just as well.

WHAT TO COMPOST
- kitchen waste
- lawn clippings (in thin layers so they do not mat down)
- chopped leaves (large leaves take a long time to break down)
- shredded branches
- garden plants
- shredded paper
- weeds (but be sure to use before they go to seed or weeds may sprout in the garden)
- straw or hay

WHAT NOT TO COMPOST
- orange and other citrus peels
- meat scraps, fatty trash (to avoid rodents and animals)
- excessive wood ashes

growing conditions in that location. Then study their placement, moving them around until it all seems to work. Think about how much space each plant will ultimately need and whether or not good air circulation is required, how the plant will look in combination with its neighbors, and similar factors. Once the herbs are all arranged, begin planting.

Soil in both the pot and the bed should be moist at planting time. The soil mix in the container or rootball should have some similarity to the mix in the planting bed. Otherwise, if there is no marriage of soils, plant growth will be limited.

Ideally, you should plant on a cloudy, cool day, which helps to minimize the stress on the new herbs. Since planting under ideal conditions is not always possible, insure that the herbs have been hardened off (gradually acclimatized to the outdoor environment) before planting them.One way to harden off herbs is to bring them outdoors each day, increasing the amount of time they're out progressively over several days.

When you take the plants out of the container, use a knife or your hands to loosen the soil around the roots. This helps break up the roots, encouraging them to grow outward into their new environment. Fill in the hole with soil, firmly tamping the soil around the roots to get rid of any air pockets. Smooth out the soil around the plants.

Plants must be watered in shortly after planting. A gentle spray of water will help the leaves acclimatize and the roots begin to establish themselves. Monitor the plants frequently to be sure they never get completely dry. The first 2 weeks are the most important time to get your plants well established in their new home.

Plants should be placed so they are at approximately the same depth as they were in the container. Remember, though, that recently dug soil is full of air holes and will settle significantly after a few weeks.

The way I see it, the day I decided to disturb the soil, I undertook an obligation to weed. For this soil is not virgin and hasn't been for centuries. It teems with hundreds of thousands of weed seeds for whom the thrust of my spade represents the knock of opportunity.
FROM *SECOND NATURE,* BY MICHAEL POLLAN

ROUTINE CARE

STAKING Most herbs, when grown under the conditions they require, hold themselves up quite well and need no staking. Some very tall herbs, like 6-foot-high monkshood, blow over in the wind without some sort of staking. Also, some plants that are overfertilized will become long, leggy, and unable to hold themselves up; these too need to be staked. Herbs grown in the shade may become leggy candidates for staking as well. Stake as plants grow, when they are very young, not after they have fallen over. Certain herbs, such as tansy, are naturally tall and floppy. Instead of staking, you can cut the plant back to the ground halfway through the growing season; the new growth will be short enough to hold itself up quite nicely.

WEEDING Weeding is a critical aspect of gardening. Weeds compete with other plants for nutrients, water, and sunshine; they need to be removed continually. Hand-weeding–going through the beds regularly and pulling any weeds you see–is the best approach. This way, you will get to the weeds before they flower and go to seed and multiply ten- or a hundred-fold. In a short time, you'll be able to recognize weed seedlings by just their first pair of leaves. If you are working with a very large area, you can hoe weeds, although with a hoe, you run the risk of damaging the fine roots of adjacent herb plants. The best time to hoe weeds is on a hot, sunny day; the hoed weeds will wilt and die quickly. If you hoe on a cool, damp day, a lot of the hoed weeds will reroot themselves and keep on growing.

MULCHING Mulching is applying some sort of material on the surface around a plant to keep down weeds and help maintain moisture in the soil (the insulating layer prevents evaporation of water into the air). Mulch can be almost anything, most often manure, compost, wood chips, grass, shredded paper, leaves,

Right: Some tall herbs require staking. Stake as plants grow, when they are very young, not after they have fallen over. *Far right:* Applying mulch.

or straw. If you use compost as mulch, be sure that any weed seeds are thoroughly composted and no longer viable. At the Berkeley Garden, well-rotted horse manure is used as mulch. The manure sits for a year before it is used. This allows the ammonia-containing urea, which would burn the plants, to dissipate and the weed seeds to compost. Organic materials used as mulch work their way into the soil or, if a bed is turned over, are incorporated into the soil, adding texture and making the soil more moisture retentive. If you have fungus problems, do not use a mulch that encourages fungus growth, such as shredded leaves.

FERTILIZING Most herbs do not need a lot of fertilizer. Usually, fertilizing at the beginning of the growing season once or perhaps twice will suffice. Overfertilized plants will become extremely leggy and unsightly and may develop burnt foliage, especially on the edges. Overfertilization also reduces the amount of oils in the leaves. One way to fertilize is to mulch with horse manure or compost, which gradually break down into the soil. Another method is to apply a dry fertilizer to the beds. Dry fertilizer, available commercially, is usually balanced with the 3 essential nutrients–nitrogen, phosphorus, and potassium. Hand-broadcast onto the beds, or apply it around individual plants. As it rains, or the area is watered, the fertilizer slowly dissolves and releases small amounts of the nutrients. You could also mix up a liquid fertilizer and spray it onto the plants, which will absorb the nutrient solution through their foliage as well as from the soil.

THINNING Thinning seedlings is an important gardening step. Hundreds of seedlings may come up in 1 small area. If you allowed them all to grow, they would compete for nutrients, water, light, and air, and you would have a crop of very scraggly, weak, thin-stemmed seedlings. Instead, remove the majority

Left: Thin seedlings so that too many do not compete for nutrients in a small space. *Far left:* Applying dry fertilizer; try not to hit the foliage, as it might cause burning.

Right: Irrigate deeply so that soil is
moist to a depth of 6 inches; that
allows plants to anchor roots deeply.

of plants. As a first step, thin out so seedlings are ¼-½ inch apart. As the
plants become larger, thin out half of those, eventually arriving at the optimum spacing for the particular herb you are growing. Thinning in stages like
this gives you an added bonus: a steady and fresh supply of tasty young herbs
for cooking and salads.

IRRIGATING Most herbs are drought-tolerant, although a few require a little
extra water. You can irrigate by hand with a hose, which is very time-consuming, or you can set up various fan sprayers or sprinklers to cover an entire area.
Don't irrigate so the water just penetrates the first inch of soil; irrigate so the
soil is moist to a depth of perhaps 6 inches. Plants send their roots down as
deeply as water is available, so deep watering will produce better-anchored
plants that are less susceptible to wilting when the soil dries out (which it does
from the surface first). At the University of California Botanical Garden the

Above: The process of removing the growing tip is called "disbudding"; it encourages flower production. *Left:* Removing the growing tip of the plant (a process called "pinching") encourages the formation of side branches.

entire herb garden is given a very deep irrigation with an overhead sprinkler turned on 3-4 hours once a week. Three or four days later, fan sprayers are applied to plants such as sweet woodruff and the aconitums that require more moisture.

PINCHING Pinching means removing the growing tip, and it's an important technique for keeping plants looking their best. Pinching encourages side branches to form. These side branches, in turn, can also be pinched, and they will form more side branches. Pinching will produce round, manageable, attractive plants instead of long and leggy ones. It's easy to make pinching a normal routine when you harvest herbs. As you pick some to use in cooking, take out tip growth; you'll get more side branches, for a better-looking plant and a larger harvest.

DISBUDDING Disbudding is the process of removing buds to encourage production of larger or more flowers. When a plant is getting ready to flower, it may have buds on the terminal part, the end, of a branch and on many little side branches as well. If you remove all the side-branch buds, the plant will direct all the energy that would have gone to them to the main bud or buds instead. The result will be larger flowers with better color, and any fruit that forms will also be much larger.

PRUNING AND DEADHEADING Pruning and deadheading are parts of everyday garden maintenance. Pinching, as discussed above, is a form of pruning. Harvesting, too, is a form of pruning; when you need a sprig for cooking, pick a branch that needs to be removed anyway–one that is growing out into the

Above and right: Deadheading and pruning keep the garden looking neat and encourage new growth

path, for example. When pruning (removing branches), cut right above a node, which is the place where the leaf is attached to the stem. This encourages formation of side branches. You can prune plants into manageable shapes and sizes so that one plant doesn't overrun another. Prune around the perimeter of plants such as mint to keep their running stems from invading the entire garden.

Deadheading is simply removing old flowers to prevent seedpods from forming and to improve the plant's appearance. By deadheading, you are allowing the plant to put all its energy into producing more foliage or perhaps a second flowering. If you allow flowers to go to seed, the plant receives a signal that it has completed its cycle of growth and it will shut itself down.

HARVESTING

It's important to understand how and when to harvest herbs because, if improperly handled, they will lose their flavor and become useless. Don't wait until autumn to begin harvesting. You'll harm perennial herbs if you cut back more than 20 percent of the plant at one time, and many herbs are past their peak by autumn. Instead, think of harvesting as a process that goes on throughout the growing season.

The most important consideration at the time of harvest is to cut a quality crop that is healthy and vigorous. Prompt and careful handling at harvest time is also critical for preserving the quality of the stored herbs. The amount of time involved in harvesting is usually much less than the time involved in preparing herbs for drying or freezing, so cut only the amount of material that you can handle before the cut herbs wilt and begin to decline in quality. Work fast and without distraction so you can get the herbs to their place for drying without delay.

Cut herbs for harvesting in the morning after the dew has dried and before the sun is very bright. The herbs' volatile oils will be at their highest levels at this time, and the herbs will be relatively cool, which slows their rate of deterioration after being cut. If you must harvest in large quantities, select a cloudy day for cutting to help reduce the potential damage to flavor and quality. Also, on a cloudy day, tender new inside leaves will not burn from sudden exposure to the sun.

Cutting at the right time in the herb's growth cycle is also critical for maximum flavor. Most herbs have their optimum quality and quantity when they are just about to come into bloom. Plan any major harvest for that time; often, with good regrowth, a second major harvest will be possible. Both when herbs are very young and in a highly active stage of growth, or in the autumn when food reserves are making their way to the roots, herbs have less flavor and are less desirable for harvesting.

If you are doing a major harvest, follow these guidelines to avoid damaging plants from overcutting. Do not remove more than 60 percent of an annual herb's foliage at any one time. This allows for regrowth and future harvests. For short-lived annual herbs such as dill, when a second harvest is not a consideration, simply harvest the whole plant. You can harvest as much as 50 percent of a perennial herb's foliage at once, although this depends on the plant's stage of growth. For example, certain perennials such as lemon balm can have all top growth removed once you see the new growth appearing at the base. Biennial herbs vary depending on the part of the plant you want to harvest. Since they have a 2-year growth cycle, the first year is the time to cut leaves in large quantities, whereas the second year is when you harvest seeds. Some biennials (e.g., parsley) you treat and harvest as annuals.

The growing habit of the herb dictates how it is cut back. Herbs like parsley are cut at the base from the outside, leaving the younger, inner leaves to develop further. Herbs like chives, on the other hand, are cut in clumps, shearing leaves back just above ground level; a new set will regrow. The top growth of herbs with an upright growing habit can be cut by $\frac{2}{3}$ as long as healthy, green growth remains. With a short-lived annual herb, such as coriander leaves (cilantro), it is more efficient to remove the whole plant at harvest time, unless you only need a small amount.

Above: Salvia cuttings on a drying tray.

STORING

Once herbs are harvested, the best and most convenient ways to preserve them are by drying and freezing.

DRYING HERBS The purpose of drying is to remove the moisture from the herbs, so they may be preserved for future use. First, remove all damaged, discolored, or diseased leaves. You may hang herbs or lay them flat to dry. In either case, you must allow them good, uniform air circulation and avoid packing them too tightly so mildew or other fungus does not attack. Lay or hang them with little overlap in order to get uniform drying. Don't dry different kinds of herbs closely together; their flavors will blend and lose much of their individuality.

When bundling herbs for upside-down drying, keep the clumps small so air circulation remains good. If you have large quantities to hang for drying, string up a clothesline. Drying flat on screens or in baskets is preferable for herbs high in water content or that bruise easily, and for flowers and flower petals such as roses. Seeds dry best by hanging seed heads on stalks upside down, inside a paper bag so that as the ripened seeds fall they will be caught in the bag.

Keep drying herbs free of dust, enclosing them in paper bags if necessary. The paper breathes, which allows the drying process to continue. Keep drying herbs away from direct sunlight, because sun will cause color and flavor to deteriorate. The ideal conditions are a room that is dark, dry, warm, and well ventilated; a dark, windowed attic is an excellent drying place.

Microwave drying is another option. It's highly efficient and has some benefits over other methods. Herbs dried in the microwave maintain extremely good color, form, and, in some cases, flavor. Flowers and flower petals dried in the microwave can keep such good color, they still look fresh. However, certain herbs seem to cook in the microwave and get too crispy and flavorless. Timing and selection are critical; experiment with small quantities. Wash herbs for microwave drying, pat dry, and put into the oven between 2 paper towels. Herbs that dry well in the microwave include bay, tarragon, rosemary, sage, and thyme.

How can you tell if the herbs are dry? Touch them. You want to achieve a crispy dryness. If the herbs crumble to powder when touched, they have probably gotten too dry. On the other hand, if they are at all moist, they will mildew when packaged. Be careful about introducing new, freshly cut herbs near herbs that are already partially dry; the drying herbs will reabsorb moisture from the fresh ones. Check drying herbs daily; drying time will vary according to temperature, humidity, air circulation, and other environmental factors. If you are drying flowers for decoration, and the conditions remain fairly constant, you can leave the bundles in the drying area for extended periods of time.

Once the herbs are dry, package them. The less the dried plant parts are touched or crushed, the more flavor they will hold. So package whole leaves where possible, and crush just before use. Select containers that are airtight and that do not breathe. Glass is ideal as long as it is not stored in the sun. Plastic also will hold in the herb flavors.

The seemingly logical place to store dried herbs is right above the stove so they're handy for cooking. Unfortunately, this is the worst possible place to keep dried herbs because of the high temperatures and high humidity. Instead, keep herbs in a kitchen cabinet where they are protected from direct sunlight. Shelf life is highly variable depending on the plant. Dried herbs can remain useful for 6 months to 2 years. Test them periodically for flavor and discard any that have deteriorated. Always keep herbs well labeled for age and type. Occasionally insects are a problem in dried herbs, so also check periodically for this, discarding any infested herbs.

FREEZING HERBS Some herbs are noted for not holding their flavor when dry. For these herbs, the preferred method of preservation is freezing. Herbs that don't dry but do freeze well include basil, chives, French tarragon, lovage, and parsley. Frozen herbs, once thawed, are limp and therefore are limited to use strictly for flavor and not for eye appeal. When freezing herbs, it's best to chop leaves and place them in the freezer in plastic bags or containers. Be sure to label and date all herbs to prevent future confusion. Keep frozen herbs only as long as you might keep other frozen foods—no longer than 6 months.

HERB VINEGARS Some herbs can be stored in vinegars, or in oils; rosemary, basil, and thyme are examples. The vinegar and oil will take on the flavor of the herb—an added bonus—and the herbs will retain much of their flavor. A tightly stoppered bottle is all that is needed; a group of them looks lovely on a kitchen shelf.

Above and left: Among the best ways to dry herbs is to hang them upside down in a dust-free room with good air circulation. These photographs illustrate the dried-herb section at Well-Sweep Herb Farm, in Port Murray, New Jersey, where hundreds of plants are stored in an attractive display.

PESTS AND DISEASES

Herbs are among the easiest of plants to grow, partly because most of them are very pest- and disease-resistant. The wonderful tastes and smells we get from many herbs are protection that the plants have evolved. The oils and scents that we find so appealing and flavorful are very offensive to insects and other animals and also make herbs resistant to disease. Consequently, pests and diseases are seldom a problem with herbs and when they are, usually just a few plants are affected, so you can treat them on a spot basis.

This is especially fortunate because you do not want to treat herbs you are growing for culinary uses or tea with poisonous insecticides. Instead, use any of the natural methods detailed below, and practice companion planting, growing certain herbs among other ones that will repel particular insects or diseases. Pennyroyal, for example, repels ants. Nasturtium does, too, along with aphids, and it attracts whitefly to itself. Chives and garlic prevent many types of diseases from attacking roses. Sage, basil, and chamomile repel a number of harmful flying insects. Mints tend to drive away flies. By planting a large variety of herbs in one area, interspersing plants of one type with those of another, you will avoid any large-scale insect or disease problems.

When herbs are bothered by pests or disease, it is usually because the plants are growing in unfavorable conditions. Plants that are stressed–for example, by too much or too little water, or hot weather–produce compounds that attract insect pests. By keeping your herbs growing in the optimum conditions–with the correct amount of light, water, and fertilizer, and in the correct location–you'll have very few insect pests or diseases. The principal ones you might occasionally encounter are discussed below.

ANTS If you have scale and aphid problems, check your garden for ants. Ants actually cultivate aphids and scale, caring for them and then harvesting the honeydew they produce. If you treat for aphids and scale but not for ants, the ants will simply bring more scale and aphids back to your garden. To control ants, purchase ant sticks and ant bait traps.

APHIDS Aphids are sucking insects. They insert a small tube into a plant's tissue and suck the juices from it. Aphids usually appear in the spring on new growth that hasn't had a chance to harden up yet. The best way to control aphids is to shoot them all off the plants with a forceful spray from your garden hose. If you have a very bad infestation, spray insecticidal soap onto the aphids by hand or with a small sprayer. You can also make your own soap preparation by mixing dishwashing liquid with water and splashing it on the leaves. However, homemade preparations might be too strong and cause burns, while commercially prepared soaps are quality controlled for strength. The soap will cover and suffocate the aphids.

CATERPILLARS These moth and butterfly larvae eat foliage. When you find a chewed leaf, inspect the plant closely, checking under leaves and on stems, and hand-pick the culprit off the plant.

NEMATODES are microscopic organisms that cause plants to wilt; they affect lavenders and parsley. To avoid nematode infestation, rotate crops every few years. Marigolds or vincas are said to repel nematodes.

SCALE Scale is an insect that forms a usually brown hemispherical dome around itself. At first, this little dome is very soft; on a mature insect, it is very hard. Scale can be a problem on some woody trees, especially bays. A bad infestation is very difficult to get rid of, so the best protection is to catch it at any early stage when it can be wiped off or sprayed off with a strong stream of water. If necessary, spray with Domant or Horticultural oil or spray (a light oil that won't kill foliage, but will suffocate the scale).

SLUGS AND SNAILS These soft-bodied pests can be a big problem. They will mow down seedlings and do great damage to larger, more established plants. If you have a small garden, remove slugs and snails by hand. For larger areas, you can use a commercial snail bait, surround vulnerable plants with a gritty material like wood ashes, or set out shallow bowls or jar lids filled with beer that the slugs and snails will be attracted to and drown in. Thyme tends to attract slugs and snails away from other plants, so you could plant this herb near plants that are especially grazed on by these pests.

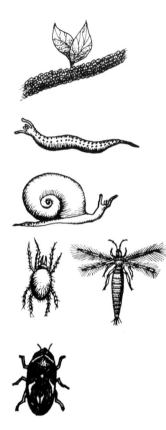

SPIDER MITES AND THRIPS These are both rasping insects; they rasp the chlorophyll off of broadleafed plants. Affected leaves appear dull and hazy; on close inspection, you will find that they are silver rather than green. To prevent or cure this problem, and to prevent a bad infestation, hose down plants regularly, washing off the foliage.

SPITTLEBUGS Spittlebugs are sucking insects that infest new spring growth. The telltale sign of this pest is a small bit of spittle, a bunch of bubbles, on a plant's stem; the spittlebug raises its young in this protective material. As with aphids, control spittlebugs by washing them off the plants.

WHITEFLIES are tiny flying insects that suck juice and weaken plants like lemon verbena, rosemary, and scented geraniums. Not more than 1/16 of an inch in size; they are too small to be seen individually and often look like a cloud of smoke. They can usually be eliminated by applying a high-pressure water spray to affected plant and removing all affected parts.

RUST Mints and a few other herbs are especially subject to rust, which appears as small orangish yellow blotches on foliage. Once you notice the affected leaves, the whole plant will be infected with the organism. The only solution is to dig up the entire plant, discard it, and replant a fresh, new plant in another area of the garden. The soil where the infected plant was growing will also contain the rust organism, so you must replant that area only with an herb that is not affected by rust (many are not; rust is very selective). Another way to deal with rust is to use the leaves of affected plants until the rust appears (it is not harmful to humans) and then cut the plant down to the ground; the new foliage will look good and be rust-free for a while.

MILDEW Mildew is the name for certain types of fungi that produce downy or powdery masses on plants. It can be a problem on certain herbs such as bergamot, hyssop, and sometimes sages. To control mildew, avoid hot, humid conditions, and irrigate with overhead spraying. If you wet down roses, be sure their foliage is completely dried off by nightfall.

Chapel Hill, North Carolina

Pretty much the same: planning for spring, projects such as drainage routes, renovating planting beds, adding fresh soil. We can often still plant perennials in January.

We begin sowing perennial seeds in the greenhouse on a seed mat set at 70° F. In the garden, we are pruning trees, shrubs, and roses that weren't pruned the previous summer. There is usually a very warm period when we hope plants won't bud out way too early; it's also too early for pruning. At this time, we dig up and divide perennials, plant roses, shrubs, and trees, and keep planting perennials.

I can begin cutting back plants such as sage, thyme, santolina, and any herbs that will put on new growth from the base of the plant. I am particularly careful to prune lavenders back early so as not to cut off the flower buds. By mid-March, I begin to pot up perennial seedlings from the greenhouse. We continue sowing the last of the perennial seeds in the greenhouse.

We're in full swing with potting perennials and divisions taken from the garden. We also begin to sow annual seeds. Most of them are sown around the first of the month and are ready to start potting up as early as one week later. We pot feverishly while outside in the garden we begin pulling back mulch from tender plants and continue cutting back perennials. Beds are amended with organic fertilizers, rock phosphates, and green sand, and mulched if necessary.

We plant annuals in the garden, continue planting perennials, and bring tender perennials out of the greenhouse and put them in the ground. There are still some annuals waiting to be potted, but we are mostly out of the greenhouse now, moving tender plants out to harden them off. Planting and shifting plants in the garden is the main activity in May.

CALENDAR OF ACTIVITIES, ITHACA, NEW YORK

January

The new year brings the annual onslaught of seed and plant catalogs beckoning us toward spring with sumptuous photos and tantalizing descriptions. This is the time for dreaming and planning. It is now that I often pull out scraps of paper with notes hastily jotted during the flurry of spring and summer activity and photos of last year's garden to remind me of changes I want to make. Then I leisurely thumb through stacks of catalogs finding plants to fill anticipated gaps, adding lists of others too inviting to ignore, always sure that with a bit of rearranging they will all find happy spots in the garden.

February

February is a month of anticipation. I've already put my plans to paper, and I've sent off the seed and plant orders. Eagerly, with maps in hand, I stomp out into the snowy garden. I might pick up a stick and trace out my planting plan in the snow, trying to visualize the summer's bounty. I'll contain my eagerness to see these plans come to life by sowing seeds of perennial herbs inside under lights.

March

The garden here in upstate New York is usually snow-covered for at least part of the month, and when it finally does thaw, the soil is generally too wet to work yet. Toward the end of the month, I'll remove pine boughs spread on sages and lavenders for winter protection and begin cutting back any herbaceous perennial herbs left standing in the fall when early snows forced me to abandon end-of-season cleanup.

While March is still a sleepy time in the garden, the greenhouse begins buzzing in anticipation of spring. Seeding has begun, though not yet in earnest, and I set to work trimming back, repotting, and fertilizing the large assortment of tender herbs carried over the winter indoors. At this time, I salvage stem cuttings to root under mist of any plants that have gotten too scraggly or that I simply want more of.

April

Seeding gets into full swing this month with two major rounds, in early and mid-April. Toward the end of the month, I begin transplanting young seedlings from seed flats into individual pots. In the garden, spring cleanup proceeds. I complete cutting back and raking, prune woody plants, do the first round of weeding, apply a top dressing of organic fertilizer, divide overgrown perennials, and if I didn't get around to edging garden beds in the fall, I will do it now. This is the month I also undertake my yearly battle with the mints. To keep them somewhat confined to their allotted spaces, I must dig them back from the edges and pull up wandering roots.

May

By now gardening has reached a fever pitch. Outside it is a race to complete the last of the spring dividing before plants are up too far. There are still more seeds yet to sow, both inside in flats and later directly in the garden. Under lights dozens of seed flats are bursting with seedling awaiting transplanting. Soon after getting pinched back and fertilized, the young transplants explode in their pots with bushy growth. I'm always afraid this is the year I've gone overboard in my gardening plans and I'll finally run out of greenhouse space, but with continual shifting, all the plants do somehow manage to fit. Then suddenly the space crunch is over–during the third week of May, I empty out the greenhouse, setting all the plants in a sheltered location to harden off for about a week before transplanting them to the garden. The next challenge is to second-guess the date of the last spring frost.

June
I used to plant out annuals and tender perennials during the last week of May, but too many times I've had to rush to cover them with ramie or bedsheets after hearing a frost warning. So to play it a bit safer, I wait until the first week of June to plant, and even then frosts here are not unheard of. To ensure vigorous growth, I add compost and 4-2-4 organic fertilizer when transplanting, and I'm sure to water in the plants well afterward.

July
Finally I can slow down a bit and enjoy the herb garden at its bountiful peak. Continuing garden tasks include weeding, watering when necessary, and occasional deadheading of spent flowers. I make successional sowings of some herbs and do much harvesting for drying. After a heavy harvest, I apply a sidedressing of compost and fertilizer to ensure a lush second flush of growth.

August
General maintenance tasks and harvesting continue as in July. Toward the middle of the month, I already begin preparations for the next year. I take cuttings of tender perennials, plus cuttings of sages and lavenders as backups in case of a particularly harsh winter or to replace woody old plants. I collect seeds as they ripen and store them in the refrigerator until next spring.

September
Seed collecting and routine maintenance continue. A last light harvest of woody herbs can be taken no later than early September to allow new growth time to harden off before frost. Toward the middle of the month, I begin the fall division of perennials.

October
Sometime during early October the first frost is expected, so I move tender plants in pots and others dug from the garden inside. I begin fall cleanup by pulling out annual and tender plants hit by frost, then proceed with cutting back perennials, completing a final round of weeding, raking fallen leaves, and edging garden beds. To prepare for a winter windowsill garden I sow seeds of annual herbs indoors and pot up divisions of garden perennials. Some plants I bring directly inside, while others I leave out in the cold for a couple of months, letting them benefit from a dormant period before they resume growth. Another task is to pot up and pinch back cuttings taken in August.

November
I just might get all the fall cleanup finished if cold weather and snow don't cut me short.

December
Around the first of December, after the ground has frozen, I cover a few plants with pine boughs for winter protection. After that I don't think about the garden at all . . . until the first new catalog arrives in the mail.

BY DIANE MISKE

Chapel Hill, North Carolina

In the first part of the month, there are still some annuals and perennials to go in the garden, but we can be pushing it by this time because of the heat. The garden is beginning to bloom and is absolutely beautiful. By the middle of the month, it is at its peak, lush and almost junglelike. We continue to mulch and take time to enjoy the garden.

We begin harvesting, trying to get as much dried as possible. The heat is usually so overwhelming by this time that we work outside only in the morning and late afternoon. It's general maintenance, lots of watering, and lots of cold herb tea. I watch plants for signs that they need an extra dose of fertilizer or water, and begin to collect seeds.

I continue harvesting seeds, leaves, and flowers. We are usually watering at least 3 days a week. I begin to take cuttings at this time from the perennials. August is a month of mostly basic maintenance.

We continue harvesting, collecting seeds and cuttings. Some hardy perennials, such as catnip, are sown to germinate in the greenhouse and overwinter in a protected spot. September can be hot, and we continue watering.

We begin the fall garden cleanup, cutting back perennials, cleaning and raking nooks and corners, mulching beds that need it and perennials that will stay out over winter. By the end of the month, we dig up tender perennials and give them a few days to sit outside before they go to the greenhouse for winter. I cut back any perennial foliage that I want to dry (such as lemon verbena) if I know it will get zapped by frost. We continue potting cuttings.

We rake fallen leaves, sow seeds of perennials that will germinate in spring, dig up plants and store them under beds of leaves while we renovate the beds. We begin pruning trees and shrubs.

A month of respite. We finish any renovations, order seeds, take cuttings of santolinas and rosemaries–and then it's time to rest.

BY REBECCA WELLBORN

SPECIAL CONDITIONS 5

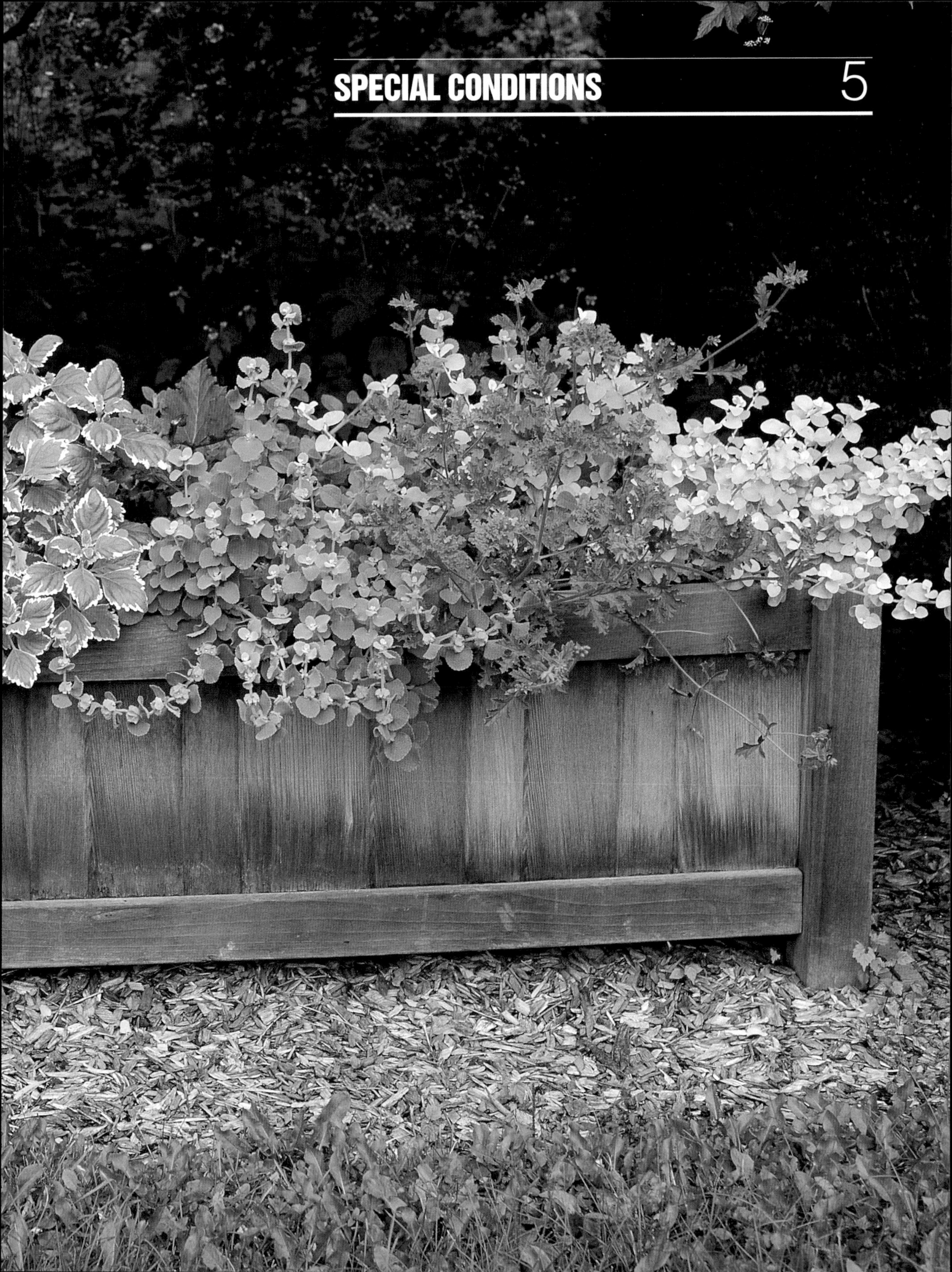

HERBS THAT DO WELL INDOORS

Aloe thrives as a houseplant, even when you ignore it. Be careful not to overwater and provide good drainage so that roots do not remain soggy.

Basil is one of the better herbs to grow indoors under lights, though you can't neglect it even for a day–it needs consistent heat, warmth, and moisture. Bush basil, lemon basil, and sweet basil are the best candidates for indoor growing; camphor and lettuce leaf do less well indoors, and purple basil rarely survives. Harvest will be modest for all basils.

Chives will not produce any growth indoors, but will survive if kept at cold temperature.

Parsley needs space for its large root system; fertilize once a month with organic matter and bone meal.

Rosemary, known as one of the best indoor herbs, is not as easily grown as commonly thought. It needs night temperatures of about 50°F. and dry soil and at least 4 hours of sun every day. The prostrate form is especially suitable.

Thyme will grow indoors if it is grown in containers during the summer.

Many tender herbs need to be brought indoors during the winter. They will not produce vigorously indoors.

INDOOR GARDENING

The thought of a steady supply of fresh, fragrant herbs, growing right on the windowsill, is intoxicating to many people. Unfortunately, contrary to public opinion, herbs do not grow particularly well indoors. They require quite a bit of specialized care, and even then often do not survive. Moreover, a small pot of herbs rarely provides the abundance of sprigs needed for cooking. People who grow herbs indoors usually admit that they often replace their pots, or supplement with store-bought supplies when making herb-heavy sauces.

On the other hand, many herbs do grow indoors–perhaps not as vigorously as outdoors, but well enough to provide fragrance as well as cuttings for culinary use. Just keep your expectations low and you won't be disappointed.

The best advantages you can give indoor herbs are artificial lights and greenhouses. Another key to success is starting with the right stock. Pulling plants from the garden and putting them into pots usually shocks them to death; try growing them outdoors in containers before you bring them in, or buying plants specifically grown for indoor use from nurseries.

Containers Herbs can be grown in a wide variety of ornamental containers and hanging baskets; just be sure they are large enough to allow room for the roots to grow. All containers need drainage holes.

Soil Garden soil doesn't work for indoor plants; it dries out too fast and often is full of pests and diseases. Buy a soil mix that specifies indoor use and contains spaghum, peat moss, and bark. Some mixes also contain perlite or vermiculite, lightweight materials that improve drainage.

Potting Place a terracotta shard, curved side up, at the bottom of the pot over the drainage hole. Fill the pot with planting mix, leaving about an inch of room at the top for watering. Press down to compress and dig holes with your fingers. Lay seedlings in the soil so that the tops of the rootballs are level with the top of the soil and then cover with soil and water well. When planting in a basket, line the basket with presoaked spaghum moss before filling with soil. When plants begin to fill the pots, move to the next size.

Light The most common reason for failure with indoor herbs is inconsistent light. Even the sunniest window will sometimes be dark for days, and plants can be burned by too much sunlight on sunny days. For this reason, most herbs do best when grown under artificial lights, usually fluorescent. Available from most gardening sources, they maintain even temperatures and light.

Humidity It is difficult to provide the proper air quality in most rooms, particularly in dry heated rooms. A greenhouse will provide much better conditions for herbs and go a long way to ensuring success. There are many small, indoor greenhouses on the market.

Feeding Indoor herbs need light applications of fertilizer; be sure to use fertilizers that are designated for indoor use.

Water Don't overwater; stick your finger into the pot to see if soil is dry through and through before watering.

HERBS ON DECKS, PATIOS, PORCHES, AND WINDOWBOXES

If you feel limited in your gardening efforts by a lack of space or proper out-door beds, you should consider the broad array of possibilities for gardening with herbs in containers. Herbs are perhaps the hardiest and easiest of plants to grow in unique ways, requiring little more than a good potting soil, at least 6 hours of sunlight, and proper watering. A large terracotta container filled with a combination of different herbs can provide fresh cut herbs through the growing season in addition to providing the sophisticated beauty of subtle textures and pleasant fragrance.

The most important consideration with containerized herbs on the deck or terrace is how to make them look extraordinarily beautiful. To do this, think in terms of several pots in varying sizes. You need low and high pots to create a multidimensional effect. How you arrange them will depend on how many and what types of pots you have. Selection of containers will depend upon the style of the garden; terracotta lends itself best to a formal garden, whiskey barrels are more suited to the informal garden. Keep to a certain style of pot so that the combination does not look like a hodgepodge. Be on the lookout for unusual containers–urns, antique clay pots, even old washtubs. Be sure that the container provides drainage.

If your containers are easily moved, or if you put them on wheels, you will be able to move them around, placing the blooming ones in front, and creat-ing a constantly-changing landscape. Don't use this as an excuse to ignore foliage plants, though; as beautiful as the blooms are, they are complemented by proper use of nonblooming plants.

People who live in colder regions of the country need to be careful about the pot storage in winter so as to prevent damage from freezing and thawing. This is especially a problem with terracotta because it absorbs moistures and is more fragile than most other materials. If terracotta containers are left outside during winter in cold climates, they should be wrapped or protected in some way to prevent deep freezing and avoid cracking of the pot. Burlap, plastic, or microfoam make good thermal blankets for this. Remove coverings after the coldest part of winter has passed. If you live in warmer regions of the country, or if you use stone or weather-resistant wood containers, you need not be con-cerned with this.

Most gardeners believe their containers are seasonal and need to be dis-mantled in late autumn every year. This is true for plants grown in strawberry jars, or other small containers. Because they provide only limited growing space, they should be replanted every year. There are cases, however–particu-larly when using hardy perennials in containers–where you can expect them to come back each year so long as they are periodically divided and replanted in fresh soil. By using large containers, you have more freedom and flexibility because there is more soil for insulating the roots and for providing nutrition to the herbs.

SOME SOURCES

American Horticultural Therapy
Association
 362A Christopher Avenue,
Gaithersburg, Maryland 20879
800-634-1603

Canadian Horticultural Therapy
Association
c/o Royal Botanical Garden
PO Box 399, Hamilton, Ontario,
Canada, L8N 3H8
416-529-7618

ENABLING GARDENS

Being forced to stop gardening is one of the worst fates that can befall a gardener, but the inability to get down on one's hands and knees owing to arthritis, a bad back, a heart problem, the need to use a wheelchair–or the normal aches, pains, and fatigues of advancing age–is no reason to stop gardening. By using a few different gardening techniques, modifying tools, following new criteria in the selection of plants, and tapping into the many resources available for information and help, no one should ever have to stop gardening.

Begin by thoroughly and frankly assessing your situation.
•How much time can you devote to gardening?
•Do you need crutches, a cane, or wheelchair to get around?
•Can you get up and down from the ground without assistance?
•How much sun or heat is wise for you?
•Can you bend at the waist easily?
•Is your coordination impaired? balance? vision? ability to hold tools?

Consult your doctor, occupational or physical therapist, and most importantly speak to a horticultural therapist.

Horticultural therapists are specially trained in applying horticulture in therapeutic programs for people with disabilities and older adults. They have developed specialized gardening tools and techniques that make gardening easier for every situation.

Once you've decided how much you can and want to do, the garden can be planned. For example, people with relatively severe mobility impairments should have firm, level surfaces an easy distance from the house and should use containers or raised beds to bring soil up to a comfortable working height–usually somewhere around 2 feet high with a maximum width of 30 inches if worked from one side and 60 inches if both sides of the container or bed are accessible. People with more mobility can work with easily worked, light soils mounded to 8-10 inches above grade and should use lightweight, long-handled tools. Smaller containers can be hung within easy reach on poles or fences, and an overhead structure can be used to support hanging baskets on ropes and pulleys so the baskets can be lowered for care and then replaced to an out-of-reach position.

Important considerations when planning the garden layout include:
•Start small: keep it manageable
•Use or create light, easily worked soils so less force is required to work them either by hand or with tools
•Keep all equipment and tools in accessible places
•Arrange for a nearby water source–soaker hose or drip irrigation, perhaps–to minimize the difficulties in watering
•Use mulches to cut down on weeding

Herb gardens are particularly useful to people with sight and hearing disabilities; the fragrance in an herb garden will provide a great deal of sensory stimulation, in addition to its other joys.

ORGANIC GARDENING

Few gardeners today are unaware of the devastating effect pesticides and other chemicals used in the past have had on our environment. Rachel Carson's searing exploration of the subject, *Silent Spring* (1962), exposed the "needless havoc" wrought by products designed to promote healthy plants. Not only were the chemicals poisoning our environment, they were also killing the natural predators of the pests we were seeking to destroy, making it impossible for nature to come to its own defense.

In the past few decades a vast and successful effort has been made to find new ways to garden without using harmful chemicals. The approach is directed at the soil and at the measures taken to control pests.

The soil is built up through the addition of organic materials, especially compost. The addition of compost, homemade or store-bought, and other organic material such as peat moss, green cover crops, and bone meal makes the soil so fertile and productive that petrochemicals are not needed.

Pest problems are handled through a practice called Integrated Pest Management (IPM), developed by the Council on Environmental Quality. IPM is defined as "maximum use of naturally occurring pest controls, including weather, disease agents, predators, and parasitoids. In addition, IPM utilizes various biological, physical, chemical controls and habitat modification techniques. Artificial controls are imposed only as required to keep a pest from surpassing tolerable population as determined from accurate assessments of the pest damage potential and the ecological, sociological, and economic costs of the control measures." In other words, gardeners must make reasonable assessments of how much damage a particular pest will do. If the pest is just munching on foliage, let it be. If controls must be taken, nonharmful ones should be tried first. Only in extreme cases is chemical warfare waged–and then in the most nonharmful ways possible.

The weapons in the IPM arsenal include:

• Careful monitoring to identify problems beforetthey become widespread.

• Beneficial insects, such as ladybugs, praying mantises, and some nematodes, which feed on garden pests. Some of these reside naturally in your garden; others can be bought and placed there.

• Bacteria such as Bt (*Bacillus thuringiensis*) that attack garden pests. These bacteria can be bought by the pound and dusted on the plants; strains have been discovered that breed and attack many common pests.

• Insecticides such as rotenone, pyrethrum, and sabadilla and insecticidal soaps.

• Pest-repellent plants such as marigolds, which repel bean beetles and nematodes, and garlic, which repels whitefly.

• Hand-picking pests off foliage wherever they are seen in small numbers.

See pages 200-201 for more information about pest control.

Holly Shimizu created this terraced garden in her home; it transformed a difficult area into a place of beauty.

TERRACED HERB GARDENS

A terraced garden is often an excellent solution for a sloping area. It can help alleviate problems with water runoff and make a useless, unattractive area a beautiful and bountiful one. The levels of a terraced garden are attractive from every angle, from above and below, and it can allow a suitable setting for creating a gentle series of steps to connect the garden to adjacent areas. Gardens created on a terrace have good drainage, a definite advantage for herb gardening. Each terrace needs to slope slightly downward and be carefully graded to avoid pockets that would hold water.

CREATING TERRACED GARDENS Decide how many terraces the slope needs or will allow by measuring the rise and run of the slope. The rise is the height of the slope and the run is the length of the slope. To measure the rise have one person hold a carpenter's level horizontal with the top of the slope and then measure from that height down to the base of the slope. The run is the length of the slope and is measured by holding the level upright and measuring the distance, horizontally across, from the top of the slope to the bottom of the slope. Start the first terrace at the base of the slope. Once laid out use stakes and string to be sure to get the terrace horizontal. Using a sharp spade cut the area before putting at least six inches of coarse gravel behind the stones to insure excellent drainage. When the first terrace is complete, fill in the spaces with soil scraped from creating the next terrace. Use a carpenter's level to be sure the terrace is flat (slightly sloping downward) and a measuring tape to insure that you get the planned depth. Then arrange the rock, brick, or other material for the terrace.

Once the terraces are in place the soil is amended and carefully graded. Wait several days before planting to allow for the earth and materials to settle. Place lower plants in the central part of the terraces with larger plants toward the sides.

MAKING A SUNKEN GARDEN Sunken gardens and terraced gardens have a great deal in common. Their construction is similar although with a sunken garden you would want to have two or a maximum of three terraces. The bottom of the terrace could be a pool, fountain, or unusual brick or stone pattern. In the garden's construction it's critical that the bottom of the terrace has a drain or walkway. The drain must carry the excess water away to a place where it will not interfere with the garden.

The height of the wall is generally best at approximately 1½-2 feet high. If it is higher then the wall becomes too prominent and you have more of a wall garden. Walls can be made from brick, stone, or railroad ties with a walkway out of something different, such as flagstone. (Look out for cretosote problems.)

Rules of planting a sunken garden are similar to those for a terraced garden in that you do not want to use any plants that are too tall except toward the back of the garden.

1. Using a stake and a plumbline, measure the slope of the area

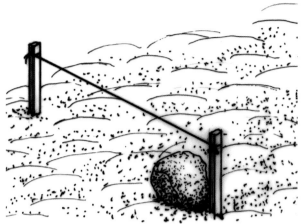

2. Drive stakes into the first level, and begin to lay stones, scooping out earth so that they rest securely.

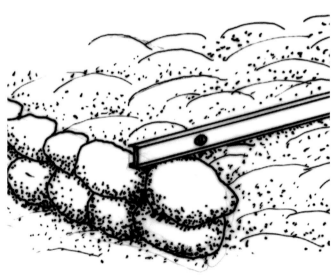

3. Once the first level is complete, fill in soil behind it, so that the entire step is level.

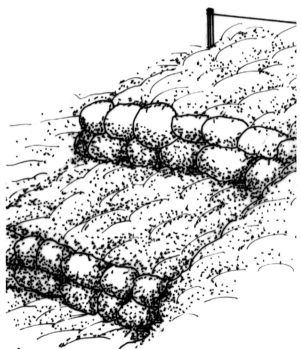

4. Repeat the process, going all the way up the slope.

COLD-HARDY HERBS

There is no scarcity of herb that will thrive in cold climates. Just a few of them are:

Mints
Oreganos
Lovage
Thymes (some)
Sages (some)
Beebalm
Catnip
Chives. Garlic chives
Costmary
Coneflowers
Sweet Goldenrod
Horehound
Lemon balm
Salad burnet
Winter savory
Sweet cicely
Sweet woodruff
Tansy
French tarragon

PROTECTING HERBS

To help marginally hardy perennial herbs (such as lavender and sages) survive the winter, apply a heavy mulch such as straw or pinestraw, or lay branches of christmas trees over the garden. It is important to mulch *after* the first frost. Remove in the early spring, even before frost is over.

A variety of devices has been developed to help the cold-climate gardener. Black plastic mulch is very effective at warming the soil at the beginning of the season, and it reduces weeds if left on all summer. But if you find it unslightly–and it is–other mulches will work almost as well. Protective devices–row covers, hot caps, cloches, and shade–protect new seedlings in the even of an unexpected cold snap.

COLD CLIMATE HERB GARDENING

Herb gardens thrive in cold climates with very little extra care. Plenty of perennial herbs are perfectly cold-hardy–even if you don't want to grow annuals from seed or overwinter tender plants indoors, you can fill a garden with herbs. Many of them do not need winter protection. Of course, there is a shorter season in the North, and some herbs that are perennial in warm climates are grown as annuals in colder regions; but most of these herbs thrive as annuals. Many books and catalogs are very conservative in assigning hardiness zones; you may be able to grow a plant listed for a warmer zone; for example, most mints in this book are listed for Zone 5 and above; many gardeners in Zone 3 report success with them.

Many herbs can be grown in cold climates simply by making sure they are not planted in the garden until the soil is warm enough and all danger of frost has passed; hardy perennials that are domant can be planted out in the garden in early spring, even before the last frost. In some cases long-season crops like sesame will not have time to mature, and fewer plantings can be done in succession. Starting seeds indoors is a useful, and often necessary practice for cold climates. It extends the growing season by allowing crops to spend some of their time indoors. Cold frames are used to allow herbs the chance to acclimate themselves to the outdoors before being placed in the garden.

If you are growing herbs in a cold region, it is best to buy your plants in that region, or to swap with friends; local selections are often more cold-hardy.

Locating the herb garden in a sheltered area will help some marginally hardy plants survive. Of course, the sunniest spot should be chosen, but try to find an area that is protected by a wall or large trees. Exposure to southern currents is advantageous as well, and these should not be blocked out.

Tender herbs can be potted up and brought indoors in winter; rosemary for example, requires a winter vacation inside. However, plants sometimes have trouble adapting to a too-quick change from life in the ground to life in an indoor container. To help them get over this double shock, leave them outdoors for a few days after they have been potted, then transfer them to a transitional area such as a patio or terrace. Most small shrubs that can't survive the winter can be grown in pots that are moved outdoors when the weather warms.

A plant will have less trouble adapting to cold if it is well-nourished in other respects; northern gardeners should pay particular attention to soil maintenance, supply sufficient water, and monitor diseases and pests. A plant that is already weak because of moisture or nutrient deficiencies or infestations will be the first to die in the event of a cold spell. Avoid fertilizing marginally hardy plants at the end of the season; the new succulent growth is most susceptible to winter injury. And don't harvest woody herbs late in the season; it will stimulate new growth that won't have a chance to harden off.

HERB GARDENING IN THE SOUTH

Contrary to a widely-held belief, growing conditions in the American South are not the same as those of the Mediterranean region in which many popular herbs originated. The humidity, hot nights, and heavy soil that Southerners deal with present a host of challenges to the herb gardener: herbs simply do not need full sun all day and twenty-four hours of heat. At the same time, the long, warm growing season makes growing many herbs a joy. So long as the gardener understands the difficulties, herb gardens–like the one that Rebecca Wellborn (who was consultant for this article) manages at North Carolina Botanical Garden in Chapel Hill, which is in USDA Climate Zone 7A–can be productive and beautiful.

There are some plants that simply cannot be expected to thrive in the Southern summer. Most members of the *Apiacaea* family–such as parsley, cilantro, anise, fennel, lovage–will usually bolt (go to seed) prematurely in the heat of a Southern summer; dill is particularly troublesome. They are best planted in early spring for a spring harvest and early fall for a fall harvest. There are some slow-bolting forms ('Tetra' dill, for example) that perform somewhat better, and more heat-tolerant varieties are expected in the coming years. Wellborn plants these varieties (particularly parsley) in the shade of other plants to give them the best possible chance. Another category that rarely performs well is gray plants–sages, lavenders, santolinas–which often are attacked by powdery mildew because of heat and humidity. And many of the small edging shrubs used in knot gardens–barberries and boxwoods–turn brown and orange in winter, probably because their growing conditions do not promote strength and health; Yaupon holly is a good substitute that does somewhat better.

Conditions in the South promote powdery mildew on many plants, but this generally does not harm the plant as a whole. Some people suggest that washing the plant with baking soda removes the mildew, but Wellborn finds that it must be done constantly to work; she just cuts out the affected parts. Some fungus diseases, particularly phytopthora, are becoming a problem, but since the only way to eliminate them is through fungicides, which should not be used near culinary herbs, the only way to deal with them is to cut out the affected parts.

To offset these drawbacks, Southern gardeners can enjoy rosemaries and calendulas that bloom through the winter, 6-7 months of basils, long seasons of winter and summer savory, thyme, perilla, and salad burnet. Annuals usually remain in the garden until the middle of November. Some tender perennials that need to be removed from northern gardens in winter–eucalyptus, lemon grass, vetiver, lemon verbena, and gardenia–can be brought through the winter successfully in North Carolina. Many tender shrubs like laurel, pomegranate, and myrtus also overwinter in North Carolina. Very few herbs require winter protection, though bay and pineapple sage benefit from it.

For information on schedules, see pages 202-203.

KEEPING PLANTS COOL

Very few herbs need or want the constant heat that the Southern climate offers. Gardeners who can keep their plants as cool as possible during the summer usually have the most success. Wellborn plans her garden so that taller plants shade the ones that are most harmed by the heat; vetiver, lemon grass and perilla all cast good shade. Young plants sometimes are shaded with tree boughs if the sun is particularly brutal. At the North Carolina Botanical Garden, one herb garden is devoted to shade; plants are constantly tested to see how they perform in various degrees of shade provided by plants and sculptures; row covers and commercial shade devices are not used because they detract from the overall look of the garden.

Another way to keep plants cool and healthy in the humid South is to allow air to circulate around them as much as possible. Wellborn prunes constantly, and recommends the practice whenever she can. She sometimes uses a mulch of sharp sand, which reflects sunlight, keeping the soil cooler and reducing fungus diseases.

DESERT HERB GARDENING

The American southwest is an ideal place to create an herb garden; just about every herb imaginable thrives in this area, which is similar in climate to the Mediterranean region where many of them originated. The warm days and usually cool nights, low humidity, and long growing season available from Arizona through Southern California allows tender perennials to live and bloom through the winter, encourages annuals to thrive for several months, and inhibits the spread of pests and diseases. Indeed, at the San Diego Wild Animal Park (where Robert Thurston, who contributed information for this article is Gardening Supervisor) over 300 different varieties of herbs are grown in an 8,000 square foot garden, and they rarely have trouble with any of them.

In order to achieve this success, 2 important factors must be dealt with: soil and water. A gardener who wishes to reap a harvest must learn to understand how these factors come into play in his garden and to take the time to observe and interact with its nature and needs. One of the easiest ways to take advantage of nature is to choose the best crop for each spot of soil; this requires knowing which area of your garden is the wettest or driest, where the sun hits most strongly, where the winds are buffered. This information can't be acquired in a few hours—it must be collected after much experience and work.

Desert herb gardeners cannot rely on any natural water at all. Of course, during some seasons rainfall provides a bonus, but any gardener who expects to harvest herbs must depend on artificial irrigation. Thurston uses 2 irrigation systems: an overhead sprinkler, turned to its lowest volume, and a hand-held hose. The sprinkler delivers the amount of water needed by the least thirsty of the plants; he is able to control which plants get more water with the hose. Basils, which sometimes suffer from dehydration get an extra dose, while marjorams get the minimum. Flooding a crop can do just as much damage as keeping it too dry. Thurston advises that gardeners take no advice about how much water their plant needs; personal observation of one's own site is the only way to judge.

Thurston's most important consideration is soil maintenance. The soil in most of the Southwest is low in organic matter and simply not fertile. Thurston "grows his soil" before he grows plants in it; properly grown soil will develop good plants with less watering. He amends his soil with compost made from straw and weeds, fertilizing twice a season. Although he occasionally adds high-nitrogen organic fertilizers like bone meal and blood meal (staying away from high-salt compounds like urea because the water in his areas is already highly saline), he is trying to build up his soil to the point where compost is all that is needed. Thurston amends his soil deeply, digging in the compost 18-24 inches, so that roots can find nourishment underground; he reminds visitors that there is more plant underground than above it. Developing good soil is not an overnight process—but it is one that leads to longterm success in desert herb gardens.

acidic soil: Soil with a pH below 7.0.

alkaline soil: Soil with a pH above 7.0; most herbs do best in a neutral to slightly alkaline soil, 7.0 or somewhat higher.

annual: A plant that lives for only year or 1 growing season.

anther: Part of a plant's stamen that bears pollen grains.

aphid: Insect that sucks the juices from a plant's tissue.

biennial: A plant that lives for 2 years or growing seasons, producing leaves the first season and flowers and seeds the second.

blackspot: Fungus disease that produces black spots on leaves, which then yellow and fall off.

blanch: Whiten a plant's leaves, stems, or shoots by excluding light: e.g., by covering with soil.

bolt: Go to seed, especially prematurely.

bract: A small, modified leaf, with or without a stem.

broadcast: Scatter seed, fertilizer, or other materials over a large area instead of placing in specific rows or planting holes.

Bt*: Bacillus thuringiensis,* a bacteria that attacks and kills many common garden pests; can be bought by the pound.

bud: Unexpanded leaf, stem, or flower that will develop at a later time.

bulb: Encased leaf or flower bud, as an onion or tulip.

calyx: All the sepals, the outer parts of a flower.

chlorophyll: Green coloring matter in plants, essential to photosynthesis.

clay soil: Soil composed of many very fine particles, sticky when wet but hard when dry; water and air have a hard time moving through clay soil.

clove: One of the segments or bulblets of a bulb like garlic.

companion planting: Practice of planting different plants near each other for their helpful effects, such as repelling insects or shading.

compost: Decomposed plant material that adds nutrients to the soil and improves soil composition.

corm: Bulblike underground stem.

corolla: The inner set of a flower's petals; the petals as a whole.

crown: The section of a plant where stem and root meet; the topmost part of a root system, from which the leaves and shoots emerge.

culinary herbs: Herbs used in cooking.

cultivar: A variety of a plant that has been created by human intervention rather than naturally.

cultivate: Stir the soil surface to eliminate the weeds, aerate the soil, and promote water absorption.

cutting: Part of a plant (stem, leaf, root) cut off and then rooted to form a new plant.

cyme: A fairly flat-topped, often branched cluster of flowers.

damping off: Fungous disease that causes seeds and seedlings to rot and die.

deadhead: Remove old flowers to prevent seedpods from forming and improve the plant's appearance.

deciduous: Shedding leaves or other plant parts each year.

die back: Process by which a plant appears to die back to the ground during its dormant period; the plant begins growing again in the spring.

direct seeding: Sowing seeds directly into the garden rather than starting seeds indoors.

disbud: Remove buds to encourage production of larger or more flowers.

division: Method of propagating by separating parts from a plant to produce new plants.

dormant oil spray: Light oil spray applied while a plant is dormant (in an inactive state) to suffocate pests.

drainage: The ability of the soil to move water so the roots of the plant don't become waterlogged, and so nutrients move through the soil.

essential oils: Volatile and fragrant oils produced by herbs.

fertilizer: Any material that supplies nutrients to plants.

*fines herbes***:** Mixture of herbs used as a seasoning or garnish.

fixative: Ingredient added to potpourri that keeps the scent strong for a long time.

friable: Term for soil that easily breaks apart or crumbles when handled.

germination: The beginning of plant growth from a seed.

harden off: The process of gradually accustoming a young, indoor-started plant to the outdoors.

herb: As commonly understood, a plant valued for its medicinal, savory, aromatic, or other household use.

herbaceous: Dying to the ground; not woody.

humus: Decayed organic matter, black and crumbly, that improves soil texture and moisture retention.

hybrid: A plant created by crossbreeding 2 or more different plants.

infuse: Steep an herb in water to extract the herb's properties.

insecticide: A product that kills insects.

knot garden: Herb garden formally planted in tight patterns.

lace bug: Insect with broad, lacy wings that sucks sap from plants.

layering: Method of propagating by putting stems of a plant in contact with soil so that roots will form, and then separating the rooted stem from its parent plant.

loam: The best garden soil, a balanced mix of silt, sand, and clay.

macerate: Soak in water or alcohol to soften.

manure: Livestock dung used as an organic fertilizer, rich in nitrogen.

mealybug: White, cottony-looking insect that attacks plants.

mildew: Fungal disease that produces white dust or downy tufts on leaves.

mordant: Substance used in dyeing to fix the coloring.

mosaic: Virus disease that causes mottled, yellow, curled leaves and discolored fruit.

mulch: Any material spread on the soil surface to conserve moisture, check weed growth, and protect the plant from excessive heat or cold.

neutral soil: Soil with a pH of 7.0.

nitrogen: One of the 3 most important plant nutrients, needed for production of leaves and stems.

node: Place where the leaf is attached to the stem of a plant.

nutrients: Elements in the soil absorbed by plants for growth.

open-pollinated: Pollinated by the wind or animals, not by human manipulation.

organic gardening: Practice of gardening without the use of synthetic chemicals.

organic matter: Part of the soil that consists of decayed or decaying plant and animal matter (humus).

panicle: Grouped flowers.

peat or **peat moss**: Decayed remains of ancient plants, added to soil to increase the soil's ability to absorb and hold moisture.

perennial: A plant that lives for more than 2 years.

perlite: Volcanic glass used in seed-starting and growing mediums.

pesticide: A product that kills garden pests.

petiole: Leaf stem or stalk.

pH: A measure of the acidity or alkalinity of the soil, on a scale of 1 (extremely acid) to 14 (extremely alkaline), with 7.0 being neutral. Herbs grow best at a pH of 7.0 or slightly higher.

phosphorus: One of 3 important plant nutrients; good organic sources are bonemeal and powdered rock phosphate.

photosynthesis: Process by which plants capture energy from the sun and convert it into compounds that fuel growth and life.

pinch: Snip back new growth, to keep plants compact and encourage bushiness.

pollination: The movement of pollen from one flower to another, necessary for fertilization and therefore fruit production.

pomander: Mixture of fragrant herbs and spices enclosed in a perforated box or bag, formerly carried as a personal scent and to ward off infection and mask unpleasant odors.

potassium: One of the 3 most important plant nutrients; good organic sources are greensand and small amounts of wood ashes.

pot-bound: Condition of a pot-grown seedling or plant whose root ball is thickly matted and contains little soil.

potherb: Herb whose leaves or stems are cooked and eaten as greens.

prune: Remove dead or living plant parts, to improve the plant's form or increase fruit or flower production.

pyrethrum: Insecticide made from chrysanthemums.

raceme: Long flower cluster, with flowers opening from the bottom first.

ray: One of the marginal flowers of the head in a composite plant.

receptacle: The end of the flower stalk which bears the flowers of a head.

rhizome: Underground stem, thick and fleshy and usually creeping.

rosette: Dense cluster of leaves on a very short stem.

rotenone: Biological insecticide.

runner: Stem that grows along the ground and takes root at its nodes or tips.

rust: Fungal disease that produces rust-colored blotches on leaves.

sabadilla: Insecticide made from a Mexican plant of the lily family.

sachet: Small bag filled with herbs and spices used to scent clothing and linens.

sacred herbs: Plants with some religious significance.

sandy soil: Soil with a high percentage of sand, or large soil particles; water travels through sandy soil very easily, so nutrients leach out quickly.

scale: Insect that forms a brown dome around itself on a plant.

scape: Leafless flowering stem that arises from the ground.

seedling: A young plant, especially one grown from seed.

set (fruit): Develop fruit or seeds after pollination.

set out: Plant a seedling in the garden.

sidedress: Apply fertilizer along a seed row or around a plant or hill.

slug: Slimy, short, worm-shaped creature that eats leaves.

soil test: Analysis of the soil to determine its pH and available nutrients.

species: Related strains of a plant that occur naturally.

spice: As commonly understood, a plant product used to season or flavor food, that comes from the tropics and is very sweet or aromatic.

spider mites: Insects that rasp chlorophyll off of broadleafed plants.

spike: Elongated flower cluster.

spittlebug: Sucking insect that deposits a small bit of spittle (a bunch of bubbles) on a plant's stem.

stamen: The pollen-bearing, or male organ, of a flower; consists of filament and anther.

steep: Soak in a liquid under the boiling point.

stem: Plant tissue that supports leaves and connects leaves with roots.

stigma: Tip of the pistil; it receives the pollen.

strewing herbs: Fragrant herbs strewn on the floor during medieval times to mask foul odors and freshen the air.

succession planting: Process of planting a new crop as soon as the earlier one is harvested.

succulent: Plant with juicy, water-storing stems or leaves.

sucker: Leafy shoot at a stem junction.

taproot: Main root that grows downward.

thin: Pull up or pinch out young plants so remaining plants have room to grow and mature.

thrips: Insect that rasps chlorophyll off of broadleafed plants.

till: Cultivate the soil, especially with a mechanical tiller.

tisane: Herb tea.

trace elements: Soil compounds essential to plant growth and development but present and needed in only very small amounts.

transplant: Move a plant to another location; also, the plant so moved.

tuber: A short, naturally swollen underground stem, as a potato.

tussie mussie: Small bouquet of aromatic herbs and flowers.

umbel: Flat-topped, umbrella-like flower cluster.

vermiculite: Lightweight, highly water-absorbent mineral used in seed-starting and growing mediums.

virus: A ultramicroscopic disease-causing organism.

white flies: Tiny flies that suck a plant's juices; often look like a cloud of smoke.

wilt: Disease that causes leaves to turn brown; often causes sudden death of plant.

SEED COMPANIES AND NURSERIES

Abundant Life Seed Foundation
PO Box 772
Port Townsend, WA 98368
206-385-5660

Agway, Inc. Seed Division
PO Box 4933
Syracuse, NY 13221

Bountiful Gardens
18001 Shafer Ranch Road
Willits, CA 95490
707-459-6410

Bonanza Seed International
PO Box V
Gilroy, CA 95020

Burgess Seed and Plant Company
905 Four Seasons Road
Bloomington, IL 61701
309-663-9551

W. Atlee Burpee & Co.
300 Park Avenue
Warminster, PA 18974
215-674-4915

Companion Plants
PO Box 88
Athens, OH 47501
614-592-4643

Caprilands Nursery
Silver Street
Coventry, CT 06238
203-742-7244

Catnip Acres Farm
67 Christian Street
Oxford, CT 06483
203-888-5649

The Cook's Garden
PO Box 535
Londonderry, VT 05148
802-824-3400

Crockett Seed Company
PO Box 237
Metamora, OH 43540

Cruickshank's, Inc.
1015 Mount Pleasant Road
Toronto, Ontario, Canada
M4P 2M1
416-488-8292

DeGiorgi Seed Co.
6011 N Street
Omaha, NE 68117
402-731-3901

Earl May Seed and Nursery
Shenandoah, IA 51603

Gurney's Seed & Nursery
110 Capitol
Yankton, SD 57079
605-665-1930

Harris Moran Seed Co.
60-A Saginaw Drive
Rochester, New York 14623
716-442-6910

Harris Moran Seed Co.
1155 Harkins Road
Salinas, CA 93901

H.G. Hastings Company
1036 White Street SW
PO Box 115535
Atlanta, Georgia 30310
404-755-6580

Henry Field's Seed and Nursery Co.
415 N. Burnett Street
Shenandoah, IA 51602
605-665-9391

Filaree Garlic Farm
Route 2, Box 162
Okanogan, Washington 98840-9774
509-422-6940

Fox Hill Farm
440 W. Michigan Avenue
Parma, MI
517-531-3179

The Gathered Herb
12114 N. State Road
Otisville, MI 48463
313-631-6572

Glock's Herbs and Spices
2214 Sue Avenue
Orlando, FL 32803 (by appt only)
407-898-5663

Hemlock Hill Herb Farm
Hemlock Hill Road
Litchfield, CT 06759-0415

High Altitude Gardens
PO Box 1048
Hailey, ID 83333

Hilltop Herb Farm
Ranch Road
PO Box 1734
Cleveland, TX 77327
713-592-5859

Horticultural Enterprises
PO Box 810082
Dallas, TX 75381

J.L. Hudson, Seedsman
PO Box 1058
Redwood, CA 94064

Jackson & Perkins
1 Rose Lane
Medford, OR 97501
503-776-2000

Johnny's Selected Seed
305 Foss Hill Road
Albion, Maine 04910
207-437-4301

Jung Seeds and Nursery
335 S. High Street
Randolph, WI 53957
414-326-3121

Le Jardin du Gourmet
PO Box 275G
St. Johnsbury Center, Vermont 05863
802-748-1446

Le Marche Seeds International
PO Box 190
Dixon, CA 95620
916-678-9244

Liberty Seed Company
PO Box 806
New Philadelphia, OH 44663
216-364-1611

Logee's Greenhouses
141 North Street
Danielson, CT 06239
203-774-8038

Meadowbrook Herb Farm
Route 138
Wyoming, RI
401-539-7603

Mellinger's
2310 W. South Range Street
North Lima, OH 44452
216-549-9861

The Meyer Seed Co.
600 S. Carolina Street
Baltimore, MD 21231
410-342-4224

Midwest Seed Growers
10559 Lackman Street
Lenexa, Kansas 66219
913-894-0050

Native Seeds/SEARCH
2509 N. Campbell, #325
Tucson, AZ 95719

Nichols Garden Nursery
1190 North Pacific Highway
Albany, OR 97321
503-928-9280

L.L. Olds Seed Co.
PO Box 1069
Madison, WI 53701
608-249-9291

Park Seed Company
Cokesbury Road
Greenwood, SC 29467
803-223-7333

Piedmont Plant Co.
PO Box 424
Albany, GA 31702
912-883-7029

Pinetree Garden Seeds
PO Box 300
New Gloucester, ME 04260
207-926-3400

Plants of the Southwest
Agua Fria Road
Route 6
PO Box 11A
Santa Fe, NM 87501

Redwood City Seed Co.
PO Box 361
Redwood City, CA 94064
415-325-7333

Richter's
357 Highway 47
Goodwood, Ontario, Canada L0C1A0
416-640-6677

Rispens, Martin & Sons
3332 Ridge Road
Lansing, IL 60438
708-474-0241

Roswell Seed Company
115-177 South Main Street
Roswell, NM 88201
505-622-7701

Sandy Mush Herb Nursery
316 Surrett Cove Road
Leicester, NC 28748
704-683-2014

Seeds Blum
Idaho City Stage
Boise, ID 83706
208-342-0858

Seeds of Change
621 Old Santa Fe Trail
Suite 10
Santa Fe, NM 88038
505-983-8956

Seed Savers Exchange
Box 239
Decorah, IA 52101

Sheperd's Garden Seeds
7389 West Zayante Road
Felton CA 95018
408-335-5400
30 Irene Street
Torrington, CT 06790

Southern Exposure Seed Exchange
PO Box 158
North Garden, VA 22959
804-973-4703

Sunnybrook Herb Farm
Box 6
Chesterland, OH 44026
216-729-7232

Talavaya Seeds
Po Box 707
Santa Cruz Station
Santa Cruz, NM 87507

Taylor's Herb Gardens
1535 Lone Oad Road
Vista, CA 92084
619-727-3485

Territorial Seed Co.
PO Box 157
Cottage Grove, OR 97424
503-942-9547

Thompson & Morgan
PO Box 1308
Jackson, NY 08527
201-363-2225

Twilley Seeds
PO Box 65
Trevose, PA 19053

Well-Sweep Herb Farm
317 Mt. Bethel Road
Port Murray, NJ 07865

Wyatt-Quarles Seed Co.
PO Box 739
Garner, NC 27529
919-772-4243

Periodicals
The Avant Gardener
PO Box 489
New York, NY 10028

Flower and Garden Magazine
4251 Pennsylvania Avenue
Kansas City, MO 64111

Horticulture
300 Mass Avenue
Boston, MA 02115

Organic Gardening and Farming
Organic Park
Emmaus, PA 18049

The Herb Companion
Interweave Press, Inc.
201 East 4th Street
Loveland, CO 80537

HerbalGram
The Journal of the American Botanical
Council and the Herb Research Foundation
PO Box 201660
Austin, TX 78720

The Joy of Herbs
PO Box 7617
Birmingham, AL 35253-0617

Organization
Herb Society of America
9019 Kirkland Chardon Road
Mentor, Ohio 44060
216-256-0514

INDEX

acid soil, 184
alkaline soils, 19, 70, 184
ancient times and herbs, 12, 14-15, 18, 26, 37, 44, 51, 55, 59, 67, 72, 82, 85, 88, 92, 98, 108, 110, 135, 154, 160
anise-flavored & -scented herbs, 28-29, 41, 104, 123-24, 149, 151
ants, 152, 200-01
aphids, 41, 58, 64, 76, 87, 157, 200-01
aphrodisiacs, 76, 108, 154
Asian herbal cuisine & gardens, 18, 62, 64, 68, 81, 85, 100, 108, 118, 128, 149, 174
baths, herbal, 12, 68, 97, 137
bees, herbs attractive to, 15, 48, 86, 96-98, 102, 110, 154
beetles, 34, 70, 121, 212
biblical herbs, 58, 92, 106
birds in the herb garden, 17, 29, 82, 102
blackspot, 33-34, 135
bone meal, 209
borers, 87
Boston Tea Party, 54, 60, 114
botanic (physic) gardens, 14
Bt (bacillus thuringiensis), 209
butterflies, herbs attractive to, 44-45, 86, 102, 110
cabbage moths, 140
calendar, 202-03
candied herbs, 38, 48, 76, 135, 162
capers, 53, 67, 157
carrot flies, 140
Carson, Rachel, 209
caterpillars, 201
chemicals in the garden, 44, 184, 200, 212
Chinese herbal medicine, 13, 15, 47, 55, 72, 75, 87, 92, 114, 160
chlorophyll, 16-17
classification of herbs, 14, 58, 85, 104
clay soil, 184
coffee & coffee substitutes, 60
cold climate gardens, 212
colonial American herb gardens, 18, 106, 128-29, 151
companion plants, 31, 33-34, 42, 48, 75-76, 140, 200, 209
compost, 19, 151, 185, 190, 193, 210, 212, 214
container plants, 19, 34, 36, 41-42, 49, 51, 53, 56, 60, 62, 67-68, 73, 75, 82, 88, 90-92, 94, 97, 101, 104, 106, 110, 116, 121, 124, 126, 128, 137, 140, 143, 146, 151, 154, 157-58, 162, 175, 188-89, 206-09
cosmetics, herbal, 13, 18, 36, 51, 54, 91, 97, 140, 143
cottage gardens, 114, 126,
county extension service, 184, 210
crown rot, 70, 129
culinary herbs, 12-15, 18, 170, 172, 175, 200 (see also individual herbs)
cuttings, 189, 191
damping off, 189
deadheading, 195-96
desert gardens, 214
Dioscorides, 14, 55, 59
disbudding, 194-95
Doctrine of Signatures, 59
dormant oil spray, 201
double digging, 185-86
drainage, 185, 210
dried flowers (everlastings), 15, 26, 29, 31, 34, 37, 42, 54-56, 79, 91, 120, 132, 140, 146, 152, 160
dried seed pods, 28, 45, 47, 108
drugs, herbal, 15-16, 70, 75, 114, 116, 158

drying herbs, 196-99
dyes, herbs for, 12-15, 34, 38, 41, 44-45, 47, 53-54, 67, 76, 79, 86, 88, 118, 121, 140, 145, 149
edging herbs, 18, 31, 34, 41, 49, 51, 116, 121, 129, 146, 150-52, 154, 160, 171, 174-75
enabling gardens, 208
erosion control, 160
evergreen herbs, 44, 49, 70, 86, 88, 104, 106, 135, 154, 211
fabrics, 94
fall-blooming herbs, 175 (see also individual herbs)
fertilizer, 19, 41, 151, 184-85, 193, 206
fiber plants, 13-15, 94
fines herbes, 41, 114
flea repellents, 15, 101
flower development process, 17
flowers, edible, 15, 29, 48, 51, 70, 102, 104, 118, 135, 140, 143, 145, 157, 162
fly repellents, 101, 200
foliar diseases, 70
folklore and herbs, 28, 38, 58, 60, 67, 72, 96-97, 150, 154, 170
freezing herbs, 198-99
fruits of herbs, 56, 58, 101-02, 132
fungal diseases, 42, 49, 92, 145, 154, 162, 193, 196, 201 (see also **mildew**)
garden design & planning, 143, 170-75, 189, 209-15
gophers, 67
grasshoppers, 58
greenhouse herbs, 36, 53, 60, 62, 68, 73, 90, 110, 124, 137, 143, 146, 154, 162, 188, 206
ground covers, 18, 42, 44, 55, 78-79, 83, 101, 129-30, 135, 137, 146, 152, 154, 160
gum, herbal, 98
hallucinogens, 96-97
hardening off, 189, 213
harvesting, 195-96
hedges, herbs as, 18, 49, 90, 104, 135, 152, 154, 174
herb, definition of, 12, 18
herb, pronunciation of, 62
herbalists, historic, 14, 55, 59, 72, 145
herbals, historic, 14, 59, 72, 145
honey, herbal, 29, 154
horticultural oil spray, 201
horticultural therapists, 208
incense, herbal, 85, 126, 154
Indian/Persian herbal cuisine, 76, 149
indoor herb gardening—see **container plants**
industrial/commercial herbs, 15
insecticidal soap, 58, 200, 209
insecticides, 15, 200, 209
insect pests, 198, 200-01 (see also specific insects)
insects, beneficial, 17, 209
integrated pest management (IPM), 209
irrigating—see water for the herb garden
knot gardens, 13, 19, 48-49, 51, 145, 152, 154, 170, 176-77
lace bug, 26
ladybugs, 209
language of flowers, 12, 15, 88, 135, 154
layering, 187
leaf mold, 210
leaves, structure of, 16
legend—see folklore and herbs
lemon-flavored & -scented herbs, 28, 36, 68, 73, 97, 104, 106, 118, 139, 154
licorice-flavored herbs, 54, 81, 123-24, 149
Linnaeus, 14
liquors and herbs, 15, 38, 60, 62, 76, 78, 85-87, 92, 98, 124, 145

CONTRIBUTORS

MAIN GARDENS
Diane Miske
Cornell Plantations
One Plantations Road
Ithaca, New York 14850

Patricia Hopkinson
Matthaei Botanical Gardens
University of Michigan
1800 North Dixboro Road
Ann Arbor, Michigan 48105

Holly Shimizu
Washington, D.C.

Jerry Parsons
University of California Botanical Gardens, Berkeley
Centennial Drive
Berkeley, California 94720

CONSULTING GARDENS
Richard Isaacson
Minnesota Landscape Arboretum
3675 Arboretum Drive
Chanhassen, Minnesota 55317

Lisa Cadey
The New York Botanical Garden
Bronx, New York 10458

Rebecca Wellborn
North Carolina Botanical Garden
CB Box 3375
University of North Carolina
Chapel Hill, North Carolina 27599-3375

Richard Thurston
San Diego Wild Animal Park
15500 San Pasqual Valley
Escondido, California 92027

Amy Greving and Dr. Donald Steinegger
University of Nebraska Horticulture Department
Lincoln, Nebraska 68588-0609

PHOTO CREDITS

©Ian Adams: 5, 13R, 26, 30BL, 30TL, 34BL, 34BR, 39BL, 40TL, 46TR, 46BL, 5-TL, 50BL, 57TR, 66TL, 57BR, 66TL, 84BL, 89BL, 93TR, 99TR, 103TR, 103TR, 107TR, 109TL, 114TL, 127BR, 142TR, TL, 173, 174B, 176, 177

©John Emmerling: 180

©Galen Gates: 40BL

©Dency Kane: 6, 10-11, 20-21, 27BR, 29, 30TR, 30BR, 39TR, 40TR, 40BR, 43TL, 43BR, 50BR, 57TR, 57BL, 61TR, 65BL, 65BR, 66TR, 69BL, 69BR, 74TR, 74BR, 76, 83BL, 85, 95TR, BR, 99BL, BR, 100TR, TL, 103TL, BL, BR, 106, 107BL, 109TR, 111, 113TR, 117BL, BR, TR, 119, 120, 125TR, BL, 127TR, 1234TL, 137TR, BL, BR, 141TL, BR, 142TL, 144TR, 147TR, 148TR, BL, 152, 153TR, 155BL, 159TR, 161TR, 168-9, 170, 171L, 174T, 180-81, 186, 187, 188, 189, 191, 198, 204-5

©Sylvia Martin: 12, 31, 34, 37, 52BR, 52BL, 53, 109BL, 110, 156BR, 185, 190

©Elvin McDonald: 28, 32BL, 43BL, 48, 55, 56, 57BR, 63TR, 64, 65TL, 65TR, 66BRT, 89BR, 100TL, 105TL, BL, 113TR, 114BL, 131BL, 137TL, 139, 141BL, 145, 147TR, 147BL, 154TR, 160, 206

©Jerry Pavia: 27BL, 32TR, 39TL, 50TR, 63BL, 74BL, 95BL, 99TL, 100TR, 117TR, 161TL, BL, 172

©Photo/NATS: Priscilla Connell: 52BR; Ann Reilly: 123BR

©Positive Image: Karen Bussollini: 181

©Sylvia and Stephen Sharnoff: 13L, 15B, 16, 27TR, 30TL, 31BR, 34TR, 34TL, 39BR, 46BR, 47, 52TR, 57TL, 57BL, 63BL, 63BR, 69TR, 71, 73, 74TR, 77TL, 77TR, BL, 80TL, TR, BL, 83TR, BL, 84TL, TR, 93BL, TL, 95TL, 105TR, 109 BR, 112, 113TL, BR, 125TL, 127TL, 131TL, TR, BR, 134 TR, TL, 136, 140, 144TL, BL, 153TL, BL, BR, 155TR, 156, 157, 158, 159TL, TR, 163, 165, 166, 178, 192, 193, 194, 195, 196

©Holly Shimizu: 210

©John Smith: 142TR, 144BR

©Albert Squillace: 27TL, 36, 42, 43TL, 43TR, 66BL, 69TL, 82, 83TR, 84TR, 89TL, BR, 105BL, 107TR, 107BR, 114TL, 125BL, 130, 148TR, 161BR, 171R, 175B

©Chani Yammer: 7, 15T, 45, 80BR, 81, 91, 93BR, 101, 116, 118, 129, 150, 135, 159BR

Illustrations on endpapers and on pages 16-17 by Delores Bego; illustration on page 23 courtesy of The United States Department of Agriculture. All other illustrations by Eric Marshall.

T=Top; B=Bottom; R=Right; L=Left

LEAF SHAPES

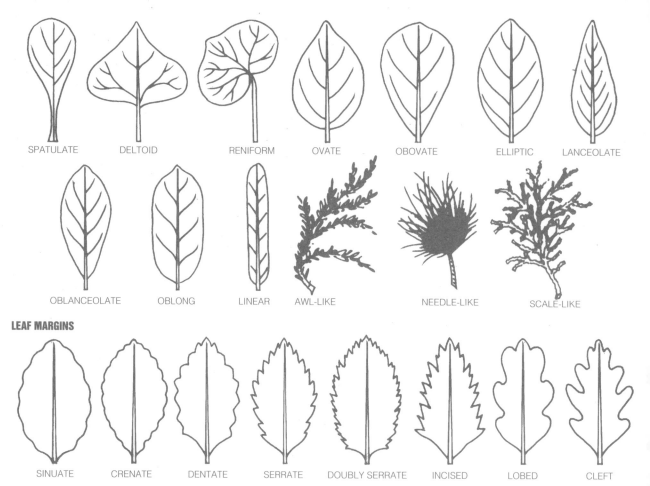

SPATULATE DELTOID RENIFORM OVATE OBOVATE ELLIPTIC LANCEOLATE

OBLANCEOLATE OBLONG LINEAR AWL-LIKE NEEDLE-LIKE SCALE-LIKE

LEAF MARGINS

SINUATE CRENATE DENTATE SERRATE DOUBLY SERRATE INCISED LOBED CLEFT

LEAF ARRANGEMENTS AND STRUCTURES

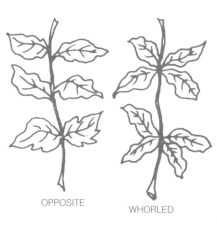

SIMPLE PALMATE COMPOUND BIPINNATE ALTERNATE OPPOSITE WHORLED